SCOTT FORESMAN ▪ ADDISON WESLEY

Mathematics

Grade 4

Homework Workbook

PEARSON
Scott
Foresman

Editorial Offices: Glenview, Illinois • Parsippany, New Jersey • New York, New York

Sales Offices: Parsippany, New Jersey • Duluth, Georgia • Glenview, Illinois
Coppell, Texas • Ontario, California • Mesa, Arizona

ISBN 0-328-07559-0

27 28 29 30   V011 18 17 16 15 14

Numbers in the Thousands

Here are some different ways to represent 2,352.

Place-value blocks:

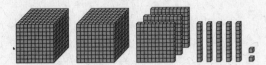

Expanded form:

2,000 + 300 + 50 + 2

2 thousands + 3 hundreds + 5 tens + 2 ones

(2 × 1,000) + (3 × 100) + (5 × 10) + (2 × 1)

Standard form: 2,352   **Word form:** two thousand, three hundred fifty-two

Each digit in 2,352 has a different *place* and *value*. The digit 3 is in the hundreds place and has a value of 300.

Write each number in standard form.

1. _____

2. 7 ten thousands + 5 thousands + 8 hundreds + 1 ten + 0 ones   _____

Write the word form and tell the value of the underlined digit for each number.

3. 4,6̲32   _____

_____

4. 7̲,129   _____

_____

5. 13,57̲2   _____

_____

6. Number Sense Write a six-digit number with a 5 in the ten thousands place and a 2 in the ones place.   _____

Name_____

Numbers in the Thousands

Write each number in standard form.

1.

_____

2. 8 ten thousands + 4 thousands +
9 hundreds + 4 tens + 7 ones

_____

Write the word form and tell the value of the underlined digit for
each number.

3. 7<u>6</u>,239 _____

_____

4. 823,<u>7</u>74 _____

_____

5. Number Sense Write the number that has 652 in
the ones period and 739 in the thousands period. _____

During a weekend at the Movie Palace Theaters, 24,875 tickets
were sold. Add the following to the number of tickets sold.

6. 100 tickets _____   **7.** 1,000 tickets _____

Test Prep

8. Which of the following numbers has a 5 in the
ten-thousands place?

A. 652,341   **B.** 562,341   **C.** 462,541   **D.** 265,401

9. Writing in Math Explain how you know the 6 in the
number 364,021 is not in the thousands place.

_____

_____

Understanding Greater Numbers

Here are different ways to represent 555,612,300.

Place-value chart:

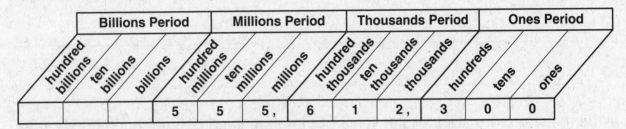

			5	5	5,	6	1	2,	3	0	0	

Expanded form: 555,612,300 = 500,000,000 + 50,000,000 +
  5,000,000 + 600,000 + 10,000 + 2,000 + 300

Word form: 555,612,300 = five hundred fifty-five million, six
  hundred twelve thousand, three hundred

The 6 is in the hundred thousands place. Its value is 600,000.

1. Write nine hundred seventy-six million,
   four hundred thirty-three thousand,
   one hundred eleven in standard form.   _____

2. Write 80,000,000 + 700,000 + 30,000 +
   200 + 90 + 7 in standard form.   _____

3. Write the word form and tell the value of the underlined
   digit in 337,123,421.

   _____

   _____

   _____

4. **Number Sense** In the number 213,954,670,
   which digit has the second greatest value?
   What is its value?   _____

Understanding Greater Numbers

Write the number in standard form and in word form.

1. 300,000,000 + 70,000,000 + 2,000,000 + 500,000 + 10,000 + 2,000 + 800 + 5

_____

_____

Write the word form and tell the value of the underlined digit for each number.

2. 4,6̲00,028   _____

_____

3. 488,423,04̲6̲   _____

_____

4. **Number Sense** Write the number that is one hundred million more than 15,146,481.   _____

5. The population in California in 2000 was 33,871,648. Write the word form.

_____

_____

Test Prep

6. Which is the expanded form for 43,287,005?

   A. 4,000,000 + 300,000 + 20,000 + 8,000 + 700 + 5

   B. 40,000,000 + 3,000,000 + 200,000 + 80,000 + 7,000 + 5

   C. 400,000,000 + 30,000,000 + 2,000,000 + 8,000 + 500

   D. 4,000,000 + 30,000 + 2,000 + 800 + 70 + 5

7. **Writing in Math** In the number 463,211,889, which digit has the greatest value? Explain.

_____

Name_____

Place-Value Patterns

Here are two different ways to show 1,400.

One Way: **Another Way:**

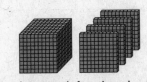

one thousand, four hundreds

fourteen hundreds

Here are two different ways to write 660.

   660 six hundred sixty   or   **66**0 sixty-six tens

Here are two different ways to write 40,000.

   40,000 forty thousand   or   **40,0**00 four hundred hundreds

---

Name each number in two different ways.

1. 700   _____

2. 1,700   _____

_____

3. Number Sense How many tens are in 6,430?   _____

The cafeteria has 900 food trays. How many stacks of trays
would there be if the trays were stacked in

4. hundreds? _____   **5.** tens? _____

6. Christopher has a collection of 1,742 pennies. If he
gets 300 more, how many total pennies will he have? _____

Look for a pattern. Find the next three numbers.

7. 2,950 3,050 3,150 _____ _____ _____

8. 1,211 1,221 1,231 _____ _____ _____

Place-Value Patterns

Name each number in two different ways.

1. 300 _____

_____

2. 2,400 _____

_____

3. 67,000 _____

_____

Reasoning Carlos has 1,300 stamps in his stamp collection.
He is planning on putting his collection into stamp books.
How many pages will he have filled if he puts

4. 10 stamps on each page? _____

5. 100 stamps on each page? _____

Look for a pattern. Find the next three numbers.

6. 4,017 4,027 4,037 _____ _____ _____

7. 11,213 11,313 11,413 _____ _____ _____

Test Prep

8. Which are the next three numbers in the pattern?
2,071 2,141 2,211

A. 2,021 2,041 2,061   **B.** 2,261 2,311 2,361

C. 2,281 2,351 2,421   **D.** 2,311 2,411 2,511

9. **Writing in Math** Describe the place-value blocks you
could use to show 1,415.

_____

_____

Name _____

Read and Understand

Seven Days There are seven days in a week. Each day has a certain number of letters. Which day of the week has the greatest number of letters?

Step 1: What do you know?

- Tell the problem in your own words.

There are seven days in a week, each with a certain number of letters.

- Identify key facts and details.

The days of the week are: Sunday, Monday, Tuesday, Wednesday, Thursday, Friday, and Saturday.

Step 2: What are you trying to find?

- Tell what the question is asking.

We want to know which day of the week has the greatest number of letters.

- Show the main idea.

Sunday	6	Thursday	8
Monday	6	Friday	6
Tuesday	7	Saturday	8
Wednesday	9		

Answer: Wednesday has the greatest number of letters.

Team Members Steve, Caroline, Heather, Brittany, Brian, Nick, Robert, Jennifer, and Susan are the players on a softball team. Are there more boys or girls on the team?

1. Identify key facts and details.

_____

_____

2. Tell what the question is asking.

_____

3. Solve the problem. Write your answer in a complete sentence.

_____

© Pearson Education, Inc. 4

4 Use with Lesson 1-4.

PROBLEM-SOLVING SKILL

Read and Understand

A zoo has 9 cows, 3 horses, 15 chickens, and
12 goats. How many animals are there in all?

1. Tell the problem in your own words.

_____

_____

2. Identify key facts and details.

_____

_____

3. Tell what the question is asking.

_____

_____

4. Show the main idea.

5. Solve the problem. Write the answer in a complete sentence.

_____

For 6 and 7, use the chart below.

6. How many more books does Elaine need
to have the same amount as Juan?

_____

Name	Number of Books
Charlotte	7
Elaine	4
Juan	9

7. How many books do Elaine, Charlotte,
and Juan have altogether?

_____

Name _____

Comparing and Ordering Numbers

You can use place value to compare two numbers. First line up the places of the numbers. Begin at the left, find the first place where the digits are different, and compare:

33,**4**14 5 hundreds > 4 hundreds,
⇓⇓ ⇓
33,**5**15 so 33,414 < 33,515.

To order numbers from greatest to least, write the numbers, lining up places. Begin at the left and find the greatest digit. If necessary, continue comparing the other digits:

42,078	Continue comparing.	Write from greatest to least.
37,544	37,**5**54	42,078
24,532	39,222	39,222
39,222	39,222 > 37,544	37,544
		24,532

Compare. Write > or < for each ◯.

1. 3,211 ◯ 4,221   **2.** 35,746 ◯ 35,645   **3.** 355,462 ◯ 535,845

4. Order the numbers from greatest to least.

62,500   62,721   63,001   61,435

_____ ; _____ ; _____ ; _____

5. Number Sense Write 3 numbers that are greater than 12,000 but less than 13,000.

_____

_____

Name_____

Comparing and Ordering Numbers

Compare. Write > or < for each ◯ .

1. 2,854,376 ◯ 2,845,763

2. 6,789 ◯ 9,876

3. 59,635 ◯ 59,536

4. 29,374,125 ◯ 30,743,225

Order the numbers from least to greatest.

5. 45,859,211   4,936,211   43,958,211

_____   _____   _____

6. Number Sense Write three numbers that are greater than 1,543,000 and less than 1,544,000.

_____   _____   _____

7. Put the planets in order from the one closest to the sun to the one farthest from the sun.

_____

_____

_____

_____

The Five Closest Planets to the Sun

Planet	Distance (miles)
Earth	93,000,000
Jupiter	483,000,000
Mars	142,000,000
Mercury	36,000,000
Venus	67,000,000

Test Prep

8. Which number has the greatest value?

A. 86,543,712   **B.** 82,691,111   **C.** 85,381,211   **D.** 86,239,121

9. Writing in Math Tell how you could use a number line to determine which of two numbers is greater.

_____

Rounding Numbers

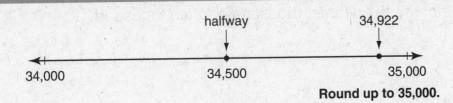

Round up to 35,000.

You can round using a number line or place value. On a number line, tell if 34,922 is closer to 34,000 or 35,000.

Using place value, find the rounding place and look at the digit to the right of it. If that digit is 5 or more, round up. If it is less than 5, round down.

For example, to round 34,922 to the nearest thousand, look at the number to the right of the thousands place. It is a 9. So, 34,922 rounds up to 35,000.

Round each number to the nearest thousand and ten thousand.

1. 13,212 _____

2. 35,645 _____

3. 55,462 _____

4. 25,845 _____

5. 367,142 _____

6. Number Sense Write three numbers that round to 1,000 when rounded to the nearest thousand.

_____

7. Round the population of Illinois to the nearest hundred thousand.

_____

> *Welcome to*
> **ILLINOIS**
> Population 12,419,000

Rounding Numbers

Round each number to the nearest thousand and ten thousand.

1. 68,354

   _____   _____

2. 857,836

   _____   _____

3. 6,172,438

   _____   _____

Round each number to the nearest hundred thousand.

4. 782,954   _____

5. 5,416,755   _____

6. Round the height of Mount
   Cameroon to the nearest
   thousand.

   _____

7. Round the height of Mount
   Kilimanjaro to the nearest ten
   thousand.

   _____

African Mountains

Mountain	Height (in feet)
Mount Kilimanjaro	19,340
Mount Cameroon	13,435
Mount Kenya	17,058
Mount Meru	14,979

Test Prep

8. Which is 346,759 rounded to the nearest ten thousand?

   A. 300,000   **B.** 346,000   **C.** 350,000   **D.** 400,000

9. **Writing in Math** Explain how you would round 265,588 to
   the nearest ten thousand.

   _____

   _____

   _____

Name_____

The Size of Numbers

R 1-7

Small groups of numbers make up larger numbers.
You know that there are 10 dimes in $1.00.

 =

How many dimes are there in $3.00? You can skip
count to find out. 10, 20, 30.

How many dimes are in $10.00? ___100___

Each dollar is equal to 100 pennies. How many pennies are in $10.00? ___1,000___

A box of chalk contains 10 pieces. How many pieces of chalk are in

1. 4 boxes? _____

2. 12 boxes? _____

3. 40 boxes? _____

4. Number Sense How many boxes of chalk would
you buy if you needed 500 pieces of chalk? _____

A jar holds 10,000 dimes.

5. How many $1 bills is this amount equal to?

_____

6. How many $100 bills is this amount equal to?

_____

7. How many $1,000 bills is this amount equal to?

_____

© Pearson Education, Inc. 4

Use with Lesson 1-7. **7**

The Size of Numbers

One freezer can hold 100 frozen yogurt bars. How many frozen yogurt bars are in

1. 10 freezers? _____

2. 3 freezers? _____

3. 60 freezers? _____

4. 100 freezers? _____

5. How many hundreds equal 1,000? _____

6. How many thousands equal 100,000? _____

7. If on average a tree drops 35 leaves a day in autumn, how many leaves would fall in 10 days? _____

8. If you took a bite of a watermelon and found 8 seeds, about how many seeds would you find in 10 bites?

_____

9. If there are 100 raisins in a box and you have 9 boxes, how many raisins do you have in all?

_____

Test Prep

10. Which of the following is equal to 1,000,000?

　A. 10 boxes with 1,000 trading cards in each box

　B. 100 boxes with 1,000 trading cards in each box

　C. 10 boxes with 10,000 trading cards in each box

　D. 100 boxes with 10,000 trading cards in each box

11. **Writing in Math** How can making small groups help you estimate large numbers?

_____

_____

_____

PROBLEM-SOLVING SKILL

Plan and Solve

Plenty of Words Each line of print in a children's book contains about 10 words. Each paragraph contains about 10 lines. Each page contains about 3 paragraphs. About how many words are on 10 pages of a book?

Here are the steps to follow when you plan and solve a problem.

Step 1: Choose a Strategy
- **Show what you know:** Draw a picture, make an organized list, make a table or a graph, act it out or use objects.

- **Look for a Pattern**

- **Try, Check, and Revise**

- **Write a Number Sentence**

- **Use Logical Reasoning**

- **Solve a Simpler Problem**

- **Work Backward**

Step 2: Stuck?
Don't give up. Try these.
- Reread the problem.

- Tell the problem in your own words.

- Tell what you know.

- Identify key facts and details.

- Try a different strategy.

- Retrace your steps.

Step 3: Answer the question in the problem.
What strategy can be used to solve the Plenty of Words problem?

A table can organize the information and make the problem easier.

Number of Words

1 line	10
1 paragraph	100
1 page	300
10 pages	3,000

The answer to the problem: Ten pages are equal to about 3,000 words.

Newspapers Sam usually delivers 22 newspapers each day. One day, 5 of his customers put a hold on the paper because they were going on vacation that week. Sam's boss told him that 2 new customers wanted delivery that week. How many papers did Sam deliver on the first day of that week?

1. What strategy might work to solve this problem?

   _____

2. Give the answer to the problem in a complete sentence.

   _____

   _____

PROBLEM-SOLVING SKILL

Plan and Solve

Rabbits At Juan's pet shop, the rabbit pen has 25 rabbits in it. Twelve of the rabbits are brown, 2 are black, and 4 are white. The rest are multi-colored. How many multi-colored rabbits are in the pen?

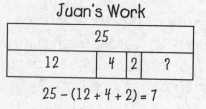

Juan's Work

25			
12	4	2	?

$25 - (12 + 4 + 2) = 7$

1. Name the strategy Juan used to solve the problem.

   _____

2. Give the answer to the problem in a complete sentence.

   _____

   _____

Frozen Yogurt Barbara sells frozen yogurt in cups or cones. The flavors are chocolate, vanilla, caramel, or strawberry. How many different ways can a customer buy frozen yogurt using one flavor and one way to serve it?

	Barbara
Cup	Cone
chocolate	chocolate
vanilla	vanilla
caramel	caramel
strawberry	strawberry
8 different ways	

3. Name the strategy Barbara used to solve the problem.

   _____

4. Give the answer to the problem in a complete sentence.

   _____

   _____

5. What other strategy might Barbara have used?

   _____

Using Money to Understand Decimals

We can use money to understand decimals. For example, a dime is one-tenth of a dollar, or 0.1. It takes 10 dimes to equal a dollar. A penny is one one-hundredth of a dollar, or 0.01, so it takes 100 pennies to equal one dollar.

| $0.01 | $0.05 | $0.10 | $0.25 | $0.50 |
| 0.01 | 0.05 | 0.1 | 0.25 | 0.5 |

The decimal point is read by saying "and." So, $1.99 is read as "one dollar *and* ninety-nine cents."

1. $3.52 = _____ dollars + _____ dimes + _____ pennies

2. $1.87 = _____ dollars + _____ dimes + _____ pennies

3. **Number Sense** Write nine and thirty-six hundredths with a decimal point. _____

How could you use only dollars, dimes, and pennies to buy

4. the baseball?

_____

_____

5. the baseball bat?

_____

_____

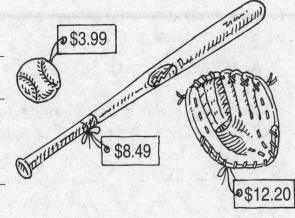

$3.99

$8.49

$12.20

Using Money to Understand Decimals

1. 2.18 = _____ ones + _____ tenths + _____ hundredths

$2.18 = _____ dollars + _____ dimes + _____ pennies

2. 9.27 = _____ ones + _____ hundredths

$9.27 = _____ dollars + _____ pennies

3. 7.39 = _____ ones + _____ tenths + _____ hundredths

$7.39 = _____ dollars + _____ dimes + _____ pennies

4. Number Sense Write 3 dollars, 9 dimes, and 5 pennies with a dollar sign and decimal point.

_____

5. Number Sense If you have 5 tenths of a dollar, how much money do you have?

_____

6. Lana wants to buy a book for $6.95. How can she pay for the book using only dollars, dimes, and nickels?

_____

Test Prep

7. How would you write sixteen and twenty-five hundredths with a decimal point?

A. 16.025   **B.** 16.25   **C.** 162.5   **D.** 1,625

8. Writing in Math Which is greater, 4 tenths and 2 hundredths or 2 tenths and 4 hundredths? Explain.

_____

_____

_____

Name_____

Counting Money

To make an amount of money with the fewest number of bills
and coins, start with the largest bill that is less than the amount
you are making. For example, to make $42.26, start with the
largest bill that is less than $42.26. Then keep using the largest
bills or coins possible. So, we need two $20 bills, two $1 bills,
1 quarter, and 1 penny to make $42.26.

Count the money. Write each amount with a dollar sign and decimal point.

1. 3 dollars, 4 dimes, 6 pennies _____

2. 3 five-dollar bills, 8 dimes, 2 pennies _____

Tell how to make each money amount with the fewest bills and coins.

3. $5.22 _____

_____

4. $16.51 _____

_____

5. Number Sense Mr. Belford has $0.59 in a tray on his desk. He
has two more dimes than quarters. What coins does he have?

_____

Counting Money

Count the money. Write each amount with a dollar sign and a decimal point.

1. 3 dollars, 5 dimes, 9 pennies = _____

2. 2 five-dollar bills, 3 dollars, 4 dimes = _____

3. 6 dollars, 4 dimes, 7 pennies = _____

4. Number Sense Larry has 3 dollars, 7 quarters, and 10 nickels. Can he buy a magazine that costs $5.00? _____

Tell how to make each amount with the fewest bills and coins.

5. $4.26 _____

_____

6. $6.50 _____

7. $10.31 _____

_____

8. $35.40 _____

_____

Test Prep

9. How much money does Lorraine have if she has three $5 bills and 5 quarters?

A. $3.50   **B.** $13.50   **C.** $15.25   **D.** $16.25

10. Writing in Math List the different ways you can make $0.25 without using pennies.

_____

_____

Making Change

An easy way to make change is to count up from the cost. For example, Chuck is making change at the convenience store. Tara buys a drink for $1.49 and pays with a $5 bill. How much change should Chuck give Tara? The chart shows how Chuck makes change.

What Chuck Does	What Chuck Says
He starts with cost of the drink.	That's $1.49
He gives one penny.	$1.50
He gives two quarters.	$1.75, $2.00
He gives three $1 bills.	$5.00
Total change given	$3.51

Chuck gives Tara $3.51 in change.

Tell how much change you would give from a $5 bill for each purchase. Give the amount with a dollar sign and a decimal point and list the bills and coins you could use.

1. $1.50 _____

_____

2. $2.73 _____

_____

3. **Reasoning** Suppose you buy an item that costs $5.03. Why might you give the salesperson $10.03?

_____

_____

_____

Making Change

Tell how you would give change from a $20.00 bill for each purchase. List the bills and coins you would use, and give the amount with a dollar sign and decimal point.

1. $13.55 _____

_____

2. $8.30 _____

_____

Tell how much change you should get from $10.00 when you buy the

$4.79 $6.28 $7.44 $8.33

3. art book. _____

4. crafts book. _____

5. music book. _____

6. sports book. _____

7. **Number Sense** Suppose you have $10. Do you have enough money to buy the music book and the art book? Explain.

_____

Test Prep

8. Which of the following is the change you would get when you buy an item that costs $1.29 with two $1 bills?

A. $0.72   **B.** $0.71   **C.** $0.69   **D.** $0.61

9. **Writing in Math** Imagine that you work in a record store. A customer gives you a $20.00 bill for a CD that costs $15.95. How much change will you give the customer? Explain.

_____

_____

More About Decimals

A grid can be used to show tenths and hundredths. To show 0.3 you would shade 3 out of the 10 parts.

0.3
3 out of 10 parts are shaded.

To show 0.30 you would shade 30 out of the 100 parts.

0.30
30 out of 100 parts are shaded.

One part of the hundredths grid can be compared to a penny, since one part of the grid is equal to 0.01 and a penny is equal to one hundredth of a dollar.

Tenths and hundredths are related. In the above examples, 3 tenths or 30 hundredths of the grids are shaded, or 0.3 and 0.30. These numbers are equal: 0.3 = 0.30.

Write the word form and decimal for each shaded part.

1.

_____

2.

_____

Shade each grid to show the decimal.

3. 0.57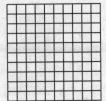

4. 0.4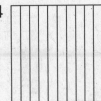

5. Number Sense Which is greater, 0.04 or 0.4? Explain.

_____

_____

_____

_____

More About Decimals

Write the word form and decimal for each shaded part.

1. _____

2. _____

For each fact, shade a grid to show the part of the population of each country that lives in cities.

3. In Jamaica, 0.5 of the people live in cities.

4. Only 0.11 of the population of Uganda live in cities.

5. In Norway, 0.72 of the people live in cities.

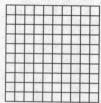

Test Prep

6. Which grid shows fourteen hundredths?

A.   **B.**   **C.**   **D.**

7. Writing in Math Explain why one column in a hundredths grid is equal to one column in a tenths grid.

_____

_____

_____

Name _____

Look Back and Check

Total Pins Shalyn bowled five frames, each time knocking down one pin more than the last frame. Shalyn knocked over three pins in the first frame. How many pins did she knock down after bowling all five frames?

Yoshi's Work

Frame	1	2	3	4	5
Pins Down	3	4	5	6	7
Total Pins	3	7	12	18	25

By the end of the fifth frame, Shalyn knocked down 25 pins.

You are not finished with a problem until you look back and check your answer. Here are the steps to follow.

Step 1: Check your answer.
Did Yoshi answer the right question?
Yes, she found the total number of pins Shalyn knocked down by the end of the fifth frame.

Step 2: Check your work.
Yoshi could use the pattern in her table to add numbers in the "total pins" column.

Did Yoshi use the correct operation?
Yoshi used addition to find the total pins knocked down.

Survey The results of a survey taken at Hillcrest School show that 140 students prefer bicycling as their favorite kind of exercise. There were 60 people who said swimming was their favorite. How many more students prefer bicycling to swimming?

Look back and check Yolanda's work on this problem.

Yolanda's Work

$$
\begin{array}{r}
14 \\
1\cancel{4}0 \\
-\ 60 \\
\hline
80
\end{array}
$$

There are 80 more students who prefer bicycling.

1. Did Yolanda answer the right question? Explain.

    _____

    _____

    _____

2. Is her work correct?

    _____

Name_____

Look Back and Check

Waterfalls Four famous waterfalls have different heights. Ruacana Falls in Angola is 406 ft high, Victoria Falls in Zambia is 343 ft high, Wentworth Falls in Australia is 614 ft high, and Akaka Falls in Hawaii is 442 ft high. What is the order of these waterfalls from the least to the greatest height?

	William
Waterfalls	Height
Wentworth Falls	614
Akaka Falls	442
Ruacana Falls	406
Victoria Falls	343

The order of the waterfalls is Wentworth Falls, Akaka Falls, Ruacana Falls, and Victoria Falls.

1. Did William answer the right question?

_____

_____

_____

2. Did William's work match the information in the problem?

_____

_____

3. Did William use a correct procedure?

_____

_____

4. Is William's answer reasonable?

_____

_____

Name_____

Go to the Door

Door County in Wisconsin has many small towns and miles of shoreline along Lake Michigan.

The chart shows the populations of four towns in Door County.

Town	Population
Forestville	1,680
Casco	2,066
New Franken	2,640
Fish Creek	1,200

Order the populations from least to greatest.

So, the order of the populations from least to greatest is

1,200   1,680   2,066   2,640

---

1. Algoma has a population of 5,387. Sturgeon Bay has a population of 16,149. Use these two populations and the ones in the table above to make a new list of populations from *greatest* to *least*.

_____

2. Write the population of Forestville in expanded form.

_____

Washington Island is near the tip of the Door County peninsula. To get there with a car or a bicycle, people have to take a ferry. Tickets for a one-way ride on the ferry cost $4.00 for adults and $2.00 for children (ages 6 to 11).

3. Jacqui bought an adult ticket and a tourist map. The total for the ticket and the map was $5.45. Jacqui paid with a $10.00 bill. How much change did she receive? _____

Name_____

In Attendance

In 2001, four baseball teams had the following home attendance totals for the season.

2,811,040   3,209,496   2,779,465   3,182,523

1. Write 3,209,496 in expanded form.

_____

2. Round each attendance total to the nearest hundred thousand.

_____

_____

3. Estimate the sum of all four attendance totals.

_____

4. **Writing in Math** Which estimate gives you more detailed information, rounding to millions or hundred thousands? Explain.

_____

_____

_____

5. Write the attendance totals in order from least to greatest.

_____

_____

6. Suppose in one month during 2001, 0.16 of the total season attendance occurred for one team. Show 16 hundredths on the grid by shading the correct number of hundredths.

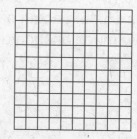

Mental Math: Adding

To add using mental math, you can break apart numbers or use compensation. The Commutative Property of Addition and the Associative Property of Addition explain why this works.

$13 + 6 = 6 + 13$ Commutative Property of Addition	$(7 + 8) + 5 = 7 + (8 + 5)$ Associative Property of Addition

With **breaking apart** you can add numbers in any order.

$235 + 158$	Break apart 158. $158 = 5 + 153$
$235 + 5 = 240$	Add one part to make a ten.
$240 + 153 = 393$	Add the other part.

With **compensation** you can add or subtract to make tens.

$235 + 158$	Add 2 to make a ten. $158 + 2 = 160$
$235 + 160 = 395$	
$395 - 2 = 393$	Subtract 2 from the answer because 2 was added earlier.

Add. Use mental math.

1. $67 + 31 =$ _____

2. $29 + 43 =$ _____

3. Reasoning How can you write $72 + (8 + 19)$ to make it easier to add? _____

Marble Collection	
red	425
blue	375
green	129
yellow	99

Use mental math to find the number of

4. red and blue marbles. _____

5. red and green marbles. _____

Mental Math: Adding

Add. Use mental math.

1. 89 + 46

2. 301 + 61

3. 400 + 157

_____

4. 722 + 158

5. 523 + 223

6. 804 + 396

_____

7. 299 + 206

8. 878 + 534

9. 1,000 + 7,000

_____

10. Reasoning How can you write
52 + (8 + 25) to make it easier to add?

_____

Use mental math to find the cost of a pound of

11. apples and a pound of oranges.

_____

12. bananas and a pound of grapefruits.

_____

Fruit	Price per Pound
Apple	$0.67
Orange	$0.98
Banana	$0.45
Grapefruit	$0.82

Test Prep

13. Stanley has $10.00. He buys bread for $3.47 and orange
juice for $2.53. How much money does Stanley have left?

A. $3.00

B. $4.00

C. $6.53

D. $8.47

14. Writing in Math Explain how you could add 678 + 303
using mental math.

_____

_____

Mental Math: Subtracting

To subtract using mental math, you can break numbers apart, use compensation, or use counting on.

Using breaking apart

88 − 15	Break apart 15.
	10 + 5 = 15
88 − 5 = 83	Subtract one part.
83 − 10 = 73	Subtract the other part.

Using compensation

162 − 48	Add 2 to make 50.
162 − 50 = 112	2 + 48 = 50
112 + 2 = 114	Since you subtracted 2 too many, add 2 to the answer.

Using counting on

400 − 185	Add 5 to make 190.
	185 + 5 = 190
190 + 10 = 200	Make the next 100.
200 + 200 = 400	Add 200 to make 400.
5 + 10 + 200 = 215	Find the total of what you added.

Subtract. Use mental math.

1. 86 − 14 = _____

2. 66 − 58 = _____

3. 141 − 46 = _____

4. 206 − 78 = _____

5. Writing in Math Subtract 164 − 94, then describe the mental math method you used.

_____

_____

_____

Mental Math: Subtracting

Subtract. Use mental math.

1. $53 - 21 =$ _____   **2.** $101 - 49 =$ _____   **3.** $224 - 26 =$ _____

4. $568 - 352 =$ _____   **5.** $120 - 33 =$ _____   **6.** $900 - 187 =$ _____

7. $141 - 98 =$ _____   **8.** $409 - 11 =$ _____   **9.** $554 - 59 =$ _____

10. Number Sense To subtract 37 from 462 using mental math, you first subtract 40 from 462 and get 422. What should you do next to get the final answer?

_____

Use mental math to find the difference in height between

11. Angel and Tugela.

_____

12. Yosemite and Cuquenan.

_____

World-Class Waterfalls

Name	Height (meters)
Angel	979
Tugela	948
Yosemite	739
Cuquenan	610

Test Prep

13. Dana has 205 cm of ribbon. She uses 64 cm of ribbon to tie a package. Which simpler problems could she use to find out how much ribbon she has left?

   A. $205 - 60$ and $145 - 4$ **B.** $205 + 64$ and $269 + 1$

   C. $205 - 60$ and $145 + 4$ **D.** $200 - 64$ and $136 - 5$

14. Writing in Math Explain how you would count on to find $350 - 156$.

_____

_____

_____

Estimating Sums and Differences

Rounding and front-end estimation can be used to estimate sums and differences.

To estimate 1,436 + 422:

Rounding

    1,436 rounds to 1,400
    422   rounds to 400
    1,400 + 400 = 1,800

Front-end estimation

    1,400 becomes 1,000
    422   becomes 400
    1,000 + 400 = 1,400

To estimate 3,635 − 1,498:

Rounding

    3,635 rounds to 3,600
    1,498 rounds to 1,500
    3,600 − 1,500 = 2,100

Front-end estimation

    3,635 becomes 3,000
    1,498 becomes 1,000
    3,000 − 1,000 = 2,000

Estimate each sum or difference.

1.   265
  + 426
	2. 348
	  + 122
		3. 562
		  − 223
			4. 824
			  − 590

5.   2,189
  +   388
	6. 1,329
	  + 5,345
		7. 877
		  − 475
			8. 9,245
			  − 4,033

9. 788 + 212 = _____

10. 9,769 − 4,879 = _____

11. 65,328 − 14,231 = _____

12. 32,910 + 4,085 = _____

13. Number Sense Is 976 − 522 more or less than 400? Explain how you can tell without actually subtracting.

_____

Estimating Sums and Differences

Estimate each sum or difference.

1.	627	2.	829	3.	987	4.	1,568
	+ 95		− 292		− 233		+ 352

5. 4,263 − 1,613 _____

6. 7,502 + 2,187 _____

7. 24,141 − 2,177

8. 64,099 − 55,555

9. 83,595 + 18,999

_____   _____   _____

10. About how much larger is the largest ocean than the smallest ocean?

_____

_____

Ocean Area

Ocean	Area (million sq km)
Arctic Ocean	13,986
Atlantic Ocean	82,217
Indian Ocean	73,481
Pacific Ocean	165,384

11. About how many million square kilometers do all the oceans together cover?

_____

Test Prep

12. Mallory is a pilot. Last week she flew the following round trips in miles: 2,020; 1,358; 952; 2,258; and 1,888. Which of the following is a good estimate of the miles Mallory flew last week?

    A. 6,000 mi   B. 6,800 mi   C. 7,600 mi   D. 8,600 mi

13. **Writing in Math** Explain how you would use front-end estimation to subtract 189 from 643.

_____

_____

Overestimates and Underestimates

When you estimate, you come close to the exact answer.
If your estimate is greater than the exact answer, it is called
an overestimate. If your estimate is less than the exact answer,
it is called an underestimate.

An Overestimate		
3,770	rounds to	4,000
+ 5,829	rounds to	6,000
		10,000

Both numbers were rounded up, so
10,000 is an overestimate. The exact
sum is less than 10,000.

An Underestimate		
742	rounds to	700
+ 312	rounds to	300
		1,000

Both numbers were rounded down, so
1,000 is an underestimate. The exact
sum is greater than 1,000.

Estimate each sum or difference. Then, if
possible, tell whether your estimate is an
overestimate or an underestimate.

1. 805 − 322 _____

2. 95 + 265 _____

3. 626 + 315 _____

4. 7,774 + 2,822 _____

5. 4,555 − 2,981 _____

6. 121 + 135 _____

7. 864 − 552 _____

8. 8,103 + 6,222 _____

9. Number Sense Melvin estimated
645 + 322 by adding 600 + 300. Is his
estimated sum an overestimate or an
underestimate? _____

Overestimates and Underestimates

Estimate each sum or difference. Then, if possible, tell whether
your estimate is an overestimate or an underestimate.

1. 448 + 492 _____

2. 7,926 − 4,002 _____

3. 1,922 + 4,498 _____

4. 5,647 − 2,089 _____

5. 829 − 673 _____

6. 7,122 + 2,692 _____

7. **Number Sense** Erin estimated 212 + 756
by adding 200 + 800. Is Erin's estimate an
overestimate or an underestimate? _____

8. Joel needs $285 for a video game system. He earned $95
mowing lawns and $112 delivering newspapers. About
how much more money does Joel need? Explain how you
estimated. Then tell whether your estimate is an
overestimate or an underestimate.

_____

_____

_____

Test Prep

9. Which of the following is an estimate of the difference: 3,492 − 1,429?

   A. 700   **B.** 2,000   **C.** 5,000   **D.** 9,000

10. **Writing in Math** Jeremy estimated 927 + 346 by adding 900 + 300.
    Explain why Jeremy's estimate is an underestimate.

_____

Adding Whole Numbers and Money

You can add numbers by adding the ones, then tens, then hundreds, and then thousands. For example:

Adding Larger Numbers

Add 53,482 + 38,811.

Estimate: 50,000 + 40,000 = 90,000

Add each place from right to left.

```
  1 1
 53,482
+38,811
────────
 92,293
```

Regroup the hundreds into 1 thousand and 2 hundreds.

The sum 92,293 is reasonable because it is close to the estimate of 90,000.

Adding Money

Add $88.50 + $11.75.

Estimate: $90 + $10 = $100

Add each place from right to left.

```
   1 1
 $ 88.50
+  11.75
─────────
 $100.25
```

Regroup as necessary.

Place the dollar sign and decimal point into the answer.

The sum $100.25 is reasonable because it is close to the estimate of $100.

Add.

1. $\begin{array}{r} 668 \\ +\ 343 \\ \hline \end{array}$

2. $\begin{array}{r} \$17.89 \\ +\ \ 2.71 \\ \hline \end{array}$

3. $\begin{array}{r} 14,587 \\ +\ 5,532 \\ \hline \end{array}$

4. $\begin{array}{r} 1,976 \\ +\ \ 240 \\ \hline \end{array}$

5. $\begin{array}{r} \$36.36 \\ +\ 24.84 \\ \hline \end{array}$

6. $\begin{array}{r} 25,039 \\ +\ 37,949 \\ \hline \end{array}$

7. $\begin{array}{r} \$86.50 \\ +\ \ 5.65 \\ \hline \end{array}$

8. $\begin{array}{r} 16,583 \\ +\ 83,795 \\ \hline \end{array}$

9. **Estimation** Zach adds 4,731 and 1,150. Should his sum be more or less than 6,000?

_____

Name_____

Adding Whole Numbers and Money

1.　　474
　　+　92

2.　　947
　　+ 261

3.　9,746
　+ 4,329

4.　2,868
　+　643

5.　87,643
　+　3,892

6.　17,246
　+ 42,369

7.　$46.96
　+　2.43

8.　$45.19
　+　39.46

9. 714 + 395

10. 2,002 + 3,003

11. $8.27 + $29.46

_____

12. **Number Sense** Jacob adds 4,296 and 7,127. Should his answer be greater than or less than 11,000?

_____

Zachary and Travis went out for lunch.

13. Zachary ordered a veggieburger and a large juice. How much was Zachary's total?

Menu	
Veggie burger	$2.75
Fish sandwich	$1.95
Milk	$0.95
Large juice	$2.25

_____

14. Travis ordered a fish sandwich and a milk. How much was his total?

_____

Test Prep

15. Lydia bought a baseball for $6.89 and a baseball bat for $23.46. How much did she spend altogether?

A. $25.30　　　**B.** $28.93　　　**C.** $30.35　　　**D.** $31.41

16. **Writing in Math** Samuel has 1,482 baseball cards in his collection. Maria gave Samuel 126 cards. How many cards does he have now? Explain what computation method you used and why.

_____

_____

Column Addition

You can add more than two numbers when you line up the numbers by place value and add one place at a time.

Add $3,456 + 139 + 5,547$.

Estimate: $3,000 + 100 + 6,000 = 9,100$

Step 1	**Step 2**	**Step 3**
Line up numbers by place value.	Add the tens.	Add the hundreds, then the thousands.
Add the ones.	Regroup if needed.	Continue to regroup.
Regroup if needed.		

Step 1
```
    2     22 becomes
 3,456    2 tens and
   139    2 ones.
+ 5,547
─────
     2
```

Step 2
```
   1 2
 3,456
   139
+ 5,547
─────
    42
```
Keep digits in neat columns as you add.

Step 3
```
  1 12
 3,456
   139
+ 5,547
─────
 9,142
```
9,142 is close to the estimate of 9,100.

Add.

1.
```
  945
  124
+ 343
```

2.
```
 2,588
   373
+  866
```

3.
```
 12,566
  8,222
+ 5,532
```

4.
```
 2,955
 9,017
+  248
```

5.
```
 $166.99
   33.11
+ 324.84
```

6.
```
 $38.81
  17.35
+  3.64
```

7. **Number Sense** Jill added $450 + 790 + 123$ and got 1,163. Is this sum reasonable?

_____

_____

Column Addition

Add.

1.   486
    875
+   45

2. $43.34
   49.48
+   8.90

3.   938
  1,487
+ 8,947

4.   7,226
  1,587
+ 72,984

5. $542.36
   2.23
+ 78.56

6.   80
  960
    4
+ 1,986

7. $279.87
  20.96
 150.98
+ 79.45

8.   8,738
  5,234
   836
+ 237

9. Number Sense Luke added 429 + 699 + 314 and got 950. Is this sum reasonable?

_____

10. What is the combined length of the three longest glaciers?

_____

11. What is the total combined length of the four longest glaciers in the world?

World's Longest Glaciers

Glaciers	Length (miles)
Lambert-Fisher Ice Passage	320
Novaya Zemlya	260
Arctic Institute Ice Passage	225
Nimrod-Lennox-King	180

_____

Test Prep

12. Which is the sum of 3,774 + 8,276 + 102?

A. 1,251   **B.** 12,152   **C.** 13,052   **D.** 102,152

13. Writing in Math Leona added 6,641 + 1,482 + 9,879. Should her answer be more than or less than 15,000?

Subtracting Whole Numbers and Money

Here is how to subtract across zeros.

Find 606 − 377.

Estimate: 600 − 400 = 200

Step 1	**Step 2**	**Step 3**	**Step 4**
606 − 377	5 10 6̸0̸6 − 377	9 5 10 16 6̸0̸6̸ − 377	9 5 10 16 6̸0̸6̸ − 377 ‾‾‾‾ 229
You cannot subtract 7 ones from 6 ones, so you must regroup.	Since there is a zero in the tens place, you must regroup using the hundreds. Regroup 6 hundreds as 5 hundreds and 10 tens.	Regroup 10 tens and 6 ones as 9 tens and 16 ones.	Subtract. 1 1 229 + 377 ‾‾‾‾ 606 You can check your answer by using addition.

Subtract.

1. $707
− 58

2. 950
− 47

3. 624
− 379

4. $3,506
− 866

5. $4,507
− 3,569

6. 3,076
− 1,466

7. $81.06
− 29.99

8. 6,083
− 1,492

9. Reasonableness Lexi subtracts 9,405 from 11,138.
Should her answer be greater than or less than 2,000?
Explain.

_____

_____

Subtracting Whole Numbers and Money

Subtract.

1.	906 $- \quad 45$	2.	3,091 $- \ 1,361$	3.	4,000 $- \ 2,557$	4.	7,242 $- \quad 158$

5.	$5.23 $- \quad 2.03$	6.	8,904 $- \ 3,596$	7.	$30.04 $- \quad 21.06$	8.	848 $- \ 257$

9. $74.03 - $32.54

10. 5,067 - 2,987

11. $67.97 - $12.98

_____   _____   _____

12. Robert set a goal to swim 1,000 laps in the local swimming pool during his summer break. Robert has currently finished 642 laps. How many more laps does he have to swim in order to meet his goal?

_____

Test Prep

13. Which of the following shows 22 dollars and 7 pennies subtracted from 130 dollars and 10 pennies?

   A. $152.17   **B.** $108.03   **C.** $107.31   **D.** $78.03

14. **Writing in Math** If 694 − 72 = _____, then 622 + _____ = 694. Explain the process of checking your work.

_____

_____

_____

Choose a Computation Method

Use **mental math** when the problem is easy to do in your head.

Marlo needs to buy 10 bowls for the party. Each bowl costs $3. How much money will the 10 bowls cost?

$10 \times \$3 = \$30$
The total cost is $30.

Use **pencil and paper** when the problem does not have regroupings or is too difficult to solve mentally.

Mr. Davis has $45.55. He buys a baseball bat for $13.21. How much money does Mr. Davis have left?

$$\begin{array}{r} \$45.55 \\ -\ 13.21 \\ \hline \$32.34 \end{array}$$

Mr. Davis has $32.34 left.

Use a **calculator** for more complicated problems, like those that have a lot of regrouping. For example:

The Booster Club had a total of $1,080.50 in its account. Club members spent $179.05 on decorations for the school pep rally. How much money is left in the account?

Press:

1080.50   [−]   179.05

[=]

Display: `901.45`

There is $901.45 left in the account.

Add or subtract.

1. $\begin{array}{r} 660 \\ -\ 360 \end{array}$

2. $\begin{array}{r} 3,546 \\ +\ \ \ 554 \end{array}$

3. $\begin{array}{r} 13,507 \\ -\ 8,569 \end{array}$

4. $\begin{array}{r} 1,276 \\ +\ 1,004 \end{array}$

5. **Number Sense** Explain why you would not use mental math to find $1,256 - 879$.

Name_____

Choose a Computation Method

Add or subtract. Tell what method you used.

1. $5,749
   + 8,274

2.   84,936
   − 27,946

3.   70,000
   + 30,000

4.   56,935
   + 3,964

5. $95,629
   −   7,846

6.   26,000
   − 4,000

7. $3,210 − $1,989 = _____

8. 4,440 + 560 = _____

9. An African elephant weighs 11,023 lb. An
   Asian elephant weighs 8,818 lb. What is
   the total combined weight of an African
   elephant and an Asian elephant?   _____

10. A hippopotamus weighs 4,409 lb.
    A white rhinoceros weighs 4,850 lb.
    How much less does the hippopotamus
    weigh than the white rhinoceros?   _____

Test Prep

11. Which number sentence is easiest to compute using
    mental math?

    A. 1,502 − 685   **B.** 1,530 + 120   **C.** 652 + 989   **D.** 1,596 + 3,628

12. **Writing in Math** Explain how you would use mental math
    to find 1,201 + 8,793. Solve.

    _____

    _____

    _____

Name_____

PROBLEM-SOLVING STRATEGY
Look for a Pattern

What pattern do you see?

1 A 2 B 3 C 4 D 5 E 6 F

The numbers alternate with letters of the alphabet, in order.
The pattern would continue like this:

7 G 8 H 9 I

What pattern do you see?

A	B	C
1	1	1
2	2	4
3	3	9
4	4	16
5		25

The number in column A is multiplied by the number in column B.
Column C is the product.

The last number in column B would be 5.

Look for a pattern. Draw the next two shapes.

1.

Look for a pattern. Write the three missing numbers.

2. 2, 4, 6, 8, _____ , _____ , _____

3. 2, 7, 12, 17, _____ , _____ , _____

4. 60, 52, 44, 36, _____ , _____ , _____

5. 88, 77, 66, 55, _____ , _____ , _____

Name_____

Look for a Pattern

Look for a pattern. Draw the next two shapes.

1.

2.

Look for a pattern. Write the missing numbers.

3. 5, 8, 11, 14, 17, _____, _____

4. 4, 6, 10, 16, 24, _____, _____

Look for a pattern. Complete each number sentence.

5. 80 + 8 = 88

808 + 80 = 888

8,008 + 880 = _____

80,808 + 8,080 = _____

6. 10 + 1 = 11

100 + 1 = 101

1,000 + 1 = _____

10,000 + 1 = _____

Look for a pattern. Write the missing numbers.

7. Sally went to purchase tiles for her kitchen floor. She measured the floor to find how many tiles she needed to cover the floor. Sally decided to make a pattern. She chose 10 red tiles,

20 beige tiles, 30 white tiles, _____ black tiles, and _____ gray tiles to complete a pattern for the kitchen floor.

8. **Reasoning** Fill in the missing amounts to update Carl's savings passbook.

Carl's Savings Account

Date	Deposit	Balance
4/7	$25	$945
4/14		$995
4/21	$25	
4/30	$50	
5/7		$1,095

Translating Words to Expressions

A **number expression** contains numbers and at least one operation. Here are some examples:

67×3 $12 \div 4$ $67 + 89 + 13$ $177 - 54$

When you solve word problems, you use key words in the problem to make number expressions. For example:

> Kelly has 2 pencils. Juan has 3 more pencils than Kelly. How many pencils does Juan have?

Word phrase: more than

More than refers to addition, so the number expression would be:

$2 + 3$.

Here are some other word phrases and the operations they refer to:

Word Phrase		Operation
more than total	plus combined with	addition
less than difference	fewer than minus	subtraction

Write a number expression for each phrase.

1. 37 marbles plus 52 marbles   _____

2. 30 days less than 365 days   _____

3. $45 increased by $67   _____

4. 25 tickets, with 18 tickets more   _____

5. Number Sense Jerry sees 15 bikes in the bike rack. He knows there are 35 total spaces for bikes. What operation can he use to find out how many more bikes will fit in the bike rack?

_____

PROBLEM-SOLVING SKILL

Translating Words to Expressions

Write a number expression for each phrase.

1. 1,285 is how much more than 622?

_____

2. $402 increased by $86

_____

3. 946 beads, then 80 fewer beads

_____

4. 12 adults combined with 26 children

_____

Write a number expression and then solve.

5. How many people do the 8 in. salad bowl and the 12 in. salad bowl serve together?

_____

6. How much more money does the 12 in. salad bowl cost compared to the 10 in. one?

_____

Cathy's Salads

Size	Servings	Price
8 in. bowl	4	$12.00
10 in. bowl	6	$15.00
12 in. bowl	8	$18.00

Write a number expression for the situation.

7. The bicycle museum had 220 fewer visitors this month than last month, when 980 people visited. How many people visited the museum this month?

_____

8. **Writing in Math** Write a word problem that can be solved using the expression 96 − 23.

_____

_____

_____

Matching Words
and Number Expressions

Number expressions that require more than one operation use
parentheses to indicate which operation should be done first.

Lori had 40 baseball cards. She gave 7 to Theo and 3 to Linda.
How many cards did Lori have left?

Step 1: Write a number expression.
$40 - (7 + 3)$

Step 2: Find the value of the expression.
Because this number expression has
parentheses around $7 + 3$, you would
do this part first.

$40 - (7 + 3)$
$\Downarrow$
$40 - 10 = 30$
Lori has 30 cards left.

Choose the number expression that matches the words.
Then find its value.

1. Mr. Roundtree had 20 tickets. He gave 10 to his family
and 8 to his friends.

$20 - (10 - 8)$ or $(20 - 10) - 8$ _____

2. Jane made 8 hamburgers. She sold 6, but then made
2 more.

$(8 - 6) + 2$ or $8 - (6 + 2)$ _____

3. Lonzo had 24 CDs. He lost 3 and gave 5 to a friend.
How many CDs does Lonzo have?

$(24 - 3) - 5$ or $24 - (3 - 5)$ _____

4. Number Sense Do $18 - (10 + 3)$ and $(18 - 10) + 3$ have
the same value? Explain.

_____

Matching Words and Number Expressions

Choose the number expression that matches the words. Then, find its value.

1. Jaleesa made 24 blueberry muffins. She gave 10 muffins to her friends. Then Jaleesa made 2 more muffins.

    $24 - (10 + 2)$ or $(24 - 10) + 2$

    _____

2. Antoine brought 24 bottles of juice to the picnic. The 14 people at the picnic each had 1 juice with their lunch. After the kids played soccer, Antoine's dad arrived with 12 more bottles of juice.

    $(24 - 14) + 12$ or $24 - (14 + 12)$

    _____

Choose the number expression that matches the words. Then, find its value.

3. Saturn has 18 moons, Jupiter has 16 moons, and Neptune has 8 moons. How many more moons do Saturn and Jupiter have combined than Neptune?

    $(18 + 16) - 8$ or $18 + (16 - 8)$

    _____

Test Prep

4. Which of the following is the value of the number expression $50 - (17 + 18)$?

    A. 25   **B.** 20   **C.** 15   **D.** 10

5. **Writing in Math** Explain which operation you would do first in the expression $47 - (17 + 12)$.

    _____

    _____

Evaluating Expressions

To evaluate an expression, replace the variable with a value
and then compute. For example:

Suppose $t = 5$. To evaluate $t + 20$,
substitute 5 for t.
Then add.

$t + 20$
$\Downarrow$
$5 + 20 = 25$

How can you find the missing number in this table?

n	$n + 11$
5	16
8	19
10	21
12	

$5 + 11 = 16$

$8 + 11 = 19$

Substitute 12 for n in the expression $n + 11$.
$12 + 11 = 23$. The missing number is 23.

Evaluate each expression for $a = 7$.

1. $a + 22 =$ _____

2. $a - 6 =$ _____

3. $17 + a =$ _____

4. Number Sense Does the expression
$f - 13$ have a greater value when $f = 23$
or when $f = 26$?

_____

Evaluate each expression for $n = 9$.

5. $n \div 3 =$ _____

6. $n + 15 =$ _____

7. $n - 7 =$ _____

Find the missing numbers in each table.

8.

n	$n - 5$
20	15
31	
50	45
17	

9.

★	★ + 21
7	
9	30
30	51
40	

Evaluating Expressions

Evaluate each expression for $y = 15$.

1. $y + 15$ _____

2. $y + 39$ _____

3. $85 - y$ _____

4. $51 - y$ _____

Find the missing numbers in each table.

5.

n	$n + 35$
2	
10	45
15	
95	

6.

x	$75 - x$
9	
25	50
35	
52	

7. Kiara saved $27. She bought her mother a gift. She has $13 left. How much did she spend on the gift?

_____

8. Carlos had 11 cans of paint. He used 4 cans painting the garage. He bought 2 more cans. How many cans of paint does Carlos have now?

_____

Test Prep

9. Which is the value of $a + 235$ when $a = 150$?

A. 85   **B.** 150   **C.** 385   **D.** 485

10. Writing in Math Explain how to evaluate $44 + x$ for $x = 34$.

_____

_____

Solving Addition and Subtraction Equations

An equation is a number sentence stating that two expressions are equal.

$$\underbrace{7 + 5}_{12} = 12$$
$$12 = 12$$

Some equations have variables, such as $n + 20 = 100$. To solve the equation, you must find the number the variable stands for. Solve $n + 20 = 100$.

Step 1	**Step 2**
Use mental math. What number plus 20 equals 100?	See if the number works. If it doesn't, try another number.
Try different numbers.	Does $70 + 20 = 100$?
Try $n = 70$.	No.
$70 + 20 = 90$	Try $n = 80$.
	$80 + 20 = 100$
	So, $n = 80$.

Solve each equation.

1. $a + 5 = 12$ _____

2. $n + 9 = 18$ _____

3. $e - 6 = 60$ _____

4. $j + 100 = 126$ _____

5. $w - 200 = 100$ _____

6. $88 + t = 100$ _____

7. **Number Sense** Is the solution of $100 - f = 60$ greater than or less than 60? Explain how you know.

_____

_____

8. **Reasonableness** Marty solved the equation $d + 71 = 87$ and got $d = 12$. Is this solution reasonable? Explain.

_____

Solving Addition and Subtraction Equations

Solve each equation.

1. $d - 12 = 12$ $d =$ _____

2. $82 + b = 90$ $b =$ _____

3. $f + 50 = 300$ $f =$ _____

4. $q - 800 = 200$ $q =$ _____

5. $9 + k = 18$ $k =$ _____

6. $90 - w = 88$ $w =$ _____

7. **Number Sense** Is the solution of $25 + n = 30$ greater or less than 30? Explain how you know without solving.

_____

_____

8. Andre bought a model airplane. He also bought a tube of glue for $6. He spent $22. Use the equation $a + \$6 = \$22$ to find the cost of the model airplane. _____

Test Prep

9. Which is the value of the variable in the equation $r - 126 = 19$?

   A. 245   **B.** 145   **C.** 107   **D.** 49

10. **Writing in Math** Explain how the variable b has two different values in the two equations.

    $6 - b = 5$ $b = 1$ $b + 5 = 15$ $b = 10$

_____

_____

Name_____

These Lakes Are Great!

Suppose that waves in a part of Lake Michigan caused the water temperature to change quickly from 72°F to 59°F.

How many degrees cooler did the water temperature become?

To find the difference, subtract.

$$
\begin{array}{r}
6\ 12 \\
\not{7}\not{2} \\
-\ 59 \\
\hline
13
\end{array}
$$

So, the water temperature is 13°F cooler.

In its deepest part, Lake Michigan is about 925 ft deep.
The average depth of Lake Michigan is about 279 feet.

1. Find the difference between the depths.

_____

The shoreline of Lake Michigan is 1,638 miles. The shoreline of Lake Superior is 2,726 miles. The shoreline of Lake Erie is 871 miles.

2. How many miles of shoreline do the three lakes have combined?

_____

3. How many more miles of shoreline does Lake Michigan have than Lake Erie?

_____

4. **Writing in Math** Candice says that the shoreline of Lake Erie and Lake Michigan combined is greater than the shoreline of Lake Superior. Is she correct? Explain.

_____

_____

Name_____

A Piece of History

The Statue of Liberty, located on Liberty Island in New York, was given to the United States as a present from France on July 4, 1884. The statue was still in France at the time. It was taken apart and then shipped in sections to the United States in 1885.

A total of 350 pieces of the statue were shipped on the French transport ship *Isere*. The pieces were shipped in a total of 214 crates.

1. Suppose that, after arriving in the United States, it took two days to remove the first 108 crates. How many crates were still on the ship?

   _____

2. Suppose four different pieces of the statue had the following weights: 4,219 lb; 3,182 lb; 876 lb; and 1,215 lb. Find the total weight of the four pieces.

   _____

3. Admission to the Statue of Liberty is free. In 2002, the price for three adults to ride the ferry round trip was $21. The price for five adults was $35. What is the round-trip price for one adult?

   _____

4. Suppose there are 13 children who take the ferry during one trip to the Statue of Liberty. A total of 51 people take the trip. Write a number sentence to find the number of adults who take the ferry. Solve. Write your answer in a complete sentence.

   _____

   _____

Name _____

Meanings for Multiplication

There are 4 rows of 5.

Addition sentence:

$5 + 5 + 5 + 5 = 20$

Multiplication sentence:

$4 \times 5 = 20$

There are 3 boxes. There are 7 books in each box.

There are 3 groups of 7.

Addition sentence:

$7 + 7 + 7 = 21$

Multiplication sentence:

$3 \times 7 = 21$

Write an addition sentence and a multiplication sentence for each picture.

1.

_____

2.

_____

Write a multiplication sentence for each addition sentence.

3. $10 + 10 + 10 + 10 = 40$ _____

4. $3 + 3 + 3 + 3 + 3 + 3 = 18$ _____

5. **Number Sense** Explain how multiplication can help you find $7 + 7 + 7$.

_____

Name_____

Meanings for Multiplication

Write an addition sentence and a multiplication sentence for the picture.

1.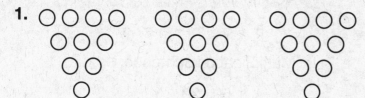

_____

Write a multiplication sentence for each addition sentence.

2. $4 + 4 + 4 + 4 = 16$ _____

3. $10 + 10 + 10 + 10 + 10 + 10 = 60$ _____

4. **Number Sense** How could you use multiplication to find $7 + 7 + 7$?

_____

5. A classroom desk has 4 legs. How many legs do
   5 desks have altogether? _____

6. Danielle planted 3 seeds in 6 different pots.
   How many seeds did she plant? _____

Test Prep

7. Which is the multiplication sentence for $2 + 2 + 2 + 2$?

   A. $4 \times 4 = 16$ **B.** $2 \times 2 = 4$ **C.** $2 \times 4 = 8$ **D.** $2 \times 6 = 12$

8. **Writing in Math** Explain how you can use multiplication to
   find $2 + 2 + 2 + 2$.

   _____

   _____

   _____

Name_____

Patterns in Multiplying by
0, 1, 2, 5, and 9

R 3-2

Pattern	Example
All multiples of two are even numbers.	2, 18, 44
All multiples of 5 end in 0 or 5.	25, 100, 220
For all multiples of nine, the sum of the digits is always a multiple of 9.	27 $2 + 7 = 9$ 63 $6 + 3 = 9$
The product of any number and zero is zero.	$17 \times 0 = 0$
The product of any number and one is that number.	$32 \times 1 = 32$
Two numbers can be multiplied in any order and the product will be the same.	$4 \times 5 = 20$ $5 \times 4 = 20$

1. $\begin{array}{r} 9 \\ \times\ 5 \\ \hline \end{array}$ 2. $\begin{array}{r} 2 \\ \times\ 8 \\ \hline \end{array}$ 3. $\begin{array}{r} 8 \\ \times\ 5 \\ \hline \end{array}$ 4. $\begin{array}{r} 9 \\ \times\ 0 \\ \hline \end{array}$

5. $\begin{array}{r} 9 \\ \times\ 3 \\ \hline \end{array}$ 6. $\begin{array}{r} 7 \\ \times\ 2 \\ \hline \end{array}$ 7. $\begin{array}{r} 0 \\ \times\ 3 \\ \hline \end{array}$ 8. $\begin{array}{r} 1 \\ \times\ 56 \\ \hline \end{array}$

9. How many baseball cards are in 4 packages?

_____

Item	Number in Package
Baseball cards	5
Stickers	2
Coupon	1

10. How many stickers do you get if you buy 9 packages?

_____

11. How many coupons do you get if you buy 7 packages?

_____

© Pearson Education, Inc. 4

30 Use with Lesson 3-2.

Patterns in Multiplying
by 0, 1, 2, 5, and 9

1. 5
    × 4

2. 2
    × 3

3. 7
    × 1

4. 5
    × 0

5. 8
    × 2

6. 5
    × 3

7. 8
    × 0

8. 4
    × 1

9. $9 \times 6 =$ _____

10. $7 \times 2 =$ _____

11. $0 \times 0 =$ _____

Algebra Find the missing number. Tell which property can help you.

12. _____ $\times 9 = 0$

_____

13. $1 \times$ _____ $= 4$

_____

14. A package of baseball cards includes
    5 cards. How many baseball cards are
    in 5 packages?   _____

Test Prep

15. What is the value of the missing number?
    $\square \times 9 = 36$

    A. 6   **B.** 4   **C.** 3   **D.** 2

16. **Writing in Math** Milton needs to find the product of two
    numbers. One of the numbers is 9. The answer also needs
    to be 9. How will he solve this problem? Explain.

    _____

    _____

Using Known Facts to Find Unknown Facts

You can use breaking apart to find a product.

Find 4×5.

4 groups of 5 are the same as 2 groups of 5 and 2 groups of 5.

$2 \times 5 = 10$

$2 \times 5 = 10$

$$4 \times 5 = 2 \times 5 + 2 \times 5$$
$$= 10 + 10$$
$$= 20$$

Use breaking apart to find each product.

1. $\begin{array}{r} 3 \\ \times\ 5 \\ \hline \end{array}$	**2.** $\begin{array}{r} 8 \\ \times\ 3 \\ \hline \end{array}$	**3.** $\begin{array}{r} 4 \\ \times\ 9 \\ \hline \end{array}$	**4.** $\begin{array}{r} 7 \\ \times\ 7 \\ \hline \end{array}$
5. $\begin{array}{r} 8 \\ \times\ 4 \\ \hline \end{array}$	**6.** $\begin{array}{r} 8 \\ \times\ 8 \\ \hline \end{array}$	**7.** $\begin{array}{r} 6 \\ \times\ 3 \\ \hline \end{array}$	**8.** $\begin{array}{r} 4 \\ \times\ 4 \\ \hline \end{array}$

Compare. Use <, >, or = to fill in each $\bigcirc$.

9. $7 \times 6 \bigcirc 5 \times 7$ **10.** $9 \times 4 \bigcirc 4 \times 9$

11. $4 \times 4 \bigcirc 2 \times 8$ **12.** $7 \times 8 \bigcirc 9 \times 5$

Name _____

Using Known Facts to Find Unknown Facts

Use breaking apart to find each product.

1. 7
   $\times\ 3$

2. 9
   $\times\ 5$

3. 8
   $\times\ 2$

4. 6
   $\times\ 4$

5. $4 \times 3 =$ _____

6. $9 \times 3 =$ _____

7. $8 \times 5 =$ _____

8. $3 \times 6 =$ _____

9. $6 \times 7 =$ _____

10. $7 \times 9 =$ _____

11. **Number Sense** Sara traced circle stencils for her project. She needs 7 rows of 9 circle stencils. She thought that 7 rows of 9 is the same as 3 rows of 9 and 2 rows of 9. Is this correct?

_____

_____

_____

Reasoning Compare. Use <, >, or = to fill in each blank $\bigcirc$.

12. $6 \times 9 \bigcirc 9 \times 6$

13. $9 \times 4 \bigcirc 6 \times 6$

14. $8 \times 8 \bigcirc 7 \times 9$

Test Prep

15. Which of the following is equal to the product of 3×3?

   A. 9×1 **B.** 3×1 **C.** 4×2 **D.** 6×3

16. **Writing in Math** Explain how the three multiplication sentences are related.

   12×2 8×3 6×4

   _____

Multiplying by 10, 11, and 12

Here are some easy ways to multiply numbers by 10, 11, and 12.

Multiples of 10

Any whole number multiplied by 10 will always equal that number with an additional zero in the ones place.

For example, $2 \times 10 = 20$, $22 \times 10 = 220$, and $220 \times 10 = 2,200$.

You can also break apart equations to help find products.

Multiples of 11

To find 12×11, think of 11 as $10 + 1$.

$12 \times 10 = 120$, $12 \times 1 = 12$, $120 + 12 = 132$, so $12 \times 11 = 132$.

Multiples of 12

To find 6×12, think of 12 as $10 + 2$.

$6 \times 10 = 60$, $6 \times 2 = 12$, $60 + 12 = 72$, so $6 \times 12 = 72$.

---

1. $5 \times 11 =$ _____   **2.** $12 \times 4 =$ _____   **3.** $10 \times 9 =$ _____

4. $7 \times 12 =$ _____   **5.** $12 \times 11 =$ _____   **6.** $8 \times 10 =$ _____

7. Number Sense Explain how 9×10 can help you find 9×11.

_____

There are 11 players on the field for each football team during a game. How many players would there be on

8. 4 teams? _____

9. 8 teams? _____

10. 10 teams? _____

11. 11 teams? _____

Multiplying by 10, 11, and 12

1. $4 \times 10 =$ _____   **2.** $12 \times 2 =$ _____   **3.** $10 \times 6 =$ _____

4. $11 \times 1 =$ _____   **5.** $4 \times 12 =$ _____   **6.** $8 \times 11 =$ _____

7. $9 \times 10 =$ _____   **8.** $12 \times 3 =$ _____   **9.** $10 \times 7 =$ _____

10. $11 \times 5 =$ _____   **11.** $10 \times 5 =$ _____   **12.** $6 \times 12 =$ _____

13. **Number Sense** Beatrice multiplied 10×9. She quickly found the answer by placing a 0 behind the 9 to get an answer of 90. Is this reasonable?

_____

_____

There are 12 months in 1 year. How many months are in

14. 2 years? _____

15. 3 years? _____

16. 5 years? _____

17. In the classroom there are 5 round tables. There are 4 students sitting at each table. How many students are sitting at the tables altogether? _____

Test Prep

18. How much money is 12 dimes?

A. $0.60   **B.** $1.00   **C.** $1.20   **D.** $2.00

19. **Writing in Math** Explain how to find 7×11.

_____

_____

PROBLEM-SOLVING STRATEGY

Make a Table

Roller Blades Bill needs $119 to buy a new pair of roller blades. He makes $15 a week delivering the Sunday paper. Will Bill have the money he needs to buy the roller blades if he saves his earnings for 8 weeks?

Read and Understand

Step 1: What do you know?

Bill makes $15 per week and needs $119 for new roller blades.

Step 2: What are you trying to find?

Will he have enough money if he works for 8 weeks?

Plan and Solve

Step 3: What strategy will you use?

Strategy: Make a Table

Week	1	2	3	4	5	6	7	8
$ Saved	$15	$30	$45	$60	$75	$90	$105	$120

Yes, he will have enough money to buy the roller blades.

Look Back and Check

Step 4: Is your work correct?

Yes, the table shows that after 8 weeks he will have $120, which is enough to buy the roller blades.

Vitamin Factory At a vitamin factory, 12 vitamins are formed every 10 sec. How many vitamins will be formed in 60 sec?

1. Complete the table for the Vitamin Factory problem.

Seconds	10	20	30			
Vitamins	12	24				

Name_____

Make a Table

Complete the table to solve the problem. Write the answer in a complete sentence.

1. The grocery store is having a sale on canned vegetables. If you buy 1 can, you get 2 free. How many cans do you need to buy to get 16 cans free?

Cans purchased	1	2	3	4	5	6	7	8	9
Free cans	2	4							

_____

2. Grandma wanted to help Jennifer learn to multiply. On the first day of Jennifer's visit, Grandma gave her 2 charms for her charm bracelet. On the second day, Grandma gave Jennifer 4 charms. On the third day, she gave Jennifer 8 charms. How many charms did Grandma give Jennifer on the sixth day of her visit?

Day	1	2	3	4	5	6	7
Charms	2	4	8				

_____

For Exercise 3, make a table. Use it to find the answer.

3. Juan decided to raise money for his camping trip by selling lemonade. He charged $1.00 for 1 glass, $1.25 for 2 glasses, $1.50 for 3 glasses, and so on. How much money did Juan charge for 5 glasses of lemonade?

_____

Meanings for Division

When you divide, you separate things into equal groups.

Doris is making 8 box lunches, each with the same number of strawberries. She has a total of 32 strawberries. How many strawberries should go in each lunch?

What you think: Doris will have to place an equal number of strawberries in each box. She must put 32 strawberries into 8 equal groups. How many strawberries are in each group?

What you show: 8 equal groups

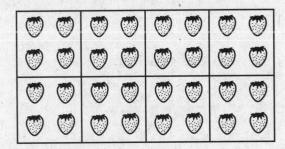

32 strawberries divided into 8 separate groups leaves 4 strawberries in each group.

What you write: $32 \div 8 = 4$

32 is the dividend, the number that is being divided.

8 is the divisor, the number the dividend is being divided by.

4 is the quotient, or the answer to the division problem.

Each lunch should have 4 strawberries.

Draw pictures to solve each problem.

1. You put 15 marbles into 3 groups.
   How many marbles are in each group?

   _____

2. You need to put 20 ice cubes into 5 glasses. How many cubes should go in each glass?

   _____

Meanings for Division

Draw pictures to solve each problem.

1. There are 12 small gift bags. Each bag can hold 1 toy and some stickers. There are 36 stickers. If an equal number of stickers is put in each bag, how many stickers will be in each bag?

   _____

2. One egg carton holds 12 eggs. How many cartons are you able to fill with 60 eggs?

   _____

3. There are 21 students in Mr. Tentler's class. The students divided themselves evenly into 3 groups. How many students are in each group?   _____

Test Prep

4. Calvin read an 18-page chapter in his social studies book in 2 hours. If he read the same number of pages each hour, how many pages did he read per hour?

   A. 3 pages   **B.** 6 pages   **C.** 9 pages   **D.** 12 pages

5. **Writing in Math** The class is planning a party. The pizza restaurant cuts each pizza into 8 slices. There are 32 students. How many pizzas does the class need to order for each student to have a slice? Explain.

   _____

   _____

Relating Multiplication and Division

Multiplication and division are related, just like addition and subtraction are related.

This is the fact family for 5, 6, and 30:

$5 \times 6 = 30$	$30 \div 6 = 5$
$6 \times 5 = 30$	$30 \div 5 = 6$

Complete each fact family.

1. $2 \times$ _____ $= 10$ $10 \div 5 =$ _____

    _____ $\times$ _____ $= 10$ $10 \div$ _____ $=$ _____

2. $9 \times$ _____ $= 27$ $27 \div 3 =$ _____

    _____ $\times$ _____ $= 27$ $27 \div$ _____ $=$ _____

3. $8 \times$ _____ $= 72$ $72 \div 8 =$ _____

    _____ $\times$ _____ $= 72$ $72 \div$ _____ $=$ _____

4. $6 \times$ _____ $= 48$ $48 \div 8 =$ _____

    _____ $\times$ _____ $= 48$ $48 \div$ _____ $=$ _____

Write a fact family for each set of numbers.

5. 7, 4, 28 _____

_____

6. 5, 8, 40 _____

_____

7. **Number Sense** What multiplication facts are part of the fact family for $12 \div 3 = 4$?

_____

Relating Multiplication and Division   P 3-7

Complete each fact family.

1. 7 × _____ = 42

_____ × _____ = 42

42 ÷ 6 = _____

42 ÷ _____ = _____

2. 9 × _____ = 36

_____ × _____ = 36

36 ÷ 4 = _____

36 ÷ _____ = _____

Write a fact family for each set of numbers.

3. 6, 3, 18

_____

4. 5, 5, 25

_____

5. Reasoning Why does the fact family for 81 and 9 have only two number sentences?

_____

_____

_____

Test Prep

6. Which number sentence completes the fact family?

9 × 6 = 54   54 ÷ 9 = 6   54 ÷ 6 = 9

A. 9 × 9 = 81   **B.** 6 × 9 = 54   **C.** 6 × 6 = 36   **D.** 8 × 6 = 48

7. Writing in Math Find two ways to divide 16 evenly. Explain.

_____

_____

Name_____

Division Facts

Thinking about multiplication facts can help when you want to divide. For example: Sunny and her father are packing oranges. They have 42 oranges. Each crate holds 6 oranges. How many crates do they need?

What You Think	**What You Say**	**What You Write**
What number times 6 = 42?	42 divided by 6 is what number?	$42 \div 6 = 7$
_____ $\times$ 6 = 42	**or**	**or**
7 times 6 equals 42 $7 \times 6 = 42$	How many times does 6 go into 42?	$6\overline{)42}$ with 7 above

---

1. $16 \div 2 =$ _____

2. $12 \div 4 =$ _____

3. $50 \div 5 =$ _____

4. $24 \div 8 =$ _____

5. $5\overline{)30}$ _____

6. $7\overline{)49}$ _____

7. $7\overline{)56}$ _____

8. $8\overline{)64}$ _____

9. Reasoning If $66 \div 6 = 11$, what is $66 \div 11$? Explain.

_____

_____

_____

10. A ticket to ride the roller coaster costs $3. How many rides can you get for $15? _____

11. Steve spends $24 on books. Books cost $8 each. How many books did Steve buy? _____

Division Facts

1. $9 \div 3 =$ _____   **2.** $21 \div 7 =$ _____   **3.** $30 \div 5 =$ _____

4. $56 \div 8 =$ _____   **5.** $72 \div 9 =$ _____   **6.** $48 \div 8 =$ _____

7. $9\overline{)81}$ _____   **8.** $6\overline{)54}$ _____   **9.** $7\overline{)49}$ _____   **10.** $3\overline{)27}$ _____

11. Reasoning If $44 \div 4 = 11$, what is $44 \div 11$? Explain.

_____

_____

_____

_____

12. Taylor bought a CD for $10. How many CDs can she buy for $40?

_____

13. Christian placed an order with the book club. He purchased 2 books for $3 each and a stamp-making kit that costs $5. What was his total?

_____

Test Prep

14. Which is the quotient of $48 \div 6$?

    A. 8   **B.** 6   **C.** 4   **D.** 9

15. Writing in Math If $9 \times 8 = 72$, then 72 divided by 8 is what number? Explain how you know without actually finding the quotient.

_____

_____

_____

_____

Special Quotients

There are special rules for dividing numbers by 1 and by 0.

Rule: A number divided by 1 is that number.

Examples: $4 \div 1 = 4$ $55 \div 1 = 55$

Rule: A number divided by itself (except 0) is 1.

Examples: $17 \div 17 = 1$ $135 \div 135 = 1$

Rule: Zero divided by a number (except 0) is 0.

Examples: $0 \div 4 = 0$ $0 \div 15 = 0$

Rule: You cannot divide a number by zero.

Examples: $7 \div 0$ cannot be done. $12 \div 0$ cannot be done.

---

1. $0 \div 2 =$ _____

2. $4 \div 4 =$ _____

3. $7\overline{)0}$ _____

4. $9\overline{)9}$ _____

5. $0 \div 3 =$ _____

6. $10\overline{)10}$ _____

7. $11\overline{)0}$ _____

8. $11 \div 1 =$ _____

Compare. Use >, <, or = for each $\bigcirc$.

9. $6 \div 6 \bigcirc 3 \div 3$

10. $7 \div 1 \bigcirc 8 \div 8$

11. $0 \div 5 \bigcirc 3 \div 1$

12. $0 \div 4 \bigcirc 0 \div 9$

13. $5 \div 5 \bigcirc 0 \div 5$

14. $7 \div 7 \bigcirc 9 \div 9$

15. $8 \div 1 \bigcirc 0 \div 8$

16. $9 \div 9 \bigcirc 9 \div 1$

17. $0 \div 12 \bigcirc 12 \div 1$

18. $0 \div 11 \bigcirc 0 \div 15$

19. Number Sense If $a \div b = 0$, what do you know about a?

_____

Special Quotients

1. $0 \div 10 =$ _____ **2.** $7 \div 1 =$ _____ **3.** $8 \div 8 =$ _____

4. $9 \div 9 =$ _____ **5.** $0 \div 5 =$ _____ **6.** $5 \div 1 =$ _____

7. $1\overline{)4}$ _____ **8.** $8\overline{)0}$ _____ **9.** $3\overline{)3}$ _____ **10.** $1\overline{)6}$ _____

11. Number Sense If $x \div 9 = 1$, how do you know what x is? Explain.

_____

_____

12. Kenneth has 22 math problems to do for homework. He has 12 problems done. How many more problems does he have left? If he completes 1 problem every minute, how many more minutes does he have to work?

_____

13. There are 8 people who would like to share a box of granola bars that contains 8 bars. How many granola bars does each person get if they share equally?

_____

Test Prep

14. Which is the quotient of $20 \div 20$?

A. 20   **B.** 2   **C.** 1   **D.** 0

15. Writing in Math Write a rule for the following number sentence: $0 \div 7 = 0$.

_____

_____

_____

_____

Name_____

Multiplication and Division Stories

Tile Floor Darren is laying a tile floor in the hallway. The pattern for the floor is shown to the right.

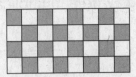

First, use Darren's tile floor to write a multiplication story for 4 × 8 = 32.

Second, use Darren's tile floor to write a division story for 32 ÷ 4 = 8.

> Darren's tile floor has 4 rows with 8 pieces of tile in each row. How many pieces of tile are there in all?

> Darren has 32 small triangles. He needs 4 for each shaded square. How many shaded squares can he make with the small triangles?

Use the data in the table to write a multiplication or a division story for each number fact. Solve.

Building Supplies	Number in a Box
Fasteners	6
Bolts	12

1. 6 × 4

_____

_____

_____

2. 12 ÷ 4

_____

_____

_____

Multiplication and Division Stories

Reasoning Write a multiplication or division story for each number fact. Solve.

1. $12 \div 3 =$ _____

_____

2. $4 \times 5 =$ _____

_____

3. $50 \div 10 =$ _____

_____

4. $3 \times 9 =$ _____

_____

Use the data in the table to write a multiplication story for the number fact. Solve.

First Aid Kit

Supply	Number in Kit
Bandages	4
Cleanser pads	6
Cotton balls	12

5. $2 \times 6 =$ _____

_____

_____

Test Prep

6. Which is the quotient of $28 \div 7$?

A. 14   **B.** 9   **C.** 6   **D.** 4

7. Writing in Math Write a division story for 12 and 3.

_____

_____

PROBLEM-SOLVING SKILL

Multiple-Step Problems

Lawn Cutting Chad and his brother Brad cut lawns in their neighborhood to make money. They charge $20 per lawn. One weekend, Brad cut 4 lawns, and Chad cut 3 lawns. How much money did they earn altogether?

Solution One

Hidden Question: How many lawns did they mow altogether?

Chad cut 3 lawns, Brad cut 4 lawns.

$$3 + 4 = 7$$

They cut 7 lawns.

Question in the Problem: How much money did they earn altogether?

$$7 \text{ lawns} \times \$20 = \$140$$

Chad and Brad earned $140.

Solution Two

Hidden Question 1: How much money did Chad get for cutting lawns?

$$3 \times \$20 = \$60$$

Hidden Question 2: How much money did Brad get for cutting lawns?

$$4 \times \$20 = \$80$$

Question in the Problem: How much money did they earn altogether?

$$\$60 + \$80 = \$140$$

Chad and Brad earned $140.

Write and answer the hidden question or questions. Then solve the problem. Write your answer in a complete sentence.

1. Keisha sold 8 ribbons. Then she sold 6 pins. The ribbons sold for $3; the pins sold for $2. How much money did Keisha make?

_____

_____

_____

_____

_____

_____

_____

Name_____

Multiple-Step Problems

Write and answer the hidden question or questions. Then solve the problem. Write your answer in a complete sentence.

1. Mario and his family went to the county fair. They bought 2 adult passes and 3 children's passes. What was the total cost for the family?

County Fair Admission	
Adults	$5.00
Students	$3.00
Children	$2.00

_____

_____

_____

2. A bus has 12 rows with 1 seat in each row on one side and 12 rows with 2 seats in each row on the other side. How many seats does the bus have altogether?

_____

_____

_____

3. **Writing in Math** Write a problem about going to the laundromat that has a hidden question. A single load of laundry costs $2 and a double load costs $4. Solve your problem.

_____

_____

_____

Writing and Evaluating Expressions

How to evaluate a multiplication expression:

Evaluate $5n$ for $n = 8$. Remember, $5n$ means the same as $5 \times n$.

First, substitute 8 for n. Then multiply.

$5 \times n = ?$
$5 \times 8 = ?$
$5 \times 8 = 40$

How to evaluate a division expression:

Evaluate $g \div 6$ for $g = 42$.

First, substitute 42 for g. Then divide.

$g \div 6 = ?$
$42 \div 6 = ?$
$42 \div 6 = 7$

How to evaluate expressions with more than one operation:

Evaluate $(4f) + 7$ for $f = 5$.

First, substitute 5 for f. Then do the computations inside the parentheses first.

$(4 \times f) + 7 = ?$
$(4 \times 5) + 7 = ?$
$20 + 7 = 27$

Evaluate each expression for $m = 4$.

1. $6m =$ _____

2. $\frac{m}{2} =$ _____

3. $20 \div m =$ _____

4. $(7m) + 2 =$ _____

5. Number Sense Write an expression that equals 50 for $n = 10$. _____

Evaluate each expression for $w = 7$.

6. $5 \times w =$ _____

7. $7 \div w =$ _____

8. $9w =$ _____

9. $3 \times (2 + w) =$ _____

Evaluate each expression.

10. $8 \times (4 + k)$ for $k = 2$ _____

11. $h \div (6 \times 1)$ for $h = 30$ _____

Writing and Evaluating Expressions

Evaluate each expression for $b = 6$.

1. $6b =$ _____   **2.** $\frac{42}{b} =$ _____   **3.** $5b =$ _____   **4.** $\frac{b}{3} =$ _____

Evaluate each expression for $c = 4$.

5. $\frac{c}{2} =$ _____   **6.** $12c$ _____   **7.** $8c$ _____   **8.** $\frac{16}{c} =$ _____

Evaluate each expression.

9. $(84 \div z) - 6$ for $z = 7$ _____   **10.** $(48 \div h) \times 2$ for $h = 8$ _____

Draw a picture that shows the main idea. Then write and evaluate an expression to solve the problem.

11. Diedre helps read to the kindergarten class. She is assigned to q students. She reads for 10 min with each student. Write an expression to represent the total number of minutes Diedre reads with kindergarten students. Evaluate the expression for $q = 5$.

_____

_____

Test Prep

12. Solve.
   $24 \div n = 12$

   A. $n = 5$ **B.** $n = 4$ **C.** $n = 3$ **D.** $n = 2$

13. Writing in Math Keith wrote the expression $10d$ to represent the number of dimes in d dollars. Is Keith's expression correct? Explain.

_____

_____

Find a Rule

Complete the table. Start with the number in the **IN** column. What rule tells you how to find the number in the **OUT** column? Write the rule.

What You Think

IN	OUT
2	10
4	20
6	30
8	
n	

$2 \times 5 = 10$

$4 \times 5 = 20$

$6 \times 5 = 30$

$8 \times 5 = 40$

A rule is *multiply by 5*.

What You Write

IN	OUT
2	10
4	20
6	30
8	40
n	$n \times 5$

The rule *multiply by 5* is written as $n \times 5$.

Complete each table. Write the rule.

1.

In	20	25	35	55	n
Out	4	5	7		

_____

2.

In	3	5	7	9	n
Out	9	15	21		

_____

3.

In	2	5	7	10	n
Out	14	35	49		

_____

Find a Rule

Complete each table. Write the rule.

1.

In	7	6	5	4	3	n
Out	21	18	15	12		

_____

2.

In	5	10	15	20	25	n
Out	1	2	3	4		

_____

In one week, Lyle read 40 pages in his book and his dad gave him 5 stickers. The next week, Lyle read 16 pages and his dad gave him 2 stickers. The third week, Lyle read 56 pages and his dad gave him 7 stickers.

Pages	40	16	56	
Stickers	5	2	7	4

3. Complete the table to show how many pages Lyle had to read to receive 4 stickers from his dad.

_____

4. Write a rule for the table.

_____

Test Prep

5. What is the rule for the table at the right?

In	2	4	6	8	10
Out	14	28	42	56	70

A. Divide by 7   **B.** Multiply by 7   **C.** Divide by 8   **D.** Multiply by 8

6. **Writing in Math** Complete the table to represent the pattern in figures. Write a rule.

Figure	1	2	3
Circles			

Figure 1   Figure 2   Figure 3

Solving Multiplication and Division Equations

To solve an equation that has a variable you need to test several numbers for the variable. Find the one number that makes the equation true.

Solve the equation $4n = 28$ by testing these values for n: 5, 6, and 7.

Try	$n = 5$	$n = 6$	$n = 7$
Find $4n$	$4 \times 5 = 20$	$4 \times 6 = 24$	$4 \times 7 = 28$
Does $4n = 28$?	No	No	Yes

The solution to the equation is $n = 7$, because $4 \times 7 = 28$.

Solve the equation $g \div 5 = 9$ by testing these values for g: 30, 45, and 60.

Try	$g = 30$	$g = 45$	$g = 60$
Find $g \div 5$	$30 \div 5 = 6$	$45 \div 5 = 9$	$60 \div 5 = 12$
Does $g \div 5 = 9$?	No	Yes	No

The solution to the equation is $g = 45$, because $45 \div 5 = 9$.

Solve each equation by testing these values for k: 2, 4, and 6.

1. $k \div 2 = 3$ _____

2. $5k = 30$ _____

3. $36 \div k = 9$ _____

4. $8k = 16$ _____

Solve each equation by testing these values for n: 12, 16, and 24.

5. $n \div 6 = 4$ _____

6. $n \div 4 = 4$ _____

7. $n \times 2 = 24$ _____

8. $n \div 4 = 3$ _____

9. Number Sense What is the value of b in the equation $b \times 7 = 63$? How do you know?

Solving Multiplication and Division Equations

Solve each equation by testing these values for y: 3, 4, 6, and 12.

1. $5 \times y = 15$ _____

2. $\frac{24}{y} = 4$ _____

Solve each equation by testing these values for a: 7, 8, 77, and 80.

3. $14 \div a = 2$ _____

4. $7 \times 11 = a$ _____

5. John's teacher made 20 First Day of School Kits. There were only 4 kits of each color. Solve the equation $4k = 20$ by testing these values for k: 2, 3, 4, and 5, to find how many different colors John's teacher used for the kits.

_____

Test Prep

6. Which is the solution for $n \div 6 = 8$?

A. 8   **B.** 16   **C.** 32   **D.** 48

7. Writing in Math Draw a picture and write an expression you could use to find the number of magazines in m rows if there are 7 magazines in each row. Use your expression to find the number of magazines in 3 rows.

Alberto is planning a party. He needs to purchase the following items:

How much will Alberto have to spend if he purchases 2 paper tablecloths?

$11 + $11 = $22

2 × $11 = $22

He will have to spend $22.

Party Supplies

Item	Price
Napkins	$2
Paper plates	$5
Cups	$9
Balloons	$10
Paper tablecloth	$11
Juice	$12

Use the chart above to answer the following questions.

1. Alberto purchased 6 packages of paper plates. The addition sentence that shows how much he spent is 5 + 5 + 5 + 5 + 5 + 5 = 30. Write the multiplication sentence for this addition sentence.

_____

2. Since many people are coming to the party, Alberto purchased 9 packages of napkins. Complete the fact family.

   2 × _____ = 18   18 ÷ 9 = _____

   18 ÷ 2 = _____   _____ × _____ = 18

How much did Alberto spend on

3. 5 bottles of juice?   _____

4. 7 packages of cups?   _____

5. 4 packages of paper plates?   _____

6. Alberto spent $50 on balloons. How many bags of balloons did he purchase?   _____

Name_____

Dr. Seuss's Books

Dr. Seuss was one of America's most famous authors and illustrators of children's books. His real name was Theodore Geisel. Geisel was born in 1904 in Springfield, Massachusetts. Geisel's first job was drawing cartoon advertisements for a company that made bug spray. Many of the cartoon characters Geisel drew for that job turned into the characters he used in his books.

1. Each Dr. Seuss hardcover book costs about $9. How much would you pay if you bought 5 books? _____

2. Oscar found a special sale on Dr. Seuss books. Each book costs the same price. He paid $36 for 6 books. How much did he pay for each book? _____

Mrs. Melvin, a librarian, found a special on-line offer for Dr. Seuss books. Each book costs $2.

3. How much did Mrs. Melvin pay for 6 books? _____

4. If Mrs. Melvin paid $20 for *n* books, how many books did she order? _____

One of Dr. Seuss's most famous books is called *The Foot Book*.

5. There are 27 pages in this book. There are about 27 drawings. On the average, about how many drawings are on each page?

_____

6. A close study of this book shows that on 6 pages the word *feet* appears 2 times. What is the total number of times the word appears on those 6 pages? _____

7. On every 9th page of this book, the word *feet* appears 3 times. Since there are 27 pages in the book, how many pages have the word *feet* written 3 times? _____

Telling Time

You can read the time shown on the analog and digital clocks as either five forty or twenty minutes to six.

A.M. includes times from midnight until noon, and P.M. includes times from noon until midnight.

Write the time shown on each clock in two ways.

1. [10:40]

2.

_____   _____

_____   _____

_____   _____

3. Write a reasonable time for leaving school. Include A.M. or P.M.

_____

4. Reasoning Would you most likely be asleep at 11:00 A.M. or 11:00 P.M.?

_____

Name_____

Telling Time

Write the time shown on each clock in two ways.

1.

_____

_____

2.

_____

_____

3. Jessica has a piano lesson on Saturday at 2:00. Is it A.M. or P.M.? _____

4. **Reasoning** The digits displayed on this clock are all the same number. List all of the times when this is true.

_____

5. **Estimation** The time is 2:57 P.M. About what time will it be in an hour and a half? _____

Test Prep

6. Which time is shown on the clock?

   A. 8:24   **B.** 8:34

   C. 8:44   **D.** 8:54

7. **Writing in Math** List two events that could happen in the A.M. and two events that could happen in the P.M.

_____

_____

_____

Units of Time

You can use the information in the table to compare different amounts of time. For example:

Which is longer, 3 years or
40 months?
According to the table,
1 year = 12 months.

1 year = 12 months
3 years = 36 months

$$\begin{array}{r} 12 \\ \times\ 3 \\ \hline 36 \end{array}$$

40 months > 36 months
40 months > 3 years

So 40 months is longer
than 3 years.

Units of Time
1 minute = 60 seconds
1 hour = 60 minutes
1 day = 24 hours
1 week = 7 days
1 month = about 4 weeks
1 year = 52 weeks
1 year = 12 months
1 year = 365 days
1 leap year = 366 days
1 decade = 10 years
1 century = 100 years
1 millennium = 1,000 years

Write <, >, or = for each ◯ .

1. 1 year ◯ 350 days

2. 25 months ◯ 2 years

3. 20 decades ◯ 2 centuries

4. 720 days ◯ 2 years

5. 8 decades ◯ 1 century

6. 72 hours ◯ 3 days

7. 240 minutes ◯ 3 hours

8. 3 years ◯ 120 months

9. **Number Sense** How many hours are in 2 days? _____

10. A score is 20 years. How many years is 5 score? _____

11. Dave's goldfish lived for 2 years, 8 months.
Chris's goldfish lived for 35 months. Whose
goldfish lived longer? _____

12. Tree A lived for 6 decades and 5 years. Tree B
lived for 58 years. Which tree lived longer? _____

Name_____

Units of Time

Write >, <, or = for each ◯.

1. 48 hours ◯ 4 days

2. 1 year ◯ 12 months

3. 60 minutes ◯ 2 hours

4. 17 days ◯ 2 weeks

5. 5 months ◯ 40 weeks

6. 1 millennium ◯ 10 centuries

7. 6 decades ◯ 1 century

8. 5 decades ◯ 48 years

9. Cheryl's grandparents have been married for 6 decades. How many years have they been married?

_____

10. Tom was in elementary school from 1997 to 2002. How much time was that in years? _____

The Declaration of Independence was signed on July 4, 1776. The United States celebrated the bicentennial on July 4, 1976. How much time was that in

11. years? _____

12. decades? _____

Test Prep

13. 49 days =

A. 5 weeks   **B.** 6 weeks   **C.** 7 weeks   **D.** 8 weeks

14. **Writing in Math** Which is longer: 180 sec or 3 min? Explain how you decided.

_____

_____

_____

_____

Name _____

Elapsed Time

Elapsed time problems can be solved in more than one way.

Find the elapsed time between 8:50 A.M. and 11:00 A.M.

One Way

8:50 to 9:00 is 10 min

9:00 to 11:00 is 2 hr

That's 2 hr and
10 min.

Another Way

8:50 to 10:50 is 2 hr

10:50 to 11:00 is
10 min

That's 2 hr and
10 min.

Find each elapsed time.

1. Start: 9:00 A.M.
Finish: 1:30 P.M.   _____

2. Start: 5:15 P.M.
Finish: 8:20 P.M.   _____

3. Start: 7:35 A.M.
Finish: 8:57 A.M.   _____

Write the time each clock will show in 35 min.

4.

_____

5.

_____

6. Number Sense Is the elapsed time from 3:35 A.M. to
11:00 A.M. more than or less than 7 hr? Explain.

_____

_____

_____

Name_____

Elapsed Time

Find each elapsed time.

1. Start: 3:52 P.M.
Finish: 4:10 P.M.

_____

2. Start: 11:35 A.M.
Finish: 12:25 P.M.

_____

3. Start: 3:15 P.M.
Finish: 5:00 P.M.

_____

4. Start: 8:20 A.M.
Finish: 2:35 P.M.

_____

Write the time each clock will show in 30 min.

5.

_____

6.

_____

7.

_____

8. Number Sense Max says that the elapsed time from
11:55 A.M. to 1:10 P.M. is more than an hour and a half. Is he
correct? Explain.

_____

Test Prep

9. Gary began eating lunch at 12:17 P.M. and finished at
1:01 P.M. Which is the elapsed time?

A. 41 min   **B.** 42 min   **C.** 43 min   **D.** 44 min

10. Writing in Math Ella went in the swimming pool
at 1:20 P.M. She swam for 1 hr and 20 min.
What time was it when she finished swimming?

_____

PROBLEM-SOLVING SKILL
Writing to Compare

Football Practice

	Start Time	Water Break	Drills	End Time
Team A	3:00	3:45	4:00	5:00
Team B	3:30	4:00	4:05	5:15

Comparison Statements	Tips for Writing Good Comparisons
Team B starts practice 30 min later than Team A, but ends 15 min later. Team A gets a water break sooner than Team B, and the break is longer.	Use comparison words such as "later," "fewer," and "same."
Team A begins practice at 3:00 and ends at 5:00. That's 2 hr. Team B begins practice at 3:30 and ends at 5:15. That's 1 hr and 45 min. Team A has a longer practice.	Sometimes you can do calculations and compare the results.

1. In which corral does the cow roping last the longest?

_____

County Fair

Event		Corral No. 1	Corral No. 2
Bronco riding	Start	9:05	8:45
	End	10:15	10:05
Cow roping	Start	10:20	10:10
	End	11:35	11:15
Hog calling	Start	11:45	11:25
	End	1:10	1:05

2. How long does the hog calling last in Corral No. 1?

_____

_____

3. In Corral No. 1, how much time is there from the start of the bronco riding to the end of the cow roping?

_____

Name_____

Writing to Compare

1. Write two statements comparing the times on the train schedule.

Train Schedule

Stop	Downtown	A	B	C	D	E	F	G	Uptown
Blue Line	8:00	8:02	8:06	8:10	8:20	8:26	8:32	8:40	8:46
Red Line	8:05	—	8:10	8:14	—	8:28	—	8:38	8:44

_____

_____

_____

_____

Summer Day-Camp Schedule

Group 1	Group 2	Times
First aid	Badminton	9:50–10:20
Swimming	Gardening	10:25–11:00
Computers	Sewing	11:05–11:35
Writing	Swimming	11:40–12:05
Lunch	Lunch	12:10–12:45

2. How long is the first-aid class?   _____

3. How long is the gardening class?   _____

4. How much time do campers have between
classes?   _____

5. Write two statements comparing the schedules of Group 1 and Group 2.

_____

_____

Calendars

Roberto is going on a business trip to Oregon on March 12. He will be gone two weeks and one day. What date will he return home?

March

S	M	T	W	T	F	S
			1	2	3	4
5	6	7	8	9	10	11
12	13	14	15	16	17	18
19	20	21	22	23	24	25
26	27	28	29	30	31	

Move down two rows for two weeks and one column to the right for one day. Roberto will return home on March 27.

Numbers such as twenty-seventh are called ordinal numbers. They are used to tell order. Some other examples of ordinal numbers are first, fourth, thirteenth, and seventy-first.

November

S	M	T	W	T	F	S
			1	2	3	4
5	6	7	8	9	10	11
12	13	14	15	16	17	18
19	20	21	22	23	24	25
26	27	28	29	30		

December

S	M	T	W	T	F	S
					1	2
3	4	5	6	7	8	9
10	11	12	13	14	15	16
17	18	19	20	21	22	23
24/31	25	26	27	28	29	30

Find the date

1. two weeks after November 7. _____

2. one week before November 13. _____

3. two weeks after December 7. _____

4. three weeks before December 26. _____

5. **Number Sense** How could you find the date two weeks after November 3, without a calendar? _____

6. Bill's birthday was three weeks before December 6. What date is Bill's birthday? _____

Calendars

Use the October and November calendars for 1–8.

October						
S	M	T	W	T	F	S
				1	2	3
4	5	6	7	8	9	10
11	12	13	14	15	16	17
18	19	20	21	22	23	24
25	26	27	28	29	30	31

November						
S	M	T	W	T	F	S
1	2	3	4	5	6	7
8	9	10	11	12	13	14
15	16	17	18	19	20	21
22	23	24	25	26	27	28
29	30					

Find the date

1. six weeks after October 9th.

2. two weeks before November 24th.

3. one week after October 30th.

4. three weeks after November 1st.

5. Suppose you have guitar lessons every Wednesday. What are the dates of your lessons in October?

6. Number Sense Find the date five days after November 30, without a calendar. _____

Test Prep

7. Which amount of time is greatest?

A. 30 days

B. the number of days in October

C. the number of days in November

D. All of the above are equal.

8. Writing in Math Use the October calendar. Explain how you can find the number of days that are between October 8th and October 23rd without counting the days.

_____

_____

Pictographs

A pictograph uses pictures or symbols to show data.

Endangered Species in the United States

Group	Number
Amphibians	🐾 🐾 🐾 🐾 🐾
Arachnids	🐾 🐾 🐾 🐾 🐾 🐾
Crustaceans	🐾 🐾 🐾 🐾 🐾 🐾 🐾 🐾 🐾
Reptiles	🐾 🐾 🐾 🐾 🐾 🐾 🐾

Each 🐾 = 2 animals

Example

	How many types of arachnids are endangered?
What you think	Look next to Arachnids. There are 6 paws. Each 🐾 = 2 animals. 2, 4, 6, 8, 10, 12
What you write	There are 12 types of arachnids in the United States that are endangered.

Favorite Ways of Communicating with a Long-Distance Friend

E-mail	☺ ☺ ☺ ☾
Telephone	☺ ☺ ☺ ☺ ☺
Letters	☺ ☾

Each ☺ = 100 people

About how many people prefer to communicate by

1. e-mail? _____

2. telephone? _____

3. letter? _____

4. About how many more people prefer to use e-mail than letters?

_____

5. **Number Sense** If each symbol on a pictograph equals 100 people, how many symbols would you need to show 750 people?

_____

Pictographs

How many people prefer a

Favorite Books

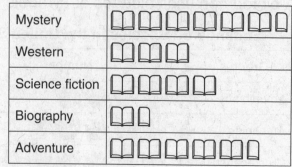

1. western book?

_____

2. mystery book?

_____

Each 📖 = 10 people.

3. About how many more people will read an adventure book than a science-fiction book?

_____

4. **Number Sense** Do more than or less than twice as many people prefer science fiction than biography?

_____

5. Make a pictograph of the data about Angela's leaf collection.

Angela's Leaf Collection	
Tamarac	11
Silver birch	7
Oak	5
Maple	10
Sassafras	15

Test Prep

Use the Favorite Books pictograph for 6 and 7.

6. Which type of book was chosen by about 15 people?

   A. Adventure   **B.** Biography   **C.** Mystery   **D.** Science fiction

7. **Writing in Math** Write your own problem for this pictograph. Then solve it.

_____

_____

Line Plots

Line plots show data along a number line. Each X represents one number in the data.

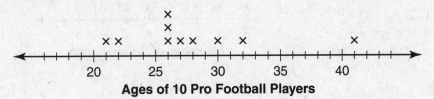

Ages of 10 Pro Football Players

Since there is one X above the 22, one of the pro football players is 22 years old.

Since there are three Xs above the 26, three of the pro football players are 26 years old.

The oldest player is 41 years old and the youngest player is 21.

The 41-year-old player is older than all of the other players. This number is called an outlier, since it is very different than the rest of the numbers.

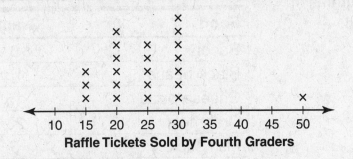

Raffle Tickets Sold by Fourth Graders

How many fourth graders sold

1. 15 raffle tickets? _____

2. 20 raffle tickets? _____

3. How many raffle tickets did most
fourth graders sell? _____

4. Number Sense Is there an outlier in the data set? Explain.

_____

_____

Line Plots

How many soccer teams scored

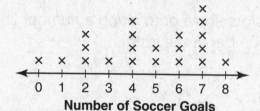

Number of Soccer Goals

1. 5 goals?

   _____

2. 2 goals?

   _____

3. 3 goals?

   _____

4. **Number Sense** Suppose the line plot was made
   in the middle of the season. For the teams that
   have scored 7 goals, how many goals do you
   predict they will score at the end of the season? _____

5. Make a line plot of the grams of
   protein in the food listed.

Grams of Protein in One Serving

Food	Grams
Bacon	6
Black beans	15
Cheese pizza	15
Crabmeat	23
Fish stick	6
Great northern beans	14

Test Prep

Use the Soccer League line plot for 6 and 7.

6. How many teams are recorded on the line plot?

   A. 18   **B.** 19   **C.** 20   **D.** 21

7. **Writing in Math** Is there an outlier in the data? Explain.

_____

Name_____

Bar Graphs

How to make a bar graph to display data

Data File

Lengths of U.S. States	
State	**Length**
Florida	500 mi
Georgia	300 mi
Kansas	400 mi
Utah	350 mi

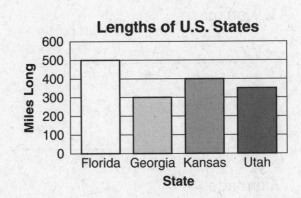

Step 1: Choose a scale.

Step 2: Draw and label the side and bottom of the graph.

Step 3: Draw a bar on the graph for each number in the data file.

Step 4: Give the graph a title. The title should be the subject of the graph.

1. Use the data at the right. Draw a bar graph with the number of points scored on the vertical axis and the players' names on the horizontal axis. Give the graph a title.

Player	Points Scored
Vito	30
Ray	25
Pat	35

Name_____

Bar Graphs

How many free-throw shots did

1. Jan make?

_____

2. Bob make?

_____

Who made

3. 35 free-throw shots?

_____

4. 15 free-throw shots?

_____

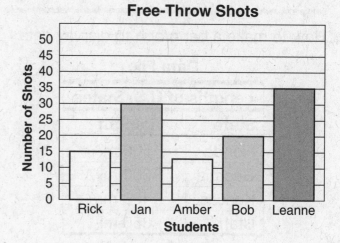

Free-Throw Shots

5. Number Sense How can you easily tell who completed about the same number of free-throw shots?

_____

_____

Test Prep

6. What are the numbers that show the units on a graph called?

   A. Scale   **B.** Intervals   **C.** Horizontal axis   **D.** Vertical axis

7. Writing in Math Describe the interval you would use for a bar graph if the data ranges from 12 to 39 units.

_____

_____

_____

Graphing Ordered Pairs

To name the location of the star on the grid:

Step 1:

Start at (0, 0).

Step 2:

Move right 3 spaces.

Step 3:

Move up 4 spaces.

The star is located at (3, 4).

The first number in an ordered pair tells how many spaces to move to the right. The second number tells how many spaces to move up. Name the ordered pair for the circle. (6, 7)

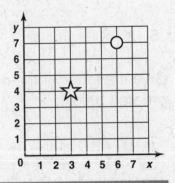

An ordered pair names a point on a grid.

Name the ordered pair for each point.

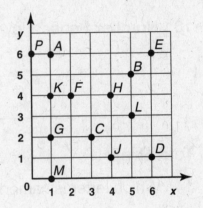

1. C _____

2. D _____

3. K _____

4. H _____

Give the letter of the point named by each ordered pair.

5. (5, 5) _____   **6.** (6, 6) _____   **7.** (2, 4) _____

Plot the following points on the coordinate grid below.

8. W(2, 4)

9. X(5, 6)

10. Y(3, 0)

11. Z(6, 1)

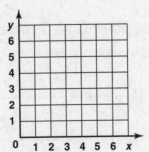

Name_____

Graphing Ordered Pairs

Name the ordered pair for each point.

1. P _____

2. H _____

3. L _____

4. F _____

5. K _____

6. Z _____

Give the letter of the point named by each ordered pair.

7. (7, 8) _____

8. (10, 1) _____

9. (2, 8) _____

10. (0, 6) _____

11. (10, 10) _____

12. (1, 10) _____

13. **Number Sense** How are the coordinates (1, 2) and (3, 2) related?

_____

_____

Test Prep

14. Which letter is named by (9, 3)?

   A. A

   B. B

   C. C

   D. D

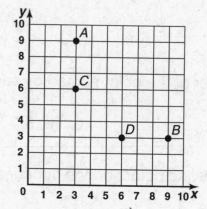

15. **Writing in Math** Explain how to plot point G (2, 7) on a coordinate grid.

_____

_____

_____

Line Graphs

Here is how to make a line graph.

Tomato Plant Growth

Day	Height (in cm)
5	5
10	7
15	10
20	20
25	30

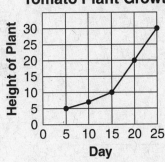

Tomato Plant Growth

Step 1	**Step 2**	**Step 3**	**Step 4**
Choose an interval for each scale. Draw and label the side and bottom of the graph. Put time on the bottom.	Plot a point for each row in the data file. Plot (5, 5), (10, 7), and so on.	Draw a line from each point to the next one, in order.	Give the graph a title. The title should describe the subject of the graph.

Jones School Recycling

Month	Bins of Paper Recycled
1	5
2	15
3	35
4	40

1. The Jones School began a recycling program. After each month, students record how many bins of paper the school recycled. Draw a line graph that shows this data. Put the months of the school year at the bottom.

Name_____

Line Graphs

In the Fourth-Grade Reading Program, how many pages were read in

1. October?

_____

2. February?

_____

3. April?

_____

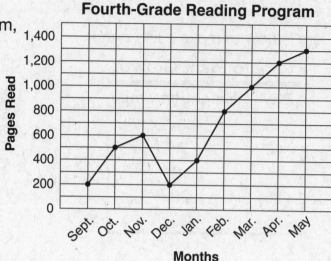

Fourth-Grade Reading Program

4. Draw a line graph showing Barbara's exercise time.

Barbara's Exercise Times

Day	Length of Time
1	25 min
2	30 min
3	40 min

5. Reasoning What is the trend in the data?

_____

_____

Test Prep

6. What is an increase or decrease on a line graph called?

  A. Trend   **B.** Median   **C.** Mode   **D.** Range

7. Writing in Math Explain how a line graph is similar to a bar graph.

_____

PROBLEM-SOLVING STRATEGY
Make a Graph

Pitcher Chris recorded 3 strikeouts in his first game, 5 in his second game, 7 in his third game, 10 in his fourth game, and 11 in his fifth game. How did his number of strikeouts change over the course of the five games he pitched?

Read and Understand

Step 1: What do you know?

I know the number of strikeouts Chris made each game.

Step 2: What are you trying to find?

How the number of strikeouts changed

Plan and Solve

Step 3: What strategy will you use?

A: Set up the bar graph.
B: Enter the known data.
C: Read the graph. Look for a pattern.

Answer: The number of strikeouts increased each game.

Strategy: Make a bar graph

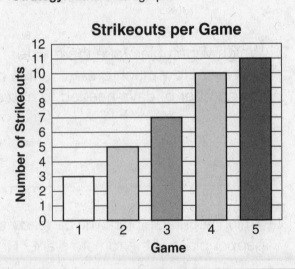

Solve. Write your answer in a complete sentence.

1. How much warmer is it, on average, in April than in January?

_____

_____

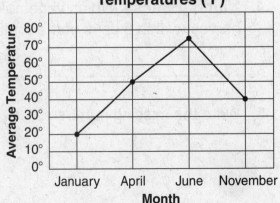

Name_____

Make a Graph

Complete the graph to solve each problem.

1.

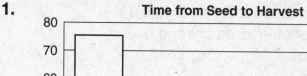

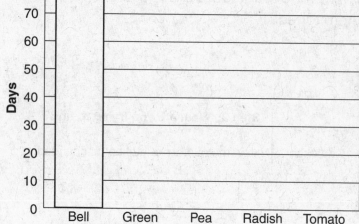

Time from Seed to Harvest

Vegetable	Days
Bell pepper	75
Green bean	56
Pea	75
Radish	23
Tomato	73

2. Which vegetables take the greatest amount of time to harvest? How much greater is this number of days than the number of days needed to harvest radishes?

_____

_____

3. Which vegetable plant will be ready to harvest earlier, the bell pepper plant or the tomato plant? How many days earlier?

_____

4. Number Sense Which vegetable plants will be ready to harvest within 5 days of the tomato plant?

_____

5. Write the missing numbers.   7, 10, 13, 16, _____, _____, _____

Name_____

Median, Mode, and Range

You can summarize data by using median, mode, and range.

Data	Median	Mode	Range
	List the data in order from smallest to largest. Then find the number in the middle.	Find the number or numbers that occur most often. A set may have more than one mode.	Subtract the least number from the greatest number.
31, 32, 35, 40, 61, 61, 62	40 is the number in the middle. The median is 40.	61 is the number that occurs most often. 61 is the mode.	62 − 31 = 31 The range is 31.
25, 25, 26, 30, 47, 47, 48	The median is 30.	The modes are 25 and 47.	48 − 25 = 23 The range is 23.

Find the median, mode, and range of each set of data.

1. 8, 9, 3, 4, 6, 8, 7

_____

2. 8, 11, 10, 12, 15, 13, 10

_____

3. Reasoning Jill said the mode of the following set is 4. Is she correct? Explain. 1, 8, 7, 4, 2, 2

_____

_____

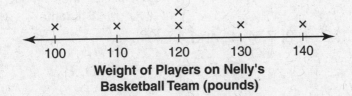

Weight of Players on Nelly's Basketball Team (pounds)

4. Find the mode, median, and range of the weights of the players on Nelly's basketball team.

_____

Name_____

Median, Mode, and Range

Find the median, mode, and range of each set of data.

1. 1, 3, 10, 8, 7, 3, 11

_____

2. 48, 50, 62, 50, 54

_____

3. 92, 99, 99, 106, 99, 97

_____

4. 80, 85, 87, 80, 89

_____

5. 10, 11, 12, 14, 10, 15, 16, 10, 11, 9, 10, 17, 10

_____

6. 5, 15, 17, 5, 11, 5, 10, 12, 5, 7, 14, 9, 5

_____

7. Number Sense Could 5 be the mode of 5, 9, 7, 5, 8, 7, 10, and 7? Explain.

_____

_____

Use the bar graph.

8. Find the median, mode, and range
of the finished journal entries.

_____

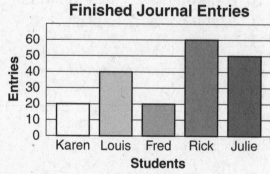

Finished Journal Entries

Test Prep

9. The range of 1, 3, 4, 6, 1, 3, 4, 2, 7, 4, 1, and 4 is

A. 5   **B.** 6   **C.** 7   **D.** 8

10. Writing in Math Tell when a set of data can have no mode.

_____

_____

Data from Surveys

To take a survey, you ask different people the same question and record their answers. Heather asked her class, "What is your favorite flavor of frozen yogurt?" Here are her results:

Favorite Flavor of Frozen Yogurt

Vanilla	IIII	4
Chocolate	~~IIII~~ IIII	9
Strawberry	III	3
Orange	I	1

We can see that Heather's classmates liked chocolate frozen yogurt the best.

Favorite Winter Olympic Sports

Bobsledding	~~IIII~~ III	
Curling	II	
Ice hockey	~~IIII~~ ~~IIII~~	
Speed skating	III	

1. How many people in the survey liked bobsledding the best? _____

2. How many people were surveyed? _____

3. According to the data, which sport is the favorite of most people? _____

4. **Number Sense** If five times as many people were surveyed, how many do you think would say they liked curling best? Explain.

_____

_____

_____

_____

Data from Surveys

Name _____

Use the data in the tally chart.

Favorite Frozen Yogurt	
Banana	|||
Blueberry	‖‖ ‖‖ ||
Strawberry	‖‖
Vanilla	‖‖ |||

1. How many people in the survey liked strawberry-flavored frozen yogurt best?

   _____

2. Which flavor of frozen yogurt received the most votes?

   _____

3. How many people liked vanilla frozen yogurt best?

   _____

4. How many people were surveyed?

   _____

5. **Number Sense** Could the frozen yogurt survey help restaurants choose flavors of frozen yogurt? Explain.

   _____

   _____

   _____

Test Prep

6. Which is the last step in taking a survey?

   A. explain the results

   B. count tallies

   C. write a survey question

   D. make a tally chart and ask the question

7. **Writing in Math** Give an example of a topic for a survey question where the results for the answers could be similar.

   _____

   _____

Misleading Graphs

Sometimes graphs can be misleading. Make sure you always look at a graph closely.

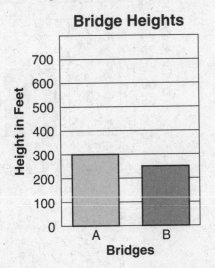

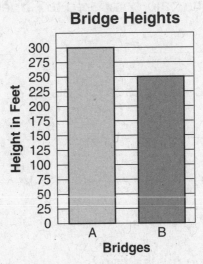

These graphs show the heights of two bridges. Look at the graph on the left. It looks as if the bridges are about the same height. However, when you look at the graph on the right, you see that Bridge A is 50 ft taller than Bridge B. The scale of the left graph is by 100s, while the scale of the right graph is by 25s.

1. Are there more students in the Math Club or in the Chemistry Club? Explain. How many students are in the Math Club? The Chemistry Club?

_____

_____

_____

_____

2. **Reasoning** Is this graph misleading? Explain.

_____

Name_____

Misleading Graphs

Use the Price Paid for CD Player bar graph for 1–4.

Price Paid for CD Player

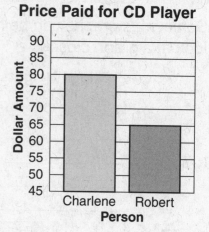

1. Looking at the graph, how much more does it seem Charlene paid compared to Robert?

_____

2. What was the cost for each CD player?

_____

_____

3. Did Charlene pay twice as much as Robert for her player? _____

4. Why is the graph misleading?

_____

Use the Party Decorations Challenge bar graph for 5–7.

Party Decorations Challenge

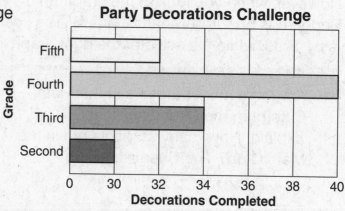

5. Looking at the graph, how many more party decorations does it seem the third grade made compared to the second grade?

_____

6. Did the fourth grade complete twice the number of party decorations compared to the third grade?

_____

Test Prep

7. **Writing in Math** Describe a better scale to use for this bar graph.

_____

_____

Name_____

Time and Money

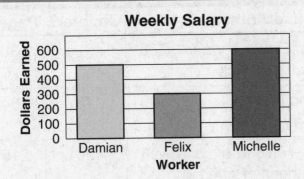

Weekly Salary

How much money does Michelle earn per week? $600

How much more money does Damian earn than Felix? $200

How can you tell by looking at the bar graph which person earned the most money? Look at the longest bar.

Clock A	**Clock B**

1. What time is shown on Clock A? _____

2. What time is shown on Clock B? _____

3. How much time has elapsed from Clock A to Clock B?

_____

Find the median, mode, and range of each set of data.

4. 17, 20, 22, 18, 19, 22, 24

_____

5. 105, 104, 104, 103, 106

_____

Name _____

The Newbery Medal

Since 1923, the Newbery Medal has been awarded by the American Library Association to authors of the most distinguished contributions to American literature for children. The award-winning books belong to a variety of genres that include biography, historical fiction, and science fiction.

Title and Author	Year	Chapters	Pages
A Year Down Yonder by Richard Peck	2001	8	130
Maniac Magee by Jerry Spinelli	1991	46	184
Jacob Have I Loved by Katherine Patterson	1981	20	215

The table above gives information about three Newbery Medal winners.

1. Complete the pictograph for the number of chapters in the three books.

Chapters in Three Newbery Medal Books

Book	Chapters
A Year Down Yonder	
Maniac Magee	

Each ■ = 2 chapters.

2. Complete the bar graph for the number of pages in each book.

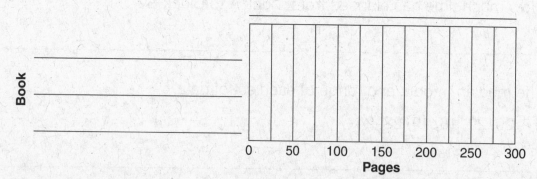

Book

0   50   100   150   200   250   300
Pages

3. Describe the pattern you see between the years the medals were awarded.

_____

Multiplying by Multiples of 10, 100, or 1,000

Patterns can help you multiply by numbers that are multiples of 10, 100, or 1,000.

$3 \times 5 = 15$	$2 \times 4 = 8$	$5 \times 7 = 35$
$3 \times 50 = 150$	$2 \times 40 = 80$	$5 \times 70 = 350$
$3 \times 500 = 1,500$	$2 \times 400 = 800$	$5 \times 700 = 3,500$
$3 \times 5,000 = 15,000$	$2 \times 4,000 = 8,000$	$5 \times 7,000 = 35,000$

To find each of the products above, first complete the basic multiplication fact, then write the same number of zeros seen in the factor that is a multiple of 10. For example:

$3 \times 500 = 1,500$

First find 3×5.   **$3 \times 5 = 15$**

Then, count the number of zeros in the multiple of 10.   **500 has 2 zeros.**

Write 2 zeros to form the product.   **1,500**

Find each product. Use mental math.

1. $8 \times 80 =$ _____

2. $6 \times 60 =$ _____

3. $7 \times 90 =$ _____

4. $5 \times 200 =$ _____

5. $3 \times 400 =$ _____

6. $7 \times 200 =$ _____

7. $5,000 \times 6 =$ _____

8. $6,000 \times 9 =$ _____

9. $3 \times 8,000 =$ _____

10. $6,000 \times 7 =$ _____

11. **Number Sense** To find 8×600, multiply 8 and 6, then write _____ zeros to form the product.

Multiplying by Multiples of 10, 100, or 1,000

Find each product. Use mental math.

1. $6 \times 70 =$ _____

2. $80 \times 2 =$ _____

3. $40 \times 9 =$ _____

4. $10 \times 3 =$ _____

5. $4 \times 500 =$ _____

6. $300 \times 9 =$ _____

7. $8 \times 600 =$ _____

8. $7 \times 400 =$ _____

9. $6 \times 2,000 =$ _____

10. $8,000 \times 5 =$ _____

11. $8 \times 6,000 =$ _____

12. $4,000 \times 3 =$ _____

13. **Number Sense** How many zeros will the product of $7 \times 5,000$ have? _____

Mr. Young has 30 times as many pencils as Jack. The whole school has 2,000 times as many pencils as Jack. If Jack has 2 pencils, how many pencils does

14. Mr. Young have?

15. the whole school have?

_____   _____

Test Prep

16. Find $3 \times 1,000$.

A. 30   **B.** 300   **C.** 3,000   **D.** 30,000

17. **Writing in Math** Wendi says that the product of 5×400 will have 2 zeros. Is she correct? Explain.

_____

_____

_____

Name_____

Estimating Products

You can use rounding or compatible numbers to estimate products.

Estimate 7 × 28.

Using rounding numbers
Round 28 to 30.
7 × 30
7 × 30 = 210

Using compatible numbers
Replace 28 with 25.
7 × 25
7 × 25 = 175

Estimate each product.

1. 6 × 88 is close to 6 × _____   **2.** 59 × 4 is close to _____ × 4

3. 7 × 31   _____   **4.** 38 × 5   _____

5. 21 × 6   _____   **6.** 3 × 53   _____

7. 5 × 790   _____   **8.** 488 × 6   _____

9. Number Sense Estimate to tell if 5 × 68 is greater than or less than 350. Tell how you decided.

_____

_____

10. Estimate how many of Part C would be made in 4 months.

_____

11. Estimate how many of Part B would be made in 3 months.

_____

12. Estimate how many of Part A would be made in 9 months.

_____

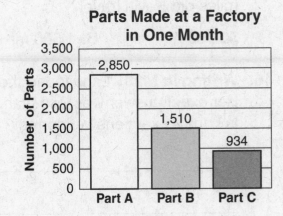

Parts Made at a Factory in One Month

Estimating Products

Estimate each product.

1. 7 × 42 is close to 7 × _____

2. 9 × 511 is close to 9 × _____

3. 5 × 79   _____

4. 6 × 32   _____

5. 4 × 63   _____

6. 8 × 102   _____

7. 9 × 354   _____

8. 3 × 428   _____

9. 7 × 493   _____

10. 5 × 814   _____

11. 2 × 3,541 _____

12. 8 × 783   _____

13. A dog weighs 27 lb. A football player weighs 9 times as much as the dog. About how many pounds does the football player weigh?

14. Nyesha has 872 stamps in her stamp collection. Her mother has 8 times as many stamps. About how many stamps does Nyesha's mother have?

_____

_____

Test Prep

15. Alma traveled 324 mi to visit her grandmother. Kevin traveled 5 times as far to see his uncle. About how many miles did Kevin travel?

A. 150 mi   **B.** 1,500 mi   **C.** 6,000 mi   **D.** 15,000 mi

16. **Writing in Math** Lana found the exact answer to 6 × 623. Her exact answer was less than her estimate of 3,600. Is Lana's exact answer correct? Explain.

_____

_____

_____

_____

Name_____

Mental Math

You can multiply mentally by breaking apart numbers or using compatible numbers.

Find 2 × 76 by breaking apart numbers.

Step 1: Use place value to break apart

76 into 70 and 6.

2 × 76

Step 2: Think of 2 × 76 as

2 × 70 and 2 × 6.

2 × 70 + 2 × 6

140 + 12

Step 3: Add the partial products to get the total.

140 + 12 = 152

2 × 76 = 152

Find 4 × 19 using compatible numbers.

Step 1: Substitute a compatible number for 19 that is easy to multiply by 4.

19 × 4

↓   Add 1 to make 20.

20 × 4

Step 2: Find the new product.

20 × 4 = 80

Step 3: Now adjust. Subtract 1 group of 4.

80 − 4 = 76.

4 × 19 = 76

Use mental math to find each product.

1. 5 × 32 = _____
2. 7 × 53 = _____
3. 66 × 2 = _____
4. 92 × 4 = _____
5. 31 × 82 = _____
6. 4 × 29 = _____
7. 18 × 5 = _____
8. 6 × 49 = _____
9. 68 × 3 = _____
10. 4 × 119 = _____
11. 107 × 5 = _____
12. 131 × 6 = _____

13. **Algebra** In $a \times b = 120$, a is a one-digit number and b is a two-digit number. What numbers could a and b represent?

_____

_____

Mental Math

Use mental math to find each product.

1. $50 \times 3 =$ _____
2. $8 \times 82 =$ _____
3. $61 \times 5 =$ _____
4. $7 \times 29 =$ _____
5. $33 \times 4 =$ _____
6. $27 \times 9 =$ _____
7. $43 \times 7 =$ _____
8. $6 \times 68 =$ _____
9. $8 \times 92 =$ _____
10. $69 \times 3 =$ _____
11. $2 \times 34 =$ _____
12. $71 \times 8 =$ _____

13. Suppose an office building is 4 times as tall as a tree that measures 52 ft. How tall is the office building? _____

14. Suppose a baseball stadium is 6 times as wide as an equipment trailer that measures 73 feet. How wide is the baseball stadium? _____

15. **Algebra** In $n \times p = 185$, n is a two-digit number and p is a one-digit number. What numbers do n and p represent?

_____

Test Prep

16. Which of the following has a greater product than 29×8?

    A. 34×5 **B.** 27×9 **C.** 38×4 **D.** 25×9

17. **Writing in Math** Explain how you would find the product of 3×75 by using the break apart method.

_____

_____

_____

Using Arrays to Multiply

You can use arrays of place-value blocks to multiply.

Find the product for 4×16.

What You Show	What You Write
$4 \times 10 = 40$ $4 \times 6 = 24$ $40 + 24 = 64$	$\begin{array}{r} 16 \\ \times\ 4 \\ \hline 24 \\ 40 \\ \hline 64 \end{array}$ $\begin{array}{l} 4 \times 6 \text{ ones} \\ 4 \times 1 \text{ tens} \end{array}$

Use the array to find the partial product and the product.
Complete the calculation.

1. $\begin{array}{r} 12 \\ \times\ 3 \\ \hline \end{array}$

2. $\begin{array}{r} 22 \\ \times\ 6 \\ \hline \end{array}$

3. $\begin{array}{r} 15 \\ \times\ 4 \\ \hline \end{array}$

4. $\begin{array}{r} 22 \\ \times\ 4 \\ \hline \end{array}$

5. $\begin{array}{r} 14 \\ \times\ 6 \\ \hline \end{array}$

6. $\begin{array}{r} 16 \\ \times\ 6 \\ \hline \end{array}$

7. $\begin{array}{r} 12 \\ \times\ 5 \\ \hline \end{array}$

8. $\begin{array}{r} 13 \\ \times\ 4 \\ \hline \end{array}$

9. $\begin{array}{r} 15 \\ \times\ 5 \\ \hline \end{array}$

10. $\begin{array}{r} 16 \\ \times\ 7 \\ \hline \end{array}$

11. Number Sense What two simpler problems can you use
to find 4×22? (Hint: Think about tens and ones.)

Using Arrays to Multiply

Use the array to find the partial products and the product.
Complete the calculation.

1.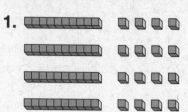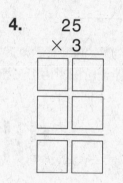

$$\begin{array}{r} 14 \\ \times\ 4 \\ \hline \end{array}$$

2.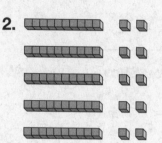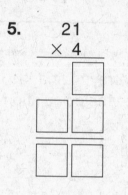

$$\begin{array}{r} 12 \\ \times\ 5 \\ \hline \end{array}$$

3. $\begin{array}{r} 17 \\ \times\ 4 \\ \hline \end{array}$

4. $\begin{array}{r} 25 \\ \times\ 3 \\ \hline \end{array}$

5. $\begin{array}{r} 21 \\ \times\ 4 \\ \hline \end{array}$

6. $4 \times 17 =$ _____

7. $5 \times 24 =$ _____

8. $3 \times 18 =$ _____

9. $5 \times 29 =$ _____

10. $23 \times 3 =$ _____

11. $21 \times 6 =$ _____

12. Clyde planted 4 rows of tomato seeds. Each row has 12 seeds. How many tomato seeds did Clyde plant? _____

Test Prep

13. Find 7×22.

A. 54   **B.** 144   **C.** 152   **D.** 154

14. Writing in Math Write a description of an array of stickers using the product of 3×15.

_____

_____

_____

Multiplying Two-Digit and One-Digit Numbers

Here is how to multiply a two-digit number by a one-digit number using paper and pencil.

Find 3 × 24.	What You **Think**	What You **Write**
Step 1 Multiply the ones. Regroup if necessary.	$3 \times 4 = 12$ ones Regroup 12 ones as 1 ten 2 ones.	$\begin{array}{r} 1 \\ 24 \\ \times\ 3 \\ \hline 2 \end{array}$
Step 2 Multiply the tens. Add any extra tens.	3×2 tens $= 6$ tens 6 tens + 1 ten = 7 tens	$\begin{array}{r} 1 \\ 24 \\ \times\ 3 \\ \hline 72 \end{array}$

Is your answer reasonable?

Exact: $3 \times 24 = 72$

Round 24 to 20.

Estimate: $3 \times 20 = 60$ Since 72 is close to 60, the answer is reasonable.

Find each product. Decide if your answer is reasonable.

1. $\begin{array}{r} 13 \\ \times\ 3 \\ \hline \end{array}$
2. $\begin{array}{r} 17 \\ \times\ 7 \\ \hline \end{array}$
3. $\begin{array}{r} 24 \\ \times\ 5 \\ \hline \end{array}$
4. $\begin{array}{r} 48 \\ \times\ 8 \\ \hline \end{array}$

5. $\begin{array}{r} 62 \\ \times\ 6 \\ \hline \end{array}$
6. $\begin{array}{r} 36 \\ \times\ 5 \\ \hline \end{array}$
7. $\begin{array}{r} 88 \\ \times\ 5 \\ \hline \end{array}$
8. $\begin{array}{r} 52 \\ \times\ 8 \\ \hline \end{array}$

9. **Estimation** Use estimation to decide which has the greater product: 813×6 or 907×5. _____

Name_____

Multiplying Two-Digit and One-Digit Numbers

Find each product. Decide if your answer is reasonable.

1.   1 9
    ×   4
    ‾‾‾‾‾‾
   7 ☐

2.   2 3
    ×   7
    ‾‾‾‾‾‾
   ☐ 6 ☐

3.   5 1
    ×   6
    ‾‾‾‾‾‾
   ☐ 0 ☐

4.   39
   × 7

5.   48
   × 5

6.   53
   × 7

7.   29
   × 8

8. $42 \times 6 = $ _____

9. $89 \times 8 = $ _____

10. $77 \times 9 = $ _____

11. $94 \times 4 = $ _____

12. **Number Sense** Penny says that $4 \times 65 = 260$. Estimate to check Penny's answer. Is she right? Explain.

_____

_____

13. A large dump truck uses about 18 gal of fuel in 1 hr of work. How many gallons of fuel are needed if the truck works for 5 hours?   _____

Test Prep

14. Which of the following is a reasonable estimate for 6×82?

    A. 48   **B.** 480   **C.** 540   **D.** 550

15. **Writing in Math** Tyrone has 6 times as many marbles as his sister Pam. Pam has 34 marbles. Louis has 202 marbles. Who has more marbles, Tyrone or Louis? Explain how you found your answer.

_____

_____

Multiplying Three-Digit and One-Digit Numbers

Here is how to multiply larger numbers.

	Example A	Example B
Step 1 Multiply the ones. Regroup if necessary.	$\begin{array}{r} 1 \\ 154 \\ \times\ 4 \\ \hline 6 \end{array}$	$\begin{array}{r} 2 \\ 214 \\ \times\ 7 \\ \hline 8 \end{array}$
Step 2 Multiply the tens. Add any extra tens. Regroup if necessary.	$\begin{array}{r} 21 \\ 154 \\ \times\ 4 \\ \hline 16 \end{array}$	$\begin{array}{r} 2 \\ 214 \\ \times\ 7 \\ \hline 98 \end{array}$
Step 3 Multiply the hundreds. Add any extra hundreds.	$\begin{array}{r} 21 \\ 154 \\ \times\ 4 \\ \hline 616 \end{array}$	$\begin{array}{r} 2 \\ 214 \\ \times\ 7 \\ \hline 1{,}498 \end{array}$

Find each product. Estimate to check reasonableness.

1. $\begin{array}{r} 185 \\ \times\ 4 \\ \hline \end{array}$
2. $\begin{array}{r} 517 \\ \times\ 4 \\ \hline \end{array}$
3. $\begin{array}{r} 741 \\ \times\ 3 \\ \hline \end{array}$
4. $\begin{array}{r} 413 \\ \times\ 6 \\ \hline \end{array}$

5. $\begin{array}{r} 625 \\ \times\ 6 \\ \hline \end{array}$
6. $\begin{array}{r} 381 \\ \times\ 5 \\ \hline \end{array}$
7. $\begin{array}{r} 711 \\ \times\ 8 \\ \hline \end{array}$
8. $\begin{array}{r} 802 \\ \times\ 5 \\ \hline \end{array}$

9. **Number Sense** How could you use the product of 108 and 4 to find the product of 324 and 4?

_____

10. A factory can make 241 footballs in 1 week. How many can it make in 9 weeks?

_____

Name _____

Multiplying Three-Digit and One-Digit Numbers

Find each product. Estimate for reasonableness.

| 1. | 352
 × 3 | 2. | 385
 × 4 | 3. | 482
 × 8 | 4. | 632
 × 5 |

1. 352
    × 3

2. 385
    × 4

3. 482
    × 8

4. 632
    × 5

5. 219
    × 6

6. 768
    × 7

7. 521
    × 4

8. 848
    × 9

9. 7 × 211 = _____

10. 6 × 517 = _____

If the baseball players in the table score the same number of runs each season, how many runs will

Runs Scored in 2001

Player	Runs Scored
A	128
B	113
C	142

11. Player A score in 5 seasons?

_____

12. Player C score in 8 seasons?

_____

Test Prep

13. How many bottles of water would Tim sell if he sold 212 bottles each week for 4 weeks?

    A. 800   **B.** 840   **C.** 848   **D.** 884

14. **Writing in Math** If you know that 8 × 300 = 2,400, how can you find 8 × 320? Explain.

_____

_____

_____

Name_____

PROBLEM-SOLVING STRATEGY

Try, Check, and Revise

Yard Sale Andrew spent $26 at his neighbor's yard sale. He bought three items. Which items did he buy?

Yard Sale	
Binoculars	$12
Shoehorn	$ 3
Bowling ball	$ 8
Army boots	$ 5
Slingshot	$ 6

Read and Understand

Step 1: What do you know?

He bought three items.
He spent $26.

Step 2: What are you trying to find?

Which three items did he buy?

Plan and Solve

Step 3: What strategy will you use?

Strategy: Try, check, and revise

Show the Main Idea

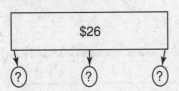

Try: The binoculars are $12. I'll try it plus two other items.

Check: Check using $12 + $8 + $5 = $25. That's too low.

Revise: I'll keep the binoculars and bowling ball, but try the slingshot instead of the army boots.

Use previous tries: $12 + $8 + $6 = $26 That's it!

Answer: He bought the binoculars, a bowling ball, and a slingshot.

Look Back and Check

Is your work correct?
Yes, the sum is $26, and he bought three items.

Use the first try to help you make a second try. Finish solving the problems.

1. Henry's dad bought 27 screws and nails at the hardware store. He bought twice as many screws as he did nails. How many of each did he buy? Try 8 nails.
   8 × 2 = 16 screws. 16 + 8 = 24. That's too low.

_____

Name_____

Try, Check, and Revise

Use the first try to help you make a second try. Finish solving
the problem.

1. Anton put 35 marbles equally into 5 jars. Each jar
   holds either 5 large marbles or 7 small marbles.
   What size of marbles did Anton put into the jars?

   5 jars
   x 5 large marbles
   _____
   25

   That's not enough.

   _____

   _____

   _____

Try, check, and revise to solve each problem. Write the answer
in a complete sentence.

2. Lenore earned $6 per hour and Dora earned $8 per hour.
   Lenore and Dora worked the same number of hours.
   Lenore earned $54. How much did Dora earn?

   _____

3. Thomas read 3 of the books.
   He read a total of 272 pages.
   Which of the books did he read?

Book	Pages
Dark Mysteries	87
History of France	146
Superhero Stories	72
Artists to Know	113

   _____

   _____

4. Heather read 2 of the books. She also read a music book
   with 211 pages. She read a total of 429 pages. Which of
   the books did she read?

   _____

   _____

Choose a Computation Method

When you compute, first try mental math.
Next, think about paper and pencil. For very
hard problems, use a calculator.

Cost of Summer Cottage Rental	
Cottage	Cost/Week
A	$ 595
B	$1,045
C	$1,887

Example A

What is the cost of a two-week stay at Cottage A?

2 × $595 = ?

This is easy to do in my head. I'll use mental math.

2 × 600 = 1,200

1,200 − 10 = 1,190

Cost: $1,190

Example B

What is the cost of a three-week stay at Cottage B?

3 × $1,045 = ?

There are a lot of regroupings. I'll use paper and pencil.

```
    1 1
  1,045
 ×    3
  3,135
```

Cost: $3,135

Example C

What is the cost of a seven-week stay at Cottage C?

7 × $1,887 = ?

There are a lot of regroupings. I'll use a calculator.

Press: **7** **1887**

Display: 13209

Cost: $13,209

Find each product. Tell what computation method you used.

1. 4,100
     ×   4

2. 5,170
     ×   4

3. 1,857
     ×   7

4. 6,253
     ×   6

5. Number Sense Gary used paper and pencil to find 6,005 × 4.
Could he have found the answer a faster way? Explain.

_____

_____

_____

Name_____

Choose a Computation Method

Find each product. Tell what computation method you used.

1. 4,701
     ×   6

  _____

2. 8,644
     ×   5

  _____

3. 4,698
     ×   8

  _____

4. 9,204
     ×   3

  _____

5. 5,920
     ×   4

  _____

6. 6,114
     ×   7

  _____

7. 7,100
     ×   4

  _____

8. 4,923
     ×   9

  _____

9. Mervin's Market sells about 1,250 lb of apples in 1 year. How many pounds of apples will Mervin's Market sell in 4 years?

_____

10. The airline flies 8,112 mi in 1 day. How many miles does the airline fly in 6 days?

_____

Test Prep

11. A theme park has 6 parking lots. If each of the parking lots holds 1,100 cars, how many total cars can park?

A. 6,000 cars   **B.** 6,100 cars   **C.** 6,500 cars   **D.** 6,600 cars

12. Writing in Math Which method would you use to find 4,202 × 8? Explain.

_____

_____

Multiplying Money

The steps for multiplying money are almost exactly the same as the steps for multiplying whole numbers.

For example, a meal deal at the local fast-food restaurant costs $4.89. How much would it cost to eat there 3 days in a row?

Step 1	Step 2
Multiply the same way as with whole numbers.	Write the answer in dollars and cents.
2 2 $4.89 × 3 ————— 14 67	2 2 $4.89 × 3 ————— $14.67
	Remember, there are two digits to the right of the decimal point when separating dollars and cents.

It costs $14.67 to eat there 3 days in a row.

Find each product.

1. $1.21
  × 3

2. $3.15
  × 4

3. $7.23
  × 5

4. $4.18
  × 4

5. $5.17 × 3 = _____

6. $70.14 × 3 = _____

7. $18.57 × 9 = _____

8. $62.53 × 4 = _____

9. Estimation If a salad costs $3.99, is $29.99 enough to buy 9 orders? Explain.

_____

Find each cost.

10. 3 boomerangs   _____

11. 4 softballs   _____

Item	Price
Boomerang	$6.49
Softball	$4.89

Multiplying Money

Find each product.

1. $2.48
   $\times$ 8

2. $3.82
   $\times$ 5

3. $45.86
   $\times$ 6

4. $22.72
   $\times$ 7

5. $4 \times \$8.23 =$ _____

6. $7 \times \$31.14 =$ _____

7. $9 \times \$25.88 =$ _____

8. $\$43.86 \times 6 =$ _____

Find each cost.

9. 5 boxes of modeling clay

_____

10. 6 boxes of colored pencils

_____

11. 4 boxes of beads

_____

Arts-N-Crafts	
Item	**Price per Box**
Beads	$3.29
Modeling clay	$4.32
Origami paper	$7.91
Colored pencils	$2.05

12. 7 boxes of origami paper

_____

Test Prep

13. Nemo wants to buy calendars for his family. Each calendar costs $5.62. How much money do 5 calendars cost?

A. $25.10

B. $28.00

C. $28.10

D. $30.10

14. Writing in Math At a local restaurant, a turkey sandwich costs $6.50. An apple juice costs $1.25. Would $15.00 be enough to buy 2 sandwiches and 2 juices? Explain.

_____

_____

Multiplying Three Factors

You can use the Commutative and Associative Properties of Multiplication to make it easier to multiply 3 factors.

Commutative Property of Multiplication:

You can multiply any two numbers in any order.

$2 \times 3 = 3 \times 2$

Associative Property of Multiplication:

You can change the grouping of the factors.

$4 \times (2 \times 3) = (4 \times 2) \times 3$

Here are three ways to find $20 \times 2 \times 3$.

Example A	Example B	Example C
Multiply 20 and 2 first.	Multiply 2 and 3 first.	Multiply 20 and 3 first.
$20 \times 2 = 40$	$2 \times 3 = 6$	$20 \times 3 = 60$
$(20 \times 2) \times 3$	$20 \times (2 \times 3)$	$(20 \times 3) \times 2$
$40 \times 3 = 120$	$20 \times 6 = 120$	$60 \times 2 = 120$

1. $5 \times 3 \times 6 =$ _____

2. $50 \times 4 \times 2 =$ _____

3. $3 \times 30 \times 5 =$ _____

4. $4 \times 5 \times 60 =$ _____

5. $8 \times 2 \times 15 =$ _____

6. $6 \times 5 \times 10 =$ _____

7. $14 \times 2 \times 3 =$ _____

8. $50 \times 7 \times 5 =$ _____

9. Number Sense For $20 \times 5 \times 6$, is it easier to find 20×5 or 20×6 mentally? Why?

_____

_____

10. Show three ways to find $4 \times 25 \times 2$.

_____

Multiplying Three Factors

1. $2 \times 4 \times 9$

_____

2. $9 \times 8 \times 3$

_____

3. $4 \times 4 \times 10$

_____

4. $6 \times 50 \times 2$

_____

5. $8 \times 60 \times 5$

_____

6. $20 \times 7 \times 3$

_____

7. $2 \times 600 \times 5$

_____

8. $80 \times 6 \times 2$

_____

9. $4 \times 70 \times 4$

_____

10. Show three ways to find $40 \times 2 \times 5$.

_____

_____

_____

11. How many building blocks did Travis use to build his city?

_____

Travis' Building Blocks
1 toy city = 4 buildings
1 building = 4 sides
1 side   = 20 blocks

Test Prep

12. How many apples would you have altogether if you have 5 apples in each of 3 bowls on each of 4 tables?

A. 60 apples   **B.** 72 apples   **C.** 81 apples   **D.** 100 apples

13. Writing in Math What is the cost of a truckload of sand if there are 25 bags per truckload, 10 lb of sand per bag, and each pound of sand costs $2? Show two different ways to solve the problem.

_____

_____

Name_____

Choose an Operation

Understanding when to choose a particular operation can help you solve problems.

READ AND UNDERSTAND **Show the main idea.**	The average male giraffe is 3 times taller than Ramon. Ramon is 6 feet tall. How tall is the average male giraffe?	A goldfish named Tish lived from 1956 to 1999. How many years did Tish live?
	□ □ □ □ Ramon's Average height giraffe's height: 3 times as tall	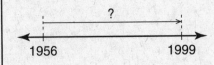 1956 1999
PLAN AND SOLVE **Choose an operation.**	Multiply to find "times as tall." 6 × 3 = 18 Ramon's Times Average height as giraffe's tall height	Subtract to compare the numbers. 1999 − 1956 = 43 Year Year Years in died born between

Draw a picture to show each main idea. Then choose an operation and solve each problem.

1. If there are 4 qt of milk in 1 gal, and 2 pt in 1 qt, how many pints are in 5 gal?

_____

2. Runner A ran 844 mi last year. Runner B ran 1,063 mi. How many more miles did Runner B run than Runner A?

Name_____

Choose an Operation

Draw a picture to show the main idea. Then choose an
operation and solve the problem.

1. A sack of potatoes weighs 20 lb and holds 200 potatoes.
   A sack of apples weighs 20 lb and holds 325 apples. How
   many more apples are there in a 20 lb sack?

   _____

2. Shawna has 35 football cards and 5 times as many
   baseball cards in her sports-card collection. How many
   baseball cards does she have?

   _____

3. A pound of peaches costs $1.29. How
   much does 4 lb of peaches cost?

   _____

4. The first modern electronic computer, called
   ENIAC, was introduced in 1946. Personal home
   computers were not available until 28 years later.
   In what year were personal home computers
   introduced?

   _____

PROBLEM-SOLVING APPLICATIONS
The Grocery Store

Caleb is preparing a meal for his friend. The chart shows the number of calories in each type of food.

Food	Amount	Grams	Calories
Seedless raisins	1 c	145	435
Salted butter	1 tbsp	14	100
Banana	1	114	105
Baked potato	1	156	145
Apple	1	138	80
Sardines	3 oz	85	175

Use mental math. How many calories are in:
  3 tbsp of salted butter? 300 calories
  4 apples? 320 calories

Use the chart above to answer the following questions.

1. How many calories are there
   in 7 baked potatoes?

   $$\begin{array}{r} \overset{3}{1\,4\,5} \\ \times\qquad 7 \\ \hline \boxed{}\;\boxed{}\,5 \end{array}$$

   _____

2. How many calories are there
   in 8 c of seedless raisins?   _____

3. How many grams are there in
   6 oz of sardines?   _____

4. Use mental math to find out how many
   calories are in 4 bananas.   _____

Name_____

Paper Problems

The business section of Caitlin's newspaper lists the performances of many stocks. There are 14 stocks listed in every 1 in. of the stock report.

1. How many stocks are listed in 6 in. of the stock report?

   _____

   _____

2. In 1 ft of the stock report, there are 168 stocks listed. How many stocks are listed in 5 ft of stock reports?

   _____

   _____

The lifestyle section of Caitlin's newspaper has a daily crossword puzzle. The puzzle has 8 rows and 8 columns.

3. How many total spaces are in the crossword puzzle?

   _____

   _____

4. There are 13 blocked (or black) spaces where you cannot write a letter. In how many spaces can you write a letter?

   _____

   _____

5. Suppose in 1 day you bought 3 copies of the newspaper for $0.50 each. How much would it cost to do this for 6 days?

   _____

   _____

Multiplying Multiples of Ten

You can multiply with mental math by using basic facts and patterns.

Example A: $5 \times 5 = 25$

$5 \times 50 = 250$

$50 \times 50 = 2{,}500$

$50 \times 5{,}000 = 250{,}000$

The product contains the number of zeros in each factor.

Example B: $5 \times 6 = 30$

$5 \times 60 = 300$

$50 \times 60 = 3{,}000$

$50 \times 600 = 30{,}000$

$50 \times 6{,}000 = 300{,}000$

When the product of a basic fact includes a zero, such as $5 \times 6 = 30$, that zero is not part of the pattern.

Multiply. Use mental math.

1. $20 \times 20 =$

2. $50 \times 10 =$

3. $40 \times 40 =$

_____

_____

_____

4. $30 \times 80 =$

5. $60 \times 600 =$

6. $50 \times 900 =$

_____

_____

_____

7. $70 \times 3{,}000 =$

8. $70 \times 6{,}000 =$

9. $40 \times 5{,}000 =$

_____

_____

_____

10. Number Sense Tell what numbers go in the blanks.

To find 90×300, multiply _____ and _____.

Then write _____ zeros at the end.

Name_____

Multiplying Multiples of Ten

Multiply. Use mental math.

1. $4 \times 30 =$ _____

2. $5 \times 90 =$ _____

3. $9 \times 200 =$ _____

4. $6 \times 500 =$ _____

5. $3 \times 600 =$ _____

6. $8 \times 6{,}000 =$ _____

7. $90 \times 70 =$ _____

8. $70 \times 400 =$ _____

9. $60 \times 8{,}000 =$ _____

10. $30 \times 800 =$ _____

11. $90 \times 5{,}000 =$ _____

12. $30 \times 4{,}000 =$ _____

13. **Number Sense** How many zeros are in the product of $60 \times 9{,}000$? Explain how you know.

_____

_____

Truck A can haul 4,000 lb in one trip. Truck B can haul 3,000 lb in one trip.

14. How many pounds can Truck A haul in 9 trips? _____

15. How many pounds can Truck B haul in 50 trips? _____

Test Prep

16. How many pounds can Truck A haul in 70 trips?

   A. 280   **B.** 2,800   **C.** 28,000   **D.** 280,000

17. **Writing in Math** There are 9 players on each basketball team in a league. Explain how you can find the total number of players in the league if there are 30 teams.

_____

_____

Estimating Products

Estimate 11 × 94.

Using rounding

    Round 11 to 10.

    Round 94 to 90.

    $10 \times 90 = 900$

    11 × 94 is about 900 days.

Using compatible numbers

    Replace 11 with 10.

    Replace 94 with 100.

    $10 \times 100 = 1,000$

    11 × 94 is about 1,000.

To find the **range**, underestimate by replacing with lesser numbers or overestimate by replacing with greater numbers. In the above examples, $10 \times 90 = 900$ is an underestimate and $15 \times 100 = 1,500$ is an overestimate. So the range for these estimates is between 900 and 1,500.

Estimate each product.

1. 62 × 82

2. 59 × 48

3. 74 × 302

_____

_____

_____

4. 47 × 790

5. 498 × 63

6. 687 × 38

_____

_____

_____

Estimate each product by finding each range.

7. 32 × 83 _____

8. 37 × 22 _____

9. 51 × 296 _____

10. Number Sense To estimate the product of 37 × 99, Chris multiplied 40 × 100. Tell how you know if this is an underestimate or an overestimate.

_____

_____

Name_____

Estimating Products

Estimate each product.

1. 38 × 29 _____

2. 71 × 47 _____

3. 54 × 76 _____

4. 121 × 62 _____

5. 548 × 28 _____

6. 823 × 83 _____

7. 67 × 289 _____

8. 183 × 34 _____

Estimate each product by finding a range.

9. 28 × 87

10. 673 × 85

_____

_____

The distance between San Francisco, California, and
Salt Lake City, Utah, is 752 miles.

11. Find a range for the number of
miles a car would drive if it made
15 trips.

12. About how many miles would
a car drive if it made 42 trips?

_____

_____

Test Prep

13. Vera has 8 boxes of paper clips. Each box has 275 paper
clips. About how many paper clips does Vera have?

A. 240   **B.** 1,600   **C.** 2,400   **D.** 24,000

14. **Writing in Math** A wind farm generates 330 kilowatts of
electricity each day. About how many kilowatts does the
wind farm produce in a week? Explain.

_____

_____

_____

Using Arrays to Multiply

Here is how to find the product of 12 × 24 using an array.

Draw a rectangle 24 units long by 12 units wide.

Divide the rectangle by tens and ones for each factor. Find the number of squares in each smaller square.

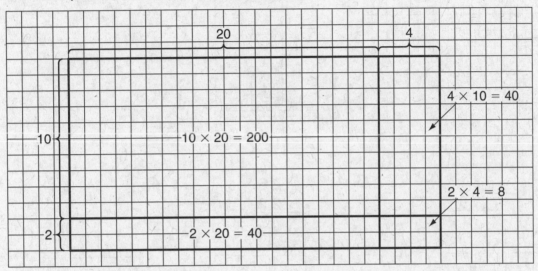

Then add the numbers of the squares in the four rectangles:

200 + 40 + 40 + 8 = 288

So, 12 × 24 = 288.

Divide the rectangle by tens and ones for each factor. Then complete the calculation.

1.

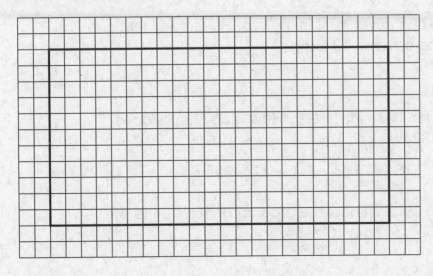

$$\begin{array}{r} 2\,2 \\ \times\ 1\,1 \\ \hline \end{array}$$

Using Arrays to Multiply

Use the grid to draw a rectangle. Then complete the calculation.

1.

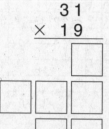

2.

$$\begin{array}{r} 3\,1 \\ \times\ 1\,9 \end{array}$$

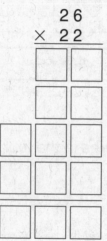

3.

$$\begin{array}{r} 2\,6 \\ \times\ 2\,2 \end{array}$$

4.

$$\begin{array}{r} 3\,3 \\ \times\ 1\,4 \end{array}$$

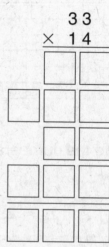

5. 24 × 57 = _____

6. 44 × 48 = _____

7. A red kangaroo can cover 40 ft in 1 jump. How many feet can the red kangaroo cover in 12 jumps? _____

Test Prep

8. Barb exercises for 14 hr in 1 week. How many hours does she exercise in 32 weeks?

A. 496 hr   **B.** 448 hr   **C.** 420 hr   **D.** 324 hr

9. Writing in Math Explain how the product of 16 × 34 is like the product of 6 × 34 plus 10 × 34.

Name_____

Make an Organized List

Theme Park Brian has four passes to a theme park. He could bring himself and three friends. The group of friends for him to choose from includes Art, Ned, Jeff, and Belinda. How many different combinations are possible?

Read and Understand

Step 1: What do you know?

There are four friends: Art, Ned, Jeff, and Belinda.

Step 2: What are you trying to find?

Find out how many different combinations of friends Brian can take.

Plan and Solve

Step 3: What strategy will you use?

Strategy: Make an Organized List

Brian, Art, Ned, Jeff, and Belinda. Brian has to be in each combination.

List the choices:
Brian, Art, Ned, Belinda
Brian, Art, Ned, Jeff
Brian, Art, Jeff, Belinda
Brian, Ned, Jeff, Belinda

Answer: There are four combinations.

Look Back and Check

Is your work correct?

Yes, because each combination uses Brian. The way the list is organized shows that all ways were found.

Finish solving the problem.

1. Ann, Mara, Jenny, Tina, and Sue are sisters. Two of the five sisters must help their father at his business each Saturday. How many combinations of two sisters are possible?

_____

_____

Ann   Mara   Jenny Tina
Ann   Jenny

Name_____

Make an Organized List

Make an organized list to solve each problem. Write each answer in a complete sentence.

1. Tonya and Lauren are designing a soccer uniform. They want to use two colors on the shirt. Their choices are green, orange, yellow, purple, blue, and silver. How many ways can they choose two colors?

_____

_____

2. Yancey collects plastic banks. He has three different banks: a pig, a cow, and a horse. How many ways can Yancey arrange his banks on a shelf?

_____

_____

3. Kevin has a rabbit, a ferret, a gerbil, and a turtle. He feeds them in a different order each day. In how many different orders can Kevin feed his pets?

_____

_____

_____

_____

Multiplying Two-Digit Numbers

There are 24 cars in the race. Each car has a 13-person crew in the pit area. How many pit-area workers are at the race?

Step 1	**Step 2**	**Step 3**
Multiply the ones.	Multiply the tens.	Add the partial products.
Regroup if necessary.	Regroup if necessary.	

Step 1

$$\begin{array}{r} 1 \\ 24 \\ \times 13 \\ \hline 72 \end{array}$$

Step 2

$$\begin{array}{r} 1 \\ 24 \\ \times 13 \\ \hline 72 \\ 240 \end{array}$$

Step 3

$$\begin{array}{r} 1 \\ 24 \\ \times 13 \\ \hline 72 \\ \underline{240} \\ 312 \end{array}$$

$24 \times 13 = 312$, so there are 312 pit-area workers at the race.

1.
$$\begin{array}{r} 38 \\ \times 26 \\ \hline \end{array}$$

2.
$$\begin{array}{r} 67 \\ \times 27 \\ \hline \end{array}$$

3.
$$\begin{array}{r} 44 \\ \times 85 \\ \hline \end{array}$$

4.
$$\begin{array}{r} 88 \\ \times 32 \\ \hline \end{array}$$

5. Number Sense Corina multiplied 62×22 and got a product of 1,042. Explain why Corina's answer is not reasonable.

_____

_____

_____

_____

Multiplying Two-Digit Numbers

1. 54
    × 17

2. 36
    × 20

3. 53
    × 12

4. 48
    × 46

5. 37
    × 83

6. 62
    × 17

7. 91
    × 49

8. 28
    × 56

9. 70
    × 39

10. 58
    × 90

11. 97
    × 42

12. 64
    × 88

13. A carton holds 24 bottles of juice. How many juice bottles are in 15 cartons?

_____

14. How much do 21 bushels of sweet corn weigh?

_____

Vegetable	Weight of 1 Bushel
Asparagus	24 lb
Beets	52 lb
Carrots	50 lb
Sweet corn	35 lb

15. How much do 18 bushels of asparagus weigh?

_____

16. How much more do 13 bushels of beets weigh than 13 bushels of carrots?

Test Prep

17. Which of the following is a reasonable answer for 92 × 98?

    A. 1,800   **B.** 9,000   **C.** 10,000   **D.** 90,000

18. **Writing in Math** Garth is multiplying 29 × 16. He has 174 after multiplying the ones and 290 after multiplying the tens. Explain how Garth can find the final product.

Multiplying Greater Numbers

Multiply 626 × 47.

Step 1	**Step 2**	**Step 3**
Estimate: 600 × 50 = 30,000	Place a zero in the ones place.	Add the partial products.
Multiply the ones.	Multiply the tens.	
Regroup if necessary.	Regroup if necessary.	

Step 1	**Step 2**	**Step 3**
	1 2	1 2
1 4	1 4	1 4
626	626	626
× 47	× 47	× 47
4,382	4,382	4,382
	25,040	25,040
		29,422

The product 29,422 is reasonable, because it is a little less than the estimate of 30,000.

---

1.   113
      × 26

2.   517
      × 44

3.   741
      × 43

---

4. Number Sense Is 11,452 a reasonable answer for 28 × 409? Explain.

_____

_____

_____

_____

Multiplying Greater Numbers

1. 242 $\times$ 30	2. 194 $\times$ 19	3. 306 $\times$ 22	4. 420 $\times$ 82
5. 324 $\times$ 38	6. 832 $\times$ 69	7. 493 $\times$ 75	8. 968 $\times$ 27
9. 828 $\times$ 34	10. 335 $\times$ 45	11. 616 $\times$ 37	12. 494 $\times$ 65

13. **Number Sense** Is 44,722 a reasonable answer for 59 $\times$ 758? Explain.

_____

_____

14. How many pencils are in 27 boxes?

_____

Supplies	Per Box
Pencils	144
Pens	115

15. How many pens are in 42 boxes?

_____

Test Prep

16. Hailey sold 122 bottles of water in 1 week. About how many bottles could she sell in 19 weeks?

  A. 1,000   **B.** 1,800   **C.** 2,400   **D.** 3,000

17. **Writing in Math** How could you use the product 10 $\times$ 414 = 4,140 to find the product of 12 $\times$ 414?

_____

_____

Name _____

Choose a Computation Method

When you multiply, first try mental math. Next, think about
pencil and paper. For very hard problems, use a calculator.

Find 12 × $1,000.

This is easy to do, so you can use mental math.

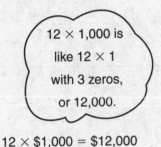

12 × 1,000 is
like 12 × 1
with 3 zeros,
or 12,000.

12 × $1,000 = $12,000

Find 810 × 15.

There are not a lot of regroupings, so you can use pencil and paper.

```
    810
×    15
  4,050
  8100
 12,150
```

810 × 15 = 12,150

Find 56 × 1,287.

There are a lot of regroupings, so you can use a calculator.

Press: **56** **1287**

ENTER
=

Display: 72072

56 × 1,287 = 72,072

Multiply. Tell what method you used.

1. 400
      × 40   _____

2. 170
      × 14   _____

3. 784
      × 33   _____

4. Number Sense The heaviest car in the world weighs 7,353 lb. How much
would 12 of these cars weigh? What computation method did you use?

_____

Name_____

Choose a Computation Method

Multiply. Tell what method you used.

1. 50
   ×90
   _____

   _____

2. 324
   × 42
   _____

   _____

3. 84
   ×39
   _____

   _____

4. 600
   × 40
   _____

   _____

5. 537
   × 88
   _____

   _____

6. 224
   × 21
   _____

   _____

How many books would you expect

7. Store B to sell in 10 weeks?

_____

8. Store A to sell in 20 weeks?

_____

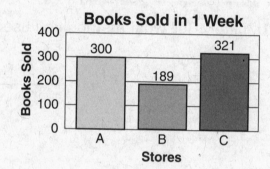

Books Sold in 1 Week

9. How many more books would you
   expect to be sold in 6 weeks in
   Store C than in Store A?

_____

Test Prep

10. Nathan has 20 friends coming to his party. If each friend
   brings 20 snacks, how many snacks are there?

   A. 400   **B.** 800   **C.** 1,000   **D.** 2,000

11. Writing in Math Explain when you would choose a calculator to multiply.

_____

_____

Multiplying Money

The steps for multiplying money are almost exactly the same as the steps for multiplying whole numbers.

Find $16 \times \$7.89$.

Step 1	Step 2	Step 3
Estimate:	Multiply the ones and then multiply the tens.	Add the partial products. Place the dollar sign and decimal point in the answer.

Step 1

Estimate:

$16 \times \$7.89$
↓ ↓
$20 \times \$8 = \$160$

The product should be less than $160.

Step 2

Multiply the ones and then multiply the tens.

```
  5 5
 $7.89
×   16
 47 34
 78 90
```

Step 3

Add the partial products. Place the dollar sign and decimal point in the answer.

```
  5 5
 $7.89
×   16
 47 34
 78 90
$126.24
```

The product $126.24 is reasonable, because it is less than the estimate of $160.00.

1.
```
  $4.68
×    14
```

2.
```
  $5.17
×    33
```

3.
```
  $9.14
×    23
```

4.
```
  $8.57
×    19
```

5. Number Sense Romario multiplies $18 \times \$5.35$. Which of the following is most likely the product: $96.30, $9.60, or $960.30? Explain.

_____

_____

_____

Multiplying Money

1. $1.26
   × 40

2. $2.30
   × 14

3. $3.96
   × 18

4. $4.21
   × 33

5. $5.54
   × 26

6. $2.28
   × 67

7. $3.37
   × 34

8. $4.82
   × 42

9. **Number Sense** Margo bought 36 shirts that cost $6.86 each. Which of the following is most likely to be the product, $24.69, $246.96, or $2,469.60? Explain.

_____

_____

How much did 42 bushels of corn cost in

10. 1970? _____

11. 2000? _____

12. How much more did 19 bushels of corn cost in 1980 than in 1990?

_____

| **Price of Corn** | |
Year	Per Bushel
1970	$1.33
1980	$3.11
1990	$2.28
2000	$1.85

Test Prep

13. The fourth-grade class rented 24 pairs of skates at the ice rink. Each pair cost $2.45. How much did it cost to rent the skates?

   A. $5.88   **B.** $49.00   **C.** $58.80   **D.** $62.48

14. **Writing in Math** Craig multiplied 43 × $5.46 and got an answer of $234.78. Do you agree? Explain.

_____

_____

Name_____

Writing to Explain

Here are some things you can do to write a good explanation in math.

Estimate the number of rectangles in all of the columns.

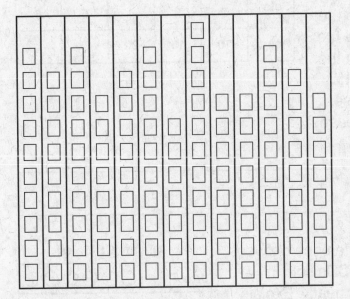

Show your computation clearly. Think about how you got your estimate. A flowchart can organize your thoughts. Write your steps in order.

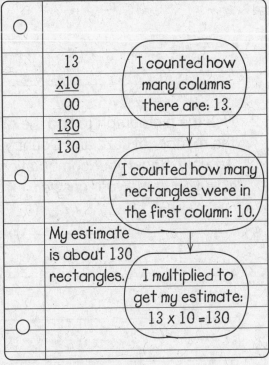

---

1. Use the pictograph to find out how many toy cars Andy has. Show your computation. You may use a flowchart to help show your thinking.

Toy Car Collection

Matthew	🚗 🚗 🚗
Andy	🚗 🚗 🚗 🚗 🚗
Ronald	🚗 🚗

Each 🚗 = 25 cars.

_____

_____

_____

Name_____

Writing to Explain

Write to explain.

1. Bonnie completed a tennis tournament. She received 5 points for each set she won. Complete the table and use the pattern to find the number of points she earned on the 4th and 5th days. Explain how the number of points earned increases as the number of sets won increases.

Day	1	2	3	4	5
Sets Won	2	3	4	5	6
Points	10	15	20		

_____

_____

2. Use the pictograph to find the difference between the number of Jazz and Country CDs sold in January. Show your computation neatly. Explain how you found your answer.

January CD Sales

Jazz	○○○○○○
Classical	○○○○
Country	○○○

Each ○ = 50 CDs.

_____

_____

_____

_____

3. Copy the table and use the pattern to complete it. Explain how the number of students changes as the number of classrooms changes.

Classrooms	2	4	6	8	10
Students	48	96	144		

_____

_____

_____

_____

PROBLEM-SOLVING APPLICATIONS

Cats

Cats are popular pets. Scientists estimate that there are over 100 million cats in the United States.

Cats should get about 70 min of exercise every week. Estimate how many minutes of exercise a cat should get in one year. Remember, there are 52 weeks in a year.

Use rounding:

70×52

↓   ↓

$70 \times 50 = 3,500$

So, cats should get about 3,500 min of exercise each year.

---

1. A pet store owner orders 98 packages of cat treats. Each package has 115 treats. What is the total number of treats ordered? _____

2. A cat breeder sells pedigree cats for $297. If he sells 24 of these cats, how much money will he make? _____

3. Jane has a new female kitten. She wants to give it a first name and a middle name. Her first name choices are Fluffy and Wiggy. Her middle name choices are Margie, Carla, and Tammy. How many different name combinations can she make? Make an organized list to solve this problem.

_____

_____

_____

_____

_____

Name_____

The Magazine

A magazine has 11 editors who supervise the writing of different parts of the magazine. Each managing editor has 28 workers.

1. Estimate how many total workers there are. Explain your estimate.

   _____

   _____

2. Find the number of workers there are
   for the 11 editors.   _____

The magazine company publishes 56 issues each year.
How many issues will the company publish in

3. 8 years?   _____

4. 15 years?   _____

5. 27 years?   _____

Each magazine costs $4.59 per issue. How much would it cost for

6. 6 issues?   _____

7. 11 issues?   _____

8. 23 issues?   _____

A subscriber receives the magazine each week at home in the mail. Subscribers pay $2.04 per issue. How much does the magazine cost for subscribers to get

9. 24 issues?   _____

10. 52 issues?   _____

11. A newsstand sells 716 issues of the magazine
    per week. How many issues does the
    newsstand sell in 1 year?   _____

Using Patterns to Divide Mentally

When dividing numbers that end in zero, you can use basic
division facts, as well as patterns, to help you divide mentally.
For example:

	Find $210 \div 7$.	Find $4{,}200 \div 6$.
What You **Think**	First, find the basic fact. $210 \div 7 =$ $21 \div 7 =$ 21 tens $\div 7 =$ 3 tens or 30	Find the basic fact. $4{,}200 \div 6 =$ $42 \div 6 =$ 42 hundreds $\div 6 =$ 7 hundreds or 700
What You **Write**	$210 \div 7 = 30$	$4{,}200 \div 6 = 700$

Divide. Use mental math.

1. $250 \div 5 =$ _____

2. $7{,}200 \div 9 =$ _____

3. $200 \div 4 =$ _____

4. $28{,}000 \div 7 =$ _____

5. $810 \div 9 =$ _____

6. $50{,}000 \div 5 =$ _____

7. **Number Sense** What basic fact would you
use to help solve $450{,}000 \div 9$? _____

8. In 1 week there are 7 days. How many weeks
are in 210 days? _____

9. How many weeks are there in 420 days? _____

Name_____

Using Patterns to Divide Mentally

Divide. Use mental math.

1. $250 \div 5 =$ _____

2. $1,400 \div 2 =$ _____

3. $300 \div 5 =$ _____

4. $1,600 \div 4 =$ _____

5. $240 \div 8 =$ _____

6. $36,000 \div 4 =$ _____

7. $16,000 \div 2 =$ _____

8. $270 \div 3 =$ _____

9. $4,200 \div 7 =$ _____

10. $640 \div 8 =$ _____

11. $2,000 \div 5 =$ _____

12. $320 \div 8 =$ _____

13. $12,000 \div 2 =$ _____

14. $1,600 \div 8 =$ _____

The fourth grade performed a play based on the story of Cinderella. There was one chair for each person present.

15. On Friday, 140 people came to the play. The chairs in the auditorium were arranged in 7 equal rows. How many chairs were in each row? _____

16. There were 8 equal rows set up for Saturday's performance. There were 240 people at the play on Saturday. How many chairs were in each row? _____

Test Prep

17. Which is the quotient of $56,000 \div 8$?

    A. 400   **B.** 4,000   **C.** 700   **D.** 7,000

18. **Writing in Math** Explain why the following answer is not correct: $1,000 \div 5 = \underline{2,000}$.

_____

_____

_____

Estimating Quotients

Estimate 460 ÷ 9.

You can use compatible numbers.

Ask yourself: What is a number close to 460 that could be easily divided by 9? Try 450.

450 ÷ 9 = 50

So, 460 ÷ 9 is about 50.

You can also estimate by thinking about multiplication.

Ask yourself: Nine times what number is about 460?

9 × 5 = 45, so 9 × 50 = 450.

So, 460 ÷ 9 is about 50.

50 is a good estimation for this problem.
Because 450 is less than 460, the estimated answer is an underestimate, that is, the actual answer is greater than 50.
An overestimate for this problem would be 540 ÷ 9 = 60.

Estimate each quotient. Tell whether you found an overestimate or an underestimate.

1. 165 ÷ 4 _____

2. 35 ÷ 4 _____

3. 715 ÷ 9 _____

4. 490 ÷ 8 _____

5. 512 ÷ 5 _____

6. 652 ÷ 8 _____

7. 790 ÷ 9 _____

8. 200 ÷ 7 _____

9. 311 ÷ 6 _____

10. **Number Sense** Find an overestimate and an underestimate for 313 ÷ 5. _____

Estimating Quotients

Estimate each quotient. Tell whether you found
an overestimate or an underestimate.

1. 82 ÷ 4   _____

2. 580 ÷ 3   _____

3. 96 ÷ 5   _____

4. 811 ÷ 2   _____

5. 194 ÷ 6   _____

6. 207 ÷ 7   _____

7. 282 ÷ 4   _____

8. 479 ÷ 8   _____

9. Jacqui is writing a book. If she needs to
   write 87 pages in 9 days, about how
   many pages will she write each day?   _____

10. Wade wants to give 412 of his marbles to
    10 of his friends. If he gives each friend
    the same number of marbles, about
    how many will each friend receive?   _____

Test Prep

11. Which is the best estimate for 502 ÷ 6?

    A. 60   **B.** 70   **C.** 80   **D.** 90

12. **Writing in Math** You are using division to determine how
    much whole wheat flour to use in a bread recipe. Is an
    estimated answer good enough?

    _____

    _____

Name_____

Dividing with Remainders

When you divide, you can think of putting items into groups.
For example:

$$60 \div 6 = 10$$

60 items   6 groups   10 items in
each group

Sometimes there are items left over. In division, the number of
"leftover" items is called the *remainder*. For example:

$$62 \div 6 = 10 \text{ R2} \longrightarrow 2 \text{ items left over}$$

62 items   6 groups   10 items in
each group

Divide. You may use counters or pictures to help.

1. $4\overline{)34}$

2. $8\overline{)65}$

3. $9\overline{)75}$

4. $6\overline{)28}$

5. $5\overline{)14}$

6. $9\overline{)37}$

7. Number Sense In division, why should the remainder not
be greater than the divisor?

© Pearson Education, Inc. 4

Use with Lesson 7-3. **83**

Dividing with Remainders

Divide. You may use counters or pictures to help.

1. $4\overline{)27}$ **2.** $6\overline{)32}$ **3.** $7\overline{)17}$ **4.** $9\overline{)29}$

5. $8\overline{)27}$ **6.** $3\overline{)27}$ **7.** $5\overline{)28}$ **8.** $4\overline{)35}$

9. $2\overline{)19}$ **10.** $7\overline{)30}$ **11.** $3\overline{)17}$ **12.** $9\overline{)16}$

If you arrange these items into equal rows, tell how many will be in each row and how many will be left over.

13. 26 shells into 3 rows _____

14. 19 pennies into 5 rows _____

15. 17 balloons into 7 rows _____

16. **Number Sense** Ms. Nikkel wants to divide her class of 23 students into 4 equal teams. Is this reasonable? Why or why not?

_____

_____

Test Prep

17. Which is the remainder for the quotient of 79 ÷ 8?

A. 7   **B.** 6   **C.** 5   **D.** 4

18. **Writing in Math** Pencils are sold in packages of 5. Explain why you need 6 packages in order to have enough for 27 students.

_____

_____

Name_____

Two-Digit Quotients

Here is how to divide two-digit quotients.

Find 37 ÷ 2.	What You **Show**	What You **Think**	What You **Write**
Step 1 Divide the tens.		There is 1 ten in each group and 1 ten left over.	$\begin{array}{r} 1 \\ 2\overline{)37} \\ -2 \\ \hline 1 \end{array}$
Step 2 Regroup by bringing down the ones.		Trade the extra ten for ten ones. The one ten and 7 ones make 17 ones.	$\begin{array}{r} 1 \\ 2\overline{)37} \\ -2 \\ \hline 17 \end{array}$
Step 3 Divide the ones.		There are 8 ones in each group and 1 one left over.	$\begin{array}{r} 18\,R1 \\ 2\overline{)37} \\ -2 \\ \hline 17 \\ -16 \\ \hline 1 \end{array}$

Use counters or draw pictures. Tell how many books are on each shelf and how many books are left over.

1. 66 books
   5 shelves _____

2. 78 books
   4 shelves _____

Divide. You may use counters or pictures to help.

3. $4\overline{)95}$ 4. $2\overline{)57}$ 5. $3\overline{)89}$

6. **Number Sense** You have 43 marbles. You divide them equally among some sacks. How many sacks must you use to get fewer than 8 marbles in each sack? _____

Name_____

Two-Digit Quotients

Use place-value blocks or draw pictures. Tell how many CDs are in each case and how many are left over.

1. 60 CDs
5 cases _____

2. 72 CDs
4 cases _____

3. 93 CDs
8 cases _____

Divide. You may use place-value blocks or pictures to help.

4. 9)97

5. 3)67

6. 6)80

7. 5)97

8. 2)54

9. 7)54

10. 8)92

11. 2)53

12. **Number Sense** Mr. Brooks brought a box of 66 acorns to class. Can he give 3 acorns to each of the 23 students in his class? Why or why not?

_____

_____

_____

Test Prep

13. Which is the quotient of 45 ÷ 4?

A. 10 R5   **B.** 11 R1   **C.** 11 R4   **D.** 12 R2

14. **Writing in Math** Explain how you can find the quotient of 84 ÷ 4.

_____

_____

_____

Dividing Two-Digit Numbers

You can find two-digit quotients by breaking apart the problem
and dividing tens, then ones.

Find 85 ÷ 5.
Estimate: 100 ÷ 5 = 20.

```
    17
5)85
  -5
   35
  -35
    0
```

Check: 17 × 5 = 85.
The answer checks.

Find 55 ÷ 3.
Estimate: 60 ÷ 3 = 20.

```
    18 R1
3)55
  -3
   25
  -24
    1
```

Check: 18 × 3 = 54.
54 + 1 = 55
The answer checks.

Find 83 ÷ 7.
Estimate: 84 ÷ 7 = 12.

```
    11 R6
7)83
  -7
   13
  - 7
    6
```

Check: 11 × 7 = 77.
77 + 6 = 83
The answer checks.

1.

```
    2 ☐
3)8 1
 -☐
   ☐ 1
  -☐ ☐
     0
```

2.

```
    1 ☐
4)7 6
 -☐
   ☐ ☐
  -☐ ☐
     0
```

3. 3)91

4. 4)86

5. 2)75

Name_____

Dividing Two-Digit Numbers

1.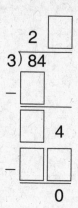

2.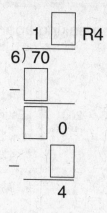

3.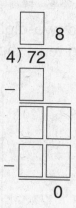

4. 2)72   **5.** 5)86   **6.** 7)94   **7.** 3)39

8. 8)99   **9.** 5)87   **10.** 2)96   **11.** 3)43

Mrs. Thomas is planning to provide snacks for 96 fourth graders when they go on a field trip to the aquarium. Each student will receive 1 of each snack. How many packages of each snack does Mrs. Thomas need?

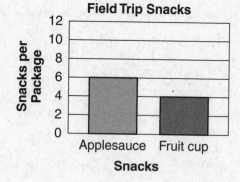

Field Trip Snacks

12. fruit cups _____

13. applesauce _____

Test Prep

14. Which is the remainder of 124 ÷ 18?

   A. 12   **B.** 16   **C.** 18   **D.** 20

15. Writing in Math Explain how to find the number of leftover pencils if Wendy wants to share 37 pencils with 9 people.

_____

_____

_____

PROBLEM-SOLVING SKILL
Interpreting Remainders

Muffins A parents' association was arranging muffins on plates for a bake sale. Each plate holds 6 muffins. There were 89 muffins baked for the sale.

When you solve a problem using division, the real-world situation tells you how to make sense of the remainder. For example:

Read and Understand	**Read and Understand**
How many plates will be filled?	How many muffins will be on the plate that is not filled?

Plan and Solve	**Plan and Solve**
Divide: $89 \div 6 = 14$ R5	Divide: $89 \div 6 = 14$ R5
The muffins will fill 14 plates.	There will be 5 muffins on the plate that is not filled.

Look Back and Check	**Look Back and Check**
14 plates will have 6 muffins each. There will be some muffins left over.	The remainder of 5 tells us that there are 5 extra muffins for another plate.

Solve.

The natural history museum has a hands-on mineral presentation. Each time the presentation is given, 8 students are permitted in the presentation area. One day, 100 students from Westbrook school were at the museum to see the presentation.

1. How many times must the presentation be given if all of the students see the presentation? _____

2. How many groups of 8 will see the presentation? _____

Name_____

Interpreting Remainders

The fourth-grade class is going camping as a nature field trip.
There are 85 students going on the trip. Solve the following
questions with this information.

1. There are 47 girls in the group. If each tent holds
   3 people, how many tents are needed for the girls? _____

2. The group will take 4 buses that can each carry
   20 children and their gear. The rest of the students
   will ride in the school van. How many students
   will ride in the van? _____

3. The teachers and parents will make 4 large pots
   of soup for dinner. About how many servings will
   each pot need to contain to feed all the students,
   4 teachers, and 6 parents? _____

4. Cups come in packages of 20. How many
   packages of cups will be needed for this meal? _____

5. One gallon of milk contains 128 fluid oz. How
   many 8 oz cups will 1 gal contain? _____

6. Each student pays $10.00 for the field trip. The chart
   shows how the money is used. If the leftover money is
   used for maintaining the camping equipment, how much
   does each student contribute for equipment?

Costs per Student

Camping fee	$2.00
Bus service	$3.50
Food	$3.75

Dividing Three-Digit Numbers

Find 454 ÷ 3.

Estimate: 450 ÷ 3 = 150.

Step 1	Step 2	Step 3	Check
Divide the hundreds.	Bring down the tens and divide.	Bring down the ones and divide.	Multiply the quotient by the divisor and add the remainder.

Step 1

Divide the hundreds.

```
    1
3)454      Multiply.
 -3        Subtract.
  1        Compare.
           1 < 3
```

Step 2

Bring down the tens and divide.

```
   15
3)454
 -3
  15       Multiply.
 -15       Subtract.
   0       Compare.
           0 < 3
```

Step 3

Bring down the ones and divide.

```
   151 R1
3)454
 -3
  15
 -15
   04      Multiply.
 -  3      Subtract.
    1      Compare.
           1 < 3
```

Check

Multiply the quotient by the divisor and add the remainder.

```
   1
  151      453
×   3    +   1
  453      454
```

The answer checks.

1.
```
   □ 9 R□
5)3 4 9
-□□
 □□
-□□
  □
```

2.

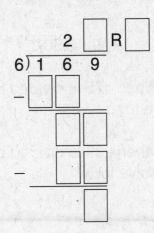
```
   2 □ R□
6)1 6 9
-□□
 □□
-□□
  □
```

3. 7)378

4. 5)227

5. 6)513

6. Number Sense When looking at the divisor and the dividend, how can you tell where to begin dividing?

_____

_____

Name_____

Dividing Three-Digit Numbers

1.
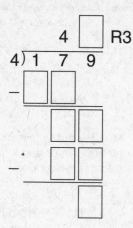

2.
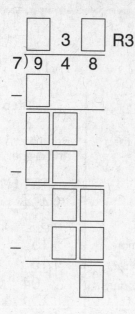

3.
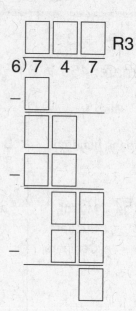

4. 7)698　　5. 8)747　　6. 2)329　　7. 9)411

8. 3)198　　9. 2)587　　10. 5)975　　11. 6)573

12. **Algebra** When 475 is divided by n, the quotient is 25. Solve for n.

_____

13. **Algebra** When 289 is divided by x, the quotient is 96 R1. Solve for x.

_____

Test Prep

14. Yvonne needs to distribute 345 stickers to 8 classrooms. How many stickers will each classroom get?

   A. 53　　　**B.** 44　　　**C.** 43　　　**D.** 38

15. **Writing in Math** Write and solve a word problem for 245 ÷ 7.

_____

_____

_____

Zeros in the Quotient

Find 956 ÷ 9.

First estimate: 900 ÷ 9 = 100.

Step 1	Step 2	Step 3	Check
Divide the hundreds.	Bring down the tens and divide.	Bring down the ones and divide.	Multiply the quotient by the divisor and add the remainder.

Step 1

$$\begin{array}{r} 1 \\ 9\overline{)956} \\ -9 \\ \hline 0 \end{array}$$

Multiply.

Compare.
0 < 9

Step 2

$$\begin{array}{r} 10 \\ 9\overline{)956} \\ -9 \\ \hline 05 \\ -0 \\ \hline 5 \end{array}$$

Multiply.
Subtract.
Compare.
5 < 9

5 can't be divided by 9. Place a zero in the quotient.

Step 3

$$\begin{array}{r} 106\,R2 \\ 9\overline{)956} \\ -9 \\ \hline 05 \\ -0 \\ \hline 56 \\ -54 \\ \hline 2 \end{array}$$

Multiply.
Subtract.
Compare.
2 < 9

Check

$$\begin{array}{r} \overset{5}{}106 \\ \times9 \\ \hline 954 \end{array} \qquad \begin{array}{r} 954 \\ +2 \\ \hline 956 \end{array}$$

The answer checks.

Divide. Check your answer.

1. $7\overline{)742}$

2. $5\overline{)520}$

3. $2\overline{)813}$

4. $4\overline{)808}$

5. Number Sense Could 540 ÷ 3 be 18? Why or why not?

_____

_____

_____

Zeros in the Quotient

Divide. Check your answer.

1. 3)921   2. 4)834   3. 5)549   4. 2)611

5. 6)627   6. 8)824   7. 7)762   8. 5)535

9. 4)810   10. 6)121   11. 7)712   12. 9)936

13. **Number Sense** When Donald divided 636 by 6, his quotient was 16. What common mistake did he make?

_____

The fourth graders in Clifton's classroom used computer games to practice their math skills. Each student's score was the same in each round.

14. Clifton scored 918 points in 9 rounds of math facts. How many points did he score in each round?   _____

15. Brionne scored 654 points in 6 rounds. How many points did she score in each round?   _____

Test Prep

16. Which is the quotient of 617 ÷ 3?

   A. 203 R2   **B.** 205   **C.** 205 R1   **D.** 205 R2

17. **Writing in Math** In Patricia's class, 7 students need to share 714 building blocks to make a building model. Each student needs an equal number of blocks. Patricia thinks each student should have 100 blocks. Is this the best plan? Explain.

_____

_____

Dividing Money Amounts

Find $1.68 ÷ 3.

Estimate: $1.50 ÷ 3 = $0.50, so $1.68 ÷ 3 should be close to $0.50.

Step 1	**Step 2**	**Check**
Divide the same way you would with whole numbers.	Show the dollar sign and decimal point in the quotient. The decimal point should be moved straight up.	Multiply the quotient by the divisor.

Step 1

```
      56
3)$1.68
  - 15
    18
  - 18
     0
```

Step 2

```
    $0.56
3)$1.68
  - 15
    18
  - 18
     0
```

Check

```
  $0.56
×     3
  $1.68
```

The answer checks.

Divide. Check your answer.

1. 6)$3.12   **2.** 5)$5.35   **3.** 4)$8.80   **4.** 7)$4.55

5. Number Sense What is a good estimate for $4.21 ÷ 2?

_____

Dividing Money Amounts

Divide. Check your answer.

1. 4)$8.12
2. 3)$1.20
3. 5)$6.55
4. 2)$9.68

5. 7)$7.21
6. 9)$8.19
7. 6)$4.74
8. 8)$9.52

Use the table at the right for Exercises 9 and 10. Find the cost of one of each type of tropical fish.

9. Neon barb

_____

10. Guppy

_____

Pete's Pets

Fish	Price
Guppies	6 for $1.44
Neon barbs	3 for $3.99
Tetras	3 for $4.98
Zebra danio	3 for $2.19
Black snail	$0.99 each

11. Marcus bought 6 cans of fish food for $7.74. How much did he spend per can?

_____

Test Prep

12. If James bought 5 trading cards for $5.25, how much did each card cost?

A. $0.88   **B.** $0.99   **C.** $1.00   **D.** $1.05

13. **Writing in Math** Explain how you can use the fact 620 ÷ 4 = 155 to find the cost of each bottle of water, if the price is $6.20 for 4 bottles.

_____

_____

_____

PROBLEM-SOLVING STRATEGY

Write a Number Sentence

The Painter Stephan spent $6.35 on paints for a painting on which he is working. He bought 5 tubes of paint. How much did each tube of paint cost?

Read and Understand

Step 1: What do you know? The 5 tubes of paint cost $6.35.

Step 2: What are you trying to find? How much each paint tube cost.

Plan and Solve

Step 3: What strategy will you use? Strategy:
Write a number sentence.

Let t = cost of one tube of paint.

$6.35 \div 5 = t$

Solve for t.

$$
\begin{array}{r}
\$1.27 \\
5)\overline{\$6.35} \\
-5 \\
\hline
13 \\
-10 \\
\hline
35 \\
-35 \\
\hline
0
\end{array}
$$

So, each tube of paint costs $1.27.

Look Back and Check

Step 4: Is your answer reasonable? Yes, $5 \times \$1.27 = \$6.35$.

Solve the number sentence.

1. There are 364 students who will be taking a field trip. The students will ride on 7 buses. An equal number of students will ride on each bus. How many students will be on each bus?
   s = the number of students on each bus
   $364 \div 7 = s$

   _____

Write a number sentence for the problem, then solve.

2. Sarah picked pears at her aunt's farm. She picked a total of 96 pears. She placed the pears into 8 baskets. How many pears did she place in each basket?

   _____

   _____

PROBLEM-SOLVING STRATEGY **P 7-10**
Write a Number Sentence

Using a Number Sentence to Solve Problems Solve the number sentence. Write the answer in a complete sentence.

1. McKinley Elementary School is holding its annual science fair. There are 140 projects to be displayed. There is room for 5 projects on each table. How many tables are needed to display all the projects?

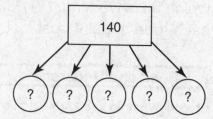

_____

_____

Writing a Number Sentence to Solve Problems Draw a picture to show the main idea for each problem. Then write a number sentence. Solve. Write the answer in a complete sentence.

2. Stanley's science fair project is on recycling. As part of the project, he and his friends collected 45 lb of aluminum cans and redeemed them at the recycling center. They received $0.31 per pound. How much did they receive for all their cans?

_____

_____

3. Brittany's project showed the size of the planet Jupiter as compared to Earth. She found that the diameter of Jupiter was about 11 times greater than the diameter of Earth. If her model of Earth has a diameter of 2 in., how large should the diameter of her model of Jupiter be?

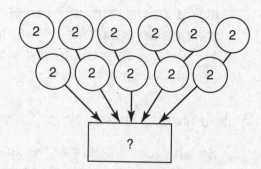

_____

_____

Divisibility Rules

You can use special rules to tell if a number is divisible by 2, 3, 5, 9, or 10.

A whole number is divisible by	Example
2 if the ones digit is even.	2, 16, 238
3 if the sum of the digits is divisible by 3.	324 $3 + 2 + 4 = 9$, $9 \div 3 = 3$
5 if the number ends in 0 or 5.	605, 310
9 if the sum of the digits is divisible by 9.	747 $7 + 4 + 7 = 18$, $18 \div 9 = 2$
10 if the number ends in 0.	60, 120, 350

Test each number to see if it is divisible by 2, 3, 5, 9, or 10.

1. 20 _____

2. 88 _____

3. 63 _____

4. 45 _____

5. 65 _____

6. 303 _____

7. 510 _____

8. 603 _____

9. 105 _____

10. 654 _____

11. Number Sense If a number is divisible by 10, is it always divisible by 2? Explain.

_____

_____

_____

_____

_____

Name_____

Divisibility Rules

Test each number to see if it is divisible by 2, 3, 5, 9, and 10.

1. 15 _____

2. 45 _____

3. 48 _____

4. 60 _____

5. 198 _____

6. 375 _____

7. 720 _____

8. 682 _____

9. Name four ways Mr. Yancey can divide his class of 20 into equal groups.

_____

_____

10. Derrick has a collection of 85 baseball cards that he wants to put into a binder. He wants to put them on pages that hold 9 cards each. Will each of the pages be filled? How do you know?

_____

_____

_____

Test Prep

11. Which of the following numbers is divisible by 2, 3, 5, 9, and 10?

A. 255   **B.** 309   **C.** 450   **D.** 535

12. Writing in Math A school bus can hold a maximum of 66 students. How do you know you can equally put 3 students in each seat?

_____

_____

Finding Averages

Follow these steps to find the average, or mean, of 13, 15, 14, and 18.

Step 1 Add the numbers: 13 + 15 + 14 + 18 = 60.	**Step 2** Count how many numbers are in the group. 4	**Step 3** Divide: 60 (the total of the numbers) ÷ 4 (how many numbers in the group) = 15 (the average, or mean, of the numbers)

Find the average, or mean, of each set of data.

1. 25, 13, 24, 34 _____

2. 16, 15, 17 _____

3. 7, 10, 9, 10 _____

4. 4, 7, 6, 7, 11 _____

5. 13, 17, 18, 20 _____

6. 30, 35, 39, 36 _____

7. Number Sense What are two numbers that have an average of 50?

_____

8. What was the average temperature of the four times shown in the chart? _____

Time	Temperature
9:00 A.M.	60°F
11:00 A.M.	62°F
1:00 P.M.	64°F
3:00 P.M.	74°F

Finding Averages

Find the average, or mean, of each set of data.

1. 6, 9, 4, 5 _____

2. 4, 8, 2, 7, 4 _____

3. 17, 25, 15 _____

4. 47, 36, 44, 29 _____

5. 9, 6, 7, 4, 3, 7 _____

6. 124, 233, 156 _____

7. 25, 16, 12, 42, 20 _____

8. 425, 125, 542 _____

9. Number Sense Could the average of three numbers be one of those three numbers? Give an example.

_____

_____

Use the table at the right for 10–14.

Find the average score for each bowler.

10. Ali _____

11. Brenda _____

12. Caitlin _____

13. Joseph _____

Bowling Scores

Bowler	Game		
	1	2	3
Ali	107	67	114
Brenda	112	115	124
Caitlin	98	125	137
Joseph	94	87	122

Test Prep

14. Which is the average of the following test scores: 98, 96, 100, 93, 83?

A. 90   **B.** 94   **C.** 96   **D.** 470

15. Writing in Math In the set 42, 43, 51, 52, and 44, explain why the average will be in the 40s.

_____

_____

Dividing by Multiples of 10

You can use basic facts to divide by multiples of 10.

There are rules for the number of zeros in the quotient.

Here are two examples:

$420 \div 70 =$	$400 \div 50 =$
What is the basic fact that will help solve this problem?	What is the basic fact that will help solve this problem?
$42 \div 7 = 6$	$40 \div 5 = 8$
Notice that there are no zeros in the numbers in the basic fact.	In this case, there is a zero in the number 40 in the basic fact.
You can apply the following rule.	You can apply the following rule.
the number of zeros in the quotient = the number of zeros in the divisor − the number of zeros in the dividend	the number of zeros in the quotient = one less than the number of zeros in the divisor − the number of zeros in the dividend
So, $420 \div 70 = 6$.	So, $400 \div 50 = 8$.

Divide. Use mental math.

1. $80 \div 40 =$ _____

2. $810 \div 90 =$ _____

3. $2,400 \div 6 =$ _____

4. $2,500 \div 5 =$ _____

5. $210 \div 30 =$ _____

6. $1,200 \div 20 =$ _____

7. Number Sense What basic fact would you use to solve $4,500 \div 90$? _____

8. There are 540 students at Middlebury school. The students are arranged into 9 teams for a sports event. How many students are on each team?

_____

Name_____

Dividing by Multiples of 10

Divide. Use mental math.

1. 360 ÷ 40 = _____   2. 450 ÷ 90 = _____   3. 270 ÷ 30 = _____

4. 630 ÷ 70 = _____   5. 1,600 ÷ 40 = _____   6. 1,000 ÷ 20 = _____

7. 250 ÷ 50 = _____   8. 490 ÷ 70 = _____   9. 1,200 ÷ 60 = _____

10. 400 ÷ 80 = _____   11. 2,100 ÷ 70 = _____   12. 1,800 ÷ 30 = _____

13. **Number Sense** If 270 ÷ 90 = 3 and 2,700 ÷ 90 = 30,
    what is 270,000 ÷ 90? _____

The whooping crane is being reintroduced to the midwestern
United States. The birds fly from Wisconsin to Florida in the fall.

14. Suppose a group of cranes covered the 1,200 mi trip
    south in about 20 flying days. How far did they fly per day? _____

15. In the spring, the birds flew the return trip back north
    in only 10 days. How many times as fast did the birds fly
    on their return trip? _____

16. Suppose that one day the flock covered 80 mi in 2 hr.
    How many miles per hour were the birds flying?

_____

Test Prep

17. Which is the quotient of 5,400 ÷ 60?

    A. 50   **B.** 60   **C.** 90   **D.** 900

18. **Writing in Math** Would it be quicker to use a calculator or
    to use mental math to answer Exercise 17? Why?

_____

_____

_____

Dividing with Two-Digit Divisors

When you divide with a two-digit divisor, an estimate is an important first step.

Find 228 ÷ 24.

Step 1 Find a reasonable estimate. You can use compatible numbers or rounding to do so.

225 ÷ 25 = 9, so 9 is a good estimate.

Step 2 Divide using the estimate.

```
        9 R12
24)228
    −216
       12
```

Step 3 Check your work.

```
  24        216
×  9      +  12
 216        228
```

The answer checks. 228 is the dividend.

Estimate each quotient. Then divide.

1. 12)264

2. 16)336

3. 45)810

4. 63)819

5. 21)672

6. 31)372

7. Number Sense What is a good estimate for 345 ÷ 26? _____

Dividing with Two-Digit Divisors

Estimate each quotient. Then divide.

1. 84 ÷ 22 _____   **2.** 271 ÷ 53 _____

3. 379 ÷ 42 _____   **4.** 294 ÷ 61 _____

5. 29)‾167   **6.** 34)‾296   **7.** 57)‾379

8. 76)‾247   **9.** 55)‾179   **10.** 82)‾396

11. Ms. Nicholas brought 189 blue beads and
189 white beads so that her class could make
bracelets. It takes 42 beads to make a bracelet.
How many bracelets could they make?   _____

12. Mr. Barkley is helping students make candles using
wax and empty milk cartons. Mr. Barkley carefully
melted 160 oz of wax. If each of the 26 students
makes a candle, about how many ounces will each
candle weigh?   _____

Test Prep

13. Trisha scored 568 points in 71 basketball games. How
many points did she score per game?

A. 9 points   **B.** 8 R41 points   **C.** 8 R22 points   **D.** 8 points

14. Writing in Math Explain why the remainder of any division
problem must be smaller than the divisor.

_____

_____

_____

_____

Name_____

The Appalachian Trail

Hiking Trip Lee and his family are planning a hiking trip on the Appalachian Trail. They are packing food in 3 lb bundles. How many bundles could they make with 51 lb of food?

What strategy can you use to solve this problem? Write a number sentence.

$51 \div 3 = b.$ b = the number of food bundles

$$
\begin{array}{r}
17 \\
3\overline{)51} \\
-3 \\
\hline
21 \\
-21 \\
\hline
0
\end{array}
$$

They can pack 17 food bundles.

---

1. The Appalachian Trail goes through 14 states. There are about 78 mi of Appalachian Trail in Georgia, about 68 mi in New Jersey, and about 82 mi in Massachusetts. What is the average number of miles of trail in these 3 states?

   _____

2. There are about 560 mi of trail in Virginia. If a person planned to hike 8 mi per day, how many days would it take to hike the Virginia portion of the trail? Write a number sentence, then solve the problem.

   _____

   _____

3. Use divisibility rules to see if the total number of miles of Appalachian Trail (2,168 mi) is divisible by 2, 3, 5, 9, or 10.

   _____

   _____

PROBLEM-SOLVING APPLICATIONS
The Divisions of Space

Solve. Write your answer in a complete sentence.

1. Astronauts eat 3 meals per day. An astronaut may require about 2,400 calories each day. If an astronaut eats the same amount of calories each meal, how many calories does the astronaut consume at each meal?

_____

_____

2. Astronauts use a space suit so they can space walk outside of a shuttle or station. A space suit's oxygen and power need to be recharged in the space shuttle after 8 hr of space walking. How many times does the space suit need to be recharged if used for 192 hr?

_____

_____

3. An astronaut is scheduled to sleep for 480 min each day. If an astronaut is sleeping in a space shuttle that is orbiting Earth, he could see the sun rise every 45 min. How many times could an astronaut see the sun rise during his scheduled sleep time?

_____

_____

4. What was the average distance from Earth for the space shuttle *Atlantis* from Wednesday until Saturday?

_____

_____

Distance from Earth for *Atlantis*

Day	Distance
Wednesday	278 mi
Thursday	323 mi
Friday	350 mi
Saturday	253 mi

Name _____

Relating Solids and Plane Figures

Solid figures have three dimensions: length, width, and height. Many solids have edges, faces, and vertices.

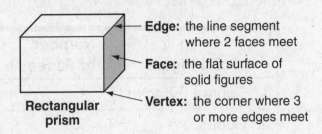

Edge: the line segment where 2 faces meet

Face: the flat surface of solid figures

Vertex: the corner where 3 or more edges meet

Rectangular prism

Spheres, cylinders, and cones have curved surfaces. Other solids have all flat surfaces.

Curved Surfaces

Sphere   Cylinder   Cone

Flat Surfaces

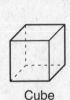

Cube   Triangular prism   Square pyramid   Rectangular pyramid

Complete the table.

Solid Figure	Number of Faces	Number of Edges	Number of Vertices	Shape(s) of Faces
1. Rectangular prism				
2. Cube				
3. Triangular prism				
4. Square pyramid				

5. Reasoning Compare rectangular pyramids and rectangular prisms. How are they alike?

_____

Name_____

Relating Solids and Plane Figures

Complete the table.

Solid Figure	Number of Faces	Number of Edges	Number of Vertices
1. Square Pyramid			
2. Cube			
3. Triangular Prism			

Identify the solid that best describes each object.

4.

_____

5.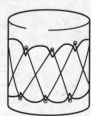

_____

6.

_____

7. How many total faces does a rectangular prism have? _____

Test Prep

8. Which solid does the figure represent?

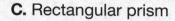

   A. Rectangular pyramid   **C.** Rectangular prism

   B. Cylinder   **D.** Square pyramid

9. Writing in Math Explain the difference between a plane figure and a solid figure.

_____

_____

_____

Polygons

Polygons are closed plane figures that are made up of line segments. All of the line segments connect. All of the sides of a polygon are straight, not curved.

Polygon
Closed figure
made of
line segments

Not a polygon
Not a closed
figure

Not a polygon
Not all of the
sides are line
segments.

Here are some common polygons. Note that the sides of polygons do not all have to be the same length.

Octagon
8 sides

Hexagon
6 sides

Pentagon
5 sides

Quadrilateral
4 sides

Triangle
3 sides

Draw an example of each type of polygon. How many sides and vertices does each one have?

1. Hexagon

_____

2. 7-sided polygon

_____

3. Pentagon

_____

4. 9-sided polygon

_____

Polygons

Draw an example of each polygon. How many sides and vertices does each one have?

1. Square

2. Octagon

3. Hexagon

_____ _____ _____

The map shows the shapes of buildings in Polygon Park. Identify the polygons that are lettered.

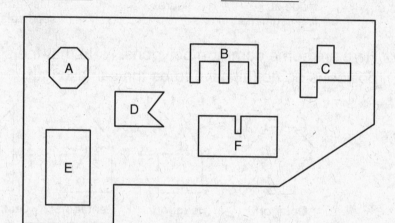

4. A

_____

5. D

_____

6. C

_____

7. B

_____

8. E

_____

9. F

_____

Test Prep

10. Which is the point where sides meet in a polygon?

    A. Edge   **B.** Endpoint   **C.** Side   **D.** Vertex

11. **Writing in Math** Describe two polygons by the number of vertices and sides each has.

_____

Lines, Line Segments, Rays, and Angles

Here are some important geometric terms.

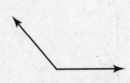

Line segment
A part of a line. It has two endpoints. This is line segment *XY*.

Ray
A part of a line. It has one endpoint and goes on and on in one direction. This is ray *AB*.

Right angle
A square corner.

Obtuse angle
Greater than a right angle.

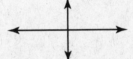

Parallel lines
Never intersect.

Intersecting lines
Pass through the same point.

Perpendicular lines
Lines that form right angles.

Use geometric terms to describe what is shown. Be as specific as possible.

1.

2.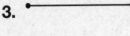

3.

_____   _____   _____

_____   _____   _____

4. Name three different rays.

_____

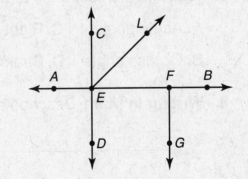

5. Name two different line segments.

_____

Lines, Line Segments, Rays, and Angles

Use geometric terms to describe what is shown. Be as specific as possible.

1.

_____

2.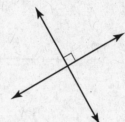

_____

3.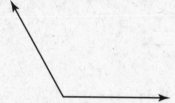

_____

4.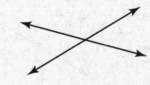

_____

5. Name two lines.

_____

6. Name two obtuse angles.

_____

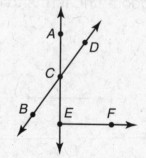

Test Prep

7. Which is the geometric term for ∠HJK?

   A. Acute angle   **C.** Right angle

   B. Obtuse angle   **D.** Straight angle

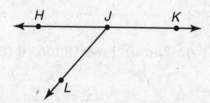

8. **Writing in Math** Describe an acute angle.

_____

_____

Equilateral triangle
All sides are the same length.

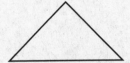

Isosceles triangle
At least two sides are the same length.

Scalene triangle
No sides are the same length.

Right triangle
One angle is a right angle.

Acute triangle
All three angles are acute angles.

Obtuse triangle
One angle is an obtuse angle.

Square
There are four right angles. All sides are the same length.

Rectangle
There are four right angles.

Parallelogram
Opposite sides are parallel.

Rhombus
Opposite sides are parallel and all sides are the same length.

Trapezoid
There is only one pair of parallel sides.

Classify each triangle by its sides and then by its angles.

1.

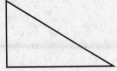

_____

2.

_____

Write the name of each quadrilateral.

3.

_____

4.

_____

Triangles and Quadrilaterals

Classify each triangle by its sides and then by its angles.

1. 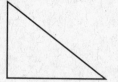 _____

2. 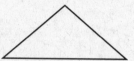 _____

3. 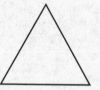 _____

Write the name of each quadrilateral.

4.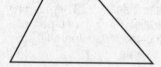

5.

_____   _____

Test Prep

6. Which is a triangle with one right angle?

   A. Scalene triangle   **C.** Right triangle

   B. Obtuse triangle   **D.** Acute triangle

7. Writing in Math Explain why a square can never be a trapezoid.

_____

_____

_____

Circles

A circle is made up of all points that are
the same distance from the center point.

A radius connects the center to any point
on the circle.

A chord connects any two points on
the circle.

A diameter connects two points on the circle
and passes through the center of the circle.

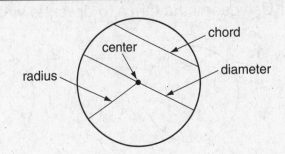

State whether the line segment shown is a radius, a chord, or a diameter.

1.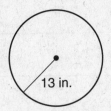

2.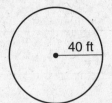

3.

4.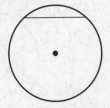

_____   _____   _____   _____

5. Writing in Math How is a chord different from a radius?

_____

_____

_____

_____

For each circle shown, find the length of the diameter.

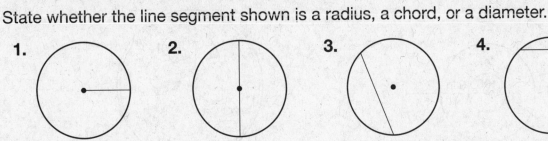

6. 13 in.

7. 40 ft

8. 11 cm

9. 5 m

_____   _____   _____   _____

Circles

Use geometric terms to describe what is shown on each circle.

1.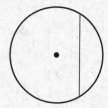

2.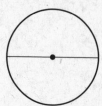

3.

_____   _____   _____

Find the length of the diameter of each circular object.

4.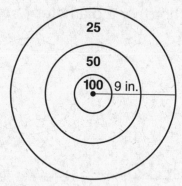

5.

_____   _____

Test Prep

6. A CD has a radius of 6 cm. Which is its diameter?

A. 3 cm   **B.** 12 cm   **C.** 18 cm   **D.** 12 in.

7. Writing in Math What is the relationship between the diameter and the radius of a circle?

_____

_____

_____

_____

Congruent Figures and Motions

When two figures have the same
shape and size, they are congruent.

Not congruent
Different size.

Congruent
Same size
and shape.

Not congruent
Different shape
and size.

Figures can be moved in three ways:
by slides, flips, or turns. When a
figure is moved, its size and shape
do not change.

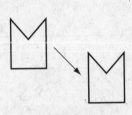 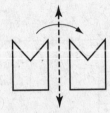 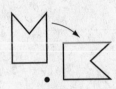

Slide
Moves the figure in
a straight direction.

Flip
Gives the figure its
mirror image. Sometimes
the object looks the
same after being flipped.

Turn
Moves a figure
about a point.

Do the figures in each pair appear to be congruent? If so, tell if
they are related by a flip, slide, or turn.

1.  **2.** 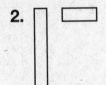 **3.**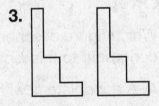

_____ _____ _____

_____ _____ _____

4. Reasoning Could the letters L and M ever be congruent? Explain.

_____

_____

Congruent Figures and Motions

Do the figures in each pair appear to be congruent? If so,
tell if they are related by a flip, slide, or turn.

1.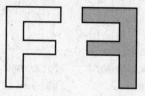

2.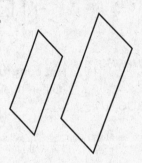

3.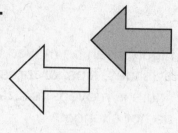

_____ _____ _____

4.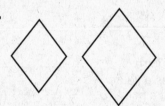

5.

6.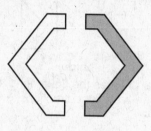

_____ _____ _____

Test Prep

7. Which figure described could be
congruent to this rectangle?

   A. A quadrilateral with equal sides   **C.** A quadrilateral with equal angles

   B. A rectangle with equal sides   **D.** A triangle with equal sides

8. Writing in Math Describe how four turns can put a figure
in its original position.

_____

_____

_____

_____

Name_____

Symmetry

R 8-7

Symmetric figures are figures that can be folded to make two halves that are congruent to each other. The lines that divide a symmetric figure into congruent halves are called lines of symmetry.

This square has 4 lines of symmetry. If you fold the square along any of the 4 dashed lines, the two halves will lie on top of each other.

How many lines of symmetry does each figure have?

1.    2.   3.   4.

_____   _____   _____   _____

5.   6.   7.   8.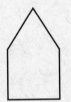

_____   _____   _____   _____

9. **Reasoning** How many lines of symmetry does the letter R have?   _____

10. Complete the drawing so that the figure is symmetric.

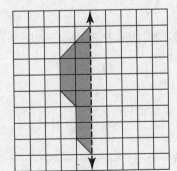

© Pearson Education, Inc. 4

102 Use with Lesson 8-7.

Symmetry

How many lines of symmetry does each figure have?

1.

_____

2.

_____

3.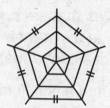

_____

4.

_____

5.

_____

6.

_____

7. Finish the drawing to make it symmetric.

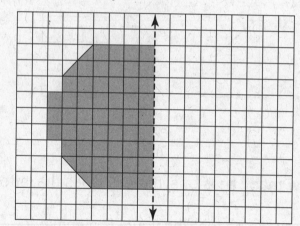

Test Prep

8. How many lines of symmetry does a rhombus that is not a square have?

   A. 0   **B.** 1   **C.** 2   **D.** 3

9. **Writing in Math** Explain why a square is always symmetric.

_____

_____

_____

Similar Figures

Similar figures are figures that have the same shape. The figures may or may not have the same size.

These triangles are about the same size, but they do not have the same shape. The triangles are NOT similar.

These shapes are similar. They have the same shape but are not the same size.

Do the figures in each pair appear to be similar? If so, are they also congruent?

1.

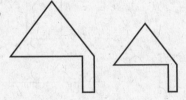

_____

2.

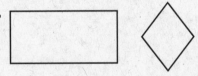

_____

3.

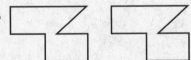

_____

4.

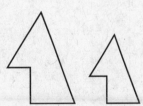

_____

5.

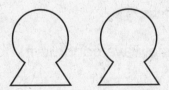

_____

6.

_____

Similar Figures

Do the figures in each pair appear to be similar? If so, are they
also congruent?

1.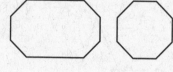

_____

2.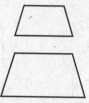

_____

3.

_____

4.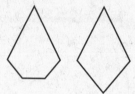

_____

5.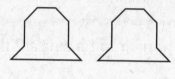

_____

6.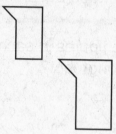

_____

Test Prep

7. Which pair of figures is similar and congruent?

A.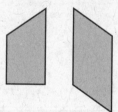

C.

B.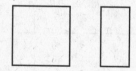

D.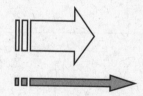

8. Writing in Math Explain why similar figures are not always congruent.

_____

_____

_____

Name_____

Writing to Describe

How would you describe the figures below?

 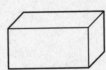

Cube　　**Rectangular pyramid**　　**Rectangular prism**

Tips for writing a math description:

- Make a list of all the geometric terms that tell about or describe how the shapes are alike.

- Choose the terms to use in your answer.

- Use geometric terms correctly when you write your description.

Example

Geometric terms that describe how the shapes are alike:

　　solid figures

　　flat surfaces

　　have rectangular faces

Since all of the shapes have height, width, and depth, they are all solid figures. They all have flat surfaces, and each of them has at least one rectangular face. They all have edges and vertices.

---

1. Write two statements to describe how the pairs of lines are alike.

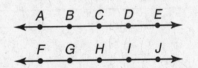 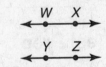

_____

_____

_____

2. Write three statements comparing rectangular prisms and rectangular pyramids.

_____

_____

_____

Name_____

Writing to Describe

Write two statements to describe how each pair of figures are alike or different. Use geometric terms.

1.

_____

_____

_____

2.

_____

_____

_____

Test Prep

3. Which statement does NOT correctly describe the figures?

   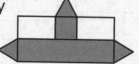 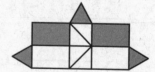

   A. The figures are similar.

   B. Both figures have five sections.

   C. One figure has 3 triangles and the other has 7 triangles.

   D. The shading of the figures is different.

4. **Writing in Math** Describe how a baseball and a basketball are alike.

_____

_____

104 Use with Lesson 8-9.

Perimeter

You can use addition to find the perimeter of a figure.

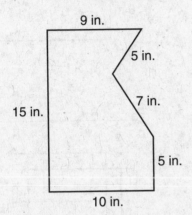

Add the lengths of the sides.

$9 + 5 + 7 + 5 + 10 + 15 = 51$ in.

Sometimes you can use a formula to find the perimeter.

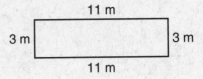

$P = 2l + 2w$

l is the length and w is the width.

$P = 2l + 2w$

$P = (2 \times 11) + (2 \times 3)$

$P = 22 + 6$

$P = 28$ m

Find the perimeter of each figure.

1.

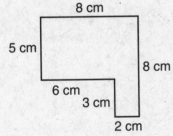

2.

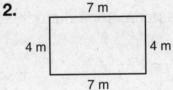

3.

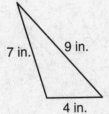

4.

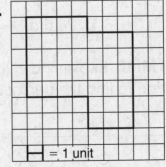

Name _____

Perimeter

Find the perimeter of each figure.

1.
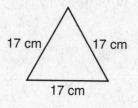
6 ft
4 ft   4 ft
5 ft   5 ft
4 ft   4 ft
6 ft

_____

2.
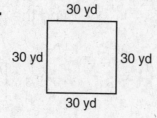
30 yd
30 yd   30 yd
30 yd

_____

3.
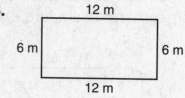
12 m
6 m   6 m
12 m

_____

4.
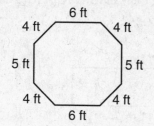
17 cm   17 cm
17 cm

_____

5.
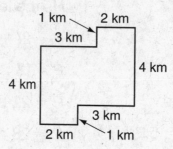
1 km   2 km
3 km
4 km
4 km
3 km
2 km   1 km

_____

6.
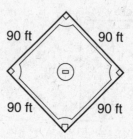
☐ = 1 unit

_____

7. What is the perimeter around the bases?

_____

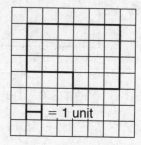
90 ft   90 ft
90 ft   90 ft

Test Prep

8. Which is the perimeter of this figure?

    A. 77 cm   **B.** 63 cm

    C. 56 cm   **D.** 28 cm

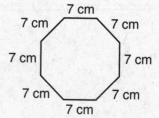
7 cm
7 cm   7 cm
7 cm   7 cm
7 cm   7 cm
7 cm

9. Writing in Math Explain how you can use multiplication to find the perimeter of a square.

_____

_____

_____

Area

What is the area of this rectangle?

Use the formula $A = lw$:

$A = 8 \times 5$

$A = 40$

The area is 40 square feet.

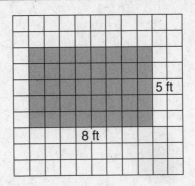

What is the area of this figure?

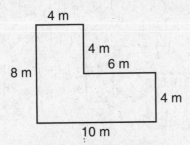

You can draw segments to divide the figure into rectangles. Then find the area of each rectangle and add.

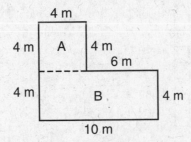

Rectangle A

$A = lw$

$A = 4 \times 4$

$\quad = 16$

Rectangle B

$A = lw$

$A = 4 \times 10$

$\quad = 40$

$16 + 40 = 56$, so the area of the original figure is 56 square meters.

Find the area of each rectangle.

1.

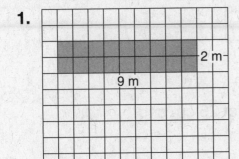

_____

2.

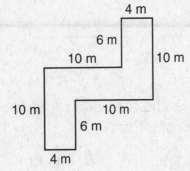

_____

3. **Reasoning** The area of a rectangle is 56 square inches. The width of the rectangle is 7 in. What is the length? _____

Area

Find the area of each figure.

1.

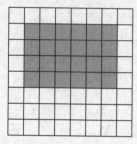

5 in.

5 in.

_____

2.

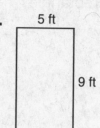

5 ft

9 ft

_____

3.

_____

4.

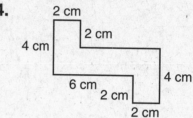

2 cm

2 cm

4 cm

6 cm

2 cm

4 cm

2 cm

_____

5. What is the area of both the bedrooms?

_____

6. What is the area of the whole house?

_____

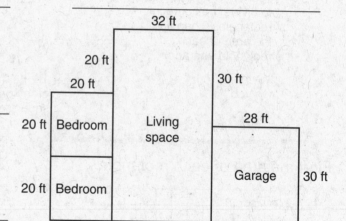

32 ft

20 ft

20 ft

30 ft

20 ft Bedroom

Living space

28 ft

20 ft Bedroom

Garage   30 ft

Test Prep

7. Which is the area of a rectangle with a length of 26 cm and a width of 34 cm?

   A. 992 cm   **B.** 884 cm   **C.** 720 cm   **D.** 324 cm

8. Writing in Math Explain how you would find the length of one side of a square if the area is 16 square units.

_____

Name_____

Act It Out

The Paper Marla wants to buy a newspaper from a newspaper vending machine on the street corner. The vending machine takes only nickels and dimes. The cost of the paper is $0.75. What is the fewest number of coins Marla can use to buy the paper?

Read and Understand

Step 1: What do you know?

A paper costs $0.75. The vending machine takes only nickels and dimes.

Step 2: What are you trying to find?

Find the least number of coins Marla will need.

Plan and Solve

Step 3: What strategy will you use?

Strategy: Act it out

Use coins to act it out. Combine different numbers of nickels and dimes to make $0.75. One combination is 5 dimes and 5 nickels, a total of 10 coins. The best combination is 7 dimes and 1 nickel, a total of 8 coins.

Look Back and Check

Step 4: Is your work correct?

Yes. Any combination must have at least 1 nickel since the amount needed for the paper ends in 5.

---

1. How many squares are needed to make the 6th design?

_____

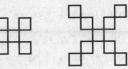 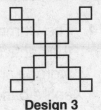

Design 1   **Design 2**   **Design 3**

2. Tom and Toby each run every day. Tom runs 4 mi each day. Toby runs 5 mi every day. How many miles has Tom run when Toby has run 65 mi?

_____

Name_____

Act It Out

Solve each problem. Write the answer in a complete sentence.

1. The Wilsons have 12 yd of fence for their garden. What are the length and width of the garden if it has the greatest possible area?

_____

2.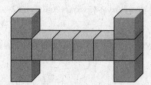

   The town of Mount Harris needs to build another bridge over Franklin Creek. If the second bridge is exactly the same as the first bridge, how many cube units are needed to build the second bridge?

_____

3. Joshua wants to build a fort in his backyard. He has 10 pieces of wood that are each 6 ft long. If Joshua arranges the wood into a rectangle to make the greatest area, what is the area of the fort?

_____

4. The Community Center wants to separate the basement of their activity hall into two rooms. One room will be used for storage and the other will have space for table tennis. The entire basement is a rectangle with a length of 48 ft and a width of 12 ft. The storage room must have an area of 144 ft. What is the perimeter and area of the table tennis room?

_____

_____

_____

Volume

The number of cubic units needed to fill a solid figure is its volume. To find the volume of a solid figure, you can count each cube. The figure to the right has a volume of 8 cubic units.

You can also use multiplication to find the volume of a solid figure.

You can use the formula $V = lwh$.

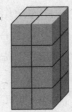

h = height of figure

w = width of figure

l = length of figure

Volume = length × width × height

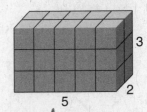

3

2

5

$V = lwh$

$V = 5 \times 2 \times 3$

    $= 30$

The volume is 30 cubic units.

Find the volume of each figure.

1.

_____

2.

_____

3.

_____

4.

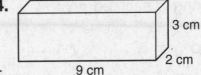

3 cm

2 cm

9 cm

_____

5. Reasoning A box with dimensions 4 in. by 4 in. by 4 in. is placed inside a box with dimensions 6 in. by 6 in. by 6 in. How much space is left inside the larger box after the smaller box is put inside?

_____

Name_____

Volume

Find the volume of each figure.

1.

_____

2.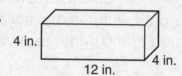

4 in.   12 in.   4 in.

_____

3.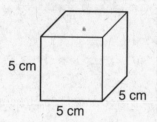

5 cm   5 cm   5 cm

_____

4.

6 ft   11 ft   3 ft

_____

5. A rectangular prism has a length of 7 cm, a width of 4 cm, and a height of 3 cm. What is the volume of the prism? _____

6. **Reasoning** The length of an edge of a cube is 5 ft. What is the total volume of two cubes of the same size? _____

7. If a cube has a volume of 64 cubic units, how long is each edge? _____

Test Prep

8. What is the volume of a cube that has an edge of 7 yd?

   A. 343 cubic yd   **B.** 98 cubic yd   **C.** 49 cubic yd   **D.** 21 cubic yd

9. **Writing in Math** If you know that a rectangular prism has a length of 256 m and a width of 192 m, can you find its volume? Explain your answer.

_____

_____

Name_____

The Living Room

Dana's parents are making some changes to their living room.
The east wall of the living room has two different paintings.

East Wall

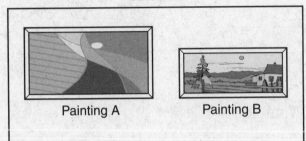

Painting A   Painting B

Are the paintings congruent?

No. They are the same shape but not the same size.

1. Dana's parents bought two round tables to be placed on each side of a couch. What is the diameter of Table X? What is the radius of Table Y?

Table X   **Table Y**

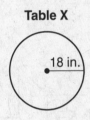

18 in.

54 in.

_____

_____

2. Are the tables similar, congruent, or both? Explain.

_____

_____

3. Dana's father thought it would be a good idea to move the living room rug. Was the rug moved by a slide, flip, or turn?

_____

4. Dana's mother made a special design on the floor using tile. How many lines of symmetry does the design have?

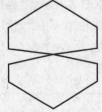

_____

Native American Math

1. Some Native American tribes used to play a game of skill in which players had to throw a lance through the center of a rolling hoop. What is the diameter of the hoop?

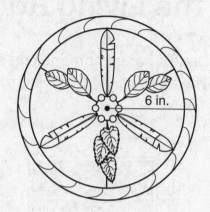

6 in.

_____

2. The Plains tribe lived in tepees. What solid figure best describes a tepee?

_____

3.

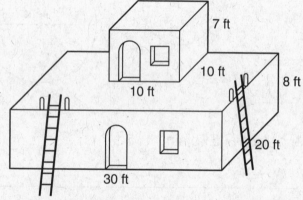

7 ft
10 ft
10 ft
8 ft
20 ft
30 ft

The Pueblo tribe lived in homes called pueblos. These houses were made of mud and brick and were built on top of each other like modern apartment buildings. People used ladders to get to the different levels. What is the total volume of the house and its upper room?

_____

4. To build an igloo, the Inuit of northern Canada use blocks of hard packed snow. If someone asked you to make a rectangular prism 7 blocks long, 5 blocks wide, and 4 blocks high, how many blocks would you need?

_____

Parts of a Region

The top number, the numerator, tells the number of equal parts described. The bottom number, the denominator, tells how many equal parts there are in all.

$\dfrac{2}{3}$ ← Numerator. 2 parts are shaded.
   ← Denominator. There are 3 parts total.

$\dfrac{2}{3}$ of the circle is shaded.

Write a fraction for the part of the region that is shaded.

1.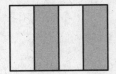

_____

2.

_____

3.

4.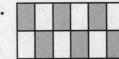

_____

Draw a model to show each fraction.

5. $\dfrac{5}{15}$

6. $\dfrac{7}{9}$

7. **Reasoning** Tara says that $\dfrac{1}{2}$ of a salad is always the same amount. Lynn says that it could be different amounts, depending on how large the salad is. Who is correct? Why?

_____

_____

_____

Name _____

Parts of a Region

Write a fraction for the part of the region below that is shaded.

1. 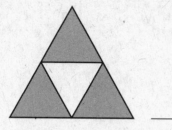 _____

2. 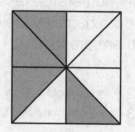 _____

Draw a model to show each fraction.

3. $\frac{2}{4}$

4. $\frac{10}{25}$

5. What fraction of the pizza is cheese?

_____

6. What fraction of the pizza is mushroom?

_____

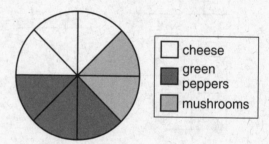

☐ cheese
■ green peppers
▨ mushrooms

7. Number Sense Is $\frac{1}{4}$ of 12 greater than $\frac{1}{4}$ of 8? Explain your answer.

_____

_____

Test Prep

8. A region has 12 equal squares. Which is the number of squares in $\frac{1}{3}$ of the region?

A. 3   **B.** 4   **C.** 6   **D.** 9

9. Writing in Math Explain why $\frac{1}{2}$ of Region A is not larger than $\frac{1}{2}$ of Region B.

_____

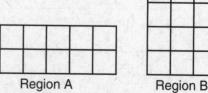

Region A   Region B

Name_____

Parts of a Set

A fraction can describe a part of a set.

What fraction of each set is shaded?

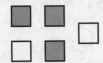

There is a total of 5 squares. 3 of them are shaded. So, $\frac{3}{5}$ of the squares are shaded.

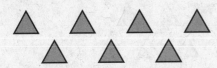

There is a total of 7 triangles. All 7 of them are shaded. So, $\frac{7}{7}$ of the triangles are shaded.

Draw a set with $\frac{3}{9}$ circles shaded.

The denominator tells how many circles are in the set, 9. So, draw 9 circles.

The numerator tells how many circles should be shaded, 3. So, shade in 3 circles.

What fraction of each set is shaded?

1.    2.   3. [squares]   4. [triangles]

_____   _____   _____   _____

Draw a picture to show each fraction as a part of a set.

5. $\frac{2}{9}$ 6. $\frac{4}{6}$

7. **Reasoning** Holly has a collection of 12 CDs. Of the 12 CDs, 7 of them are classical music. Write a fraction to show how many of the CDs are classical music.

_____

Parts of a Set

What fraction of each set is shaded?

1.  2.  3.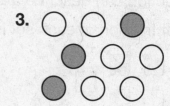

_____   _____   _____

4.  _____ 5.

_____

Draw a picture to show each fraction as part of a set.

6. $\frac{3}{6}$ 7. $\frac{2}{5}$

8. **Number Sense** $\frac{5}{5}$ of the models that Brian has are airplanes. How many are cars?

_____

Test Prep

9. What fraction of the half-circles is shaded?

A. $\frac{1}{8}$ B. $\frac{1}{2}$ C. $\frac{3}{4}$ D. $\frac{2}{8}$

10. **Writing in Math** Frank said that $\frac{1}{2}$ of the squares to the right are shaded. Is he correct? Explain.

_____

_____

Fractions, Length, and the Number Line

How to show fractions on a number line:

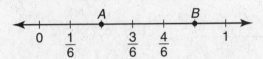

The number line is divided into 6 equal lengths because the denominator is 6. The numerators go in order from 1 to 6. $\frac{2}{6}$ should be written at point A. $\frac{5}{6}$ should be written at point B.

How to write a fraction for the part of the length that is shaded:

The length has been divided into 9 equal parts. 9 is the denominator of the fraction. Because 5 of the lengths are shaded, 5 is the numerator of the fraction. So, $\frac{5}{9}$ is shaded.

Write a fraction for the part of each length that is shaded.

1. _____

2. _____

3. _____

4. _____

What fraction should be written at each point?

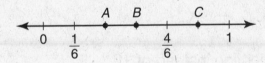

5. A _____

6. B _____

7. C _____

8. Number Sense To show $\frac{4}{5}$ on a number line, how many equal parts should be between 0 and 1? _____

Name _____

Fractions, Length, and the Number Line

Write a fraction for the part of each length that is shaded.

1. ═══════════════════ _____

2. ═══════════════════════════ _____

3. ═══════════════════ _____

4. ═══════════════════ _____

5. ═══════════════════ _____

6. ═══════════════════ _____

Which fraction should be written at each point?

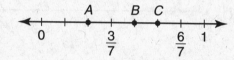

7. A _____

8. B _____

9. C _____

Reasoning Write the missing fractions.

10.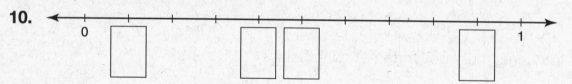

Test Prep

11. Which fraction could go on a number line instead of 1?

   A. $\frac{0}{7}$ B. $\frac{5}{7}$ C. $\frac{7}{7}$ D. $\frac{1}{2}$

12. **Writing in Math** Explain why point A
    could be written as either $\frac{1}{2}$ or $\frac{4}{8}$.

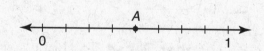

_____

_____

_____

Estimating Fractional Parts

Benchmark fractions are fractions that are commonly used, such as $\frac{1}{4}$, $\frac{1}{3}$, $\frac{1}{2}$, $\frac{2}{3}$, and $\frac{3}{4}$. They are useful when you estimate fractional parts. For example:

About $\frac{1}{2}$ of the rectangle is shaded.

Point A is at about $\frac{1}{4}$.

Point B is at about $\frac{1}{2}$.

About $\frac{1}{3}$ of the length is shaded.

Estimate the fractional part of each that is shaded.

1.

_____

2.

_____

3.

_____

4.

_____

5.

_____

6.

_____

Estimate the fraction that should be written at each point.

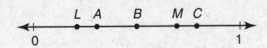

7. L _____

8. A _____

9. B _____

10. M _____

11. C _____

12. Number Sense There is a pan of food. About $\frac{1}{4}$ of the food has been eaten. About how much food is left?

_____

Name_____

Estimating Fractional Parts

Estimate the fractional part of each that is shaded.

1.

2.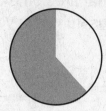

3.

_____   _____   _____

4. **Number Sense** Is $\frac{1}{6}$ a reasonable estimate for the shaded part in the region to the right? Explain.

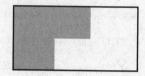

_____

_____

Estimate the fraction that should be written at each point.

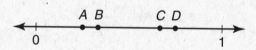

5. A _____   6. B _____   7. C _____   8. D _____

Test Prep

9. Part of the region to the right is shaded. Which is the best estimate?

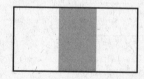

   A. $\frac{3}{3}$ **B.** $\frac{2}{3}$ **C.** $\frac{1}{3}$ **D.** $\frac{0}{3}$

10. **Writing in Math** Explain how you estimated the shaded region in Exercise 9.

_____

_____

_____

PROBLEM-SOLVING STRATEGY
Draw a Picture

The Fence A fence is 20 ft long. It has posts at each end and at every 4 ft along its length. How many fence posts are there?

Read and Understand

Step 1: What do you know?

The fence is 20 ft long.

There are fence posts at each end.

There are fence posts every 4 ft along the length of the fence.

Step 2: What are you trying to find?

How many posts the fence has

Plan and Solve

Step 3: What strategy will you use?

Strategy: Draw a picture

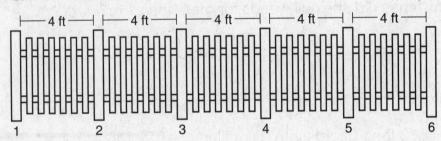

There are 6 fence posts altogether.

Look Back and Check

Step 4: Is your work correct?

Yes, the picture shows that there is a total of 6 fence posts.

Solve the problem. Write the answer in a complete sentence.

1. Tim, Kara, and Ann are working together to write a 4-page report. Each student is going to do an equal amount of writing. What fraction of the entire report does each student need to write?

Name _____

Draw a Picture

Solve each problem. Write the answer in a complete sentence.

1. Three friends divided a veggie pizza into 12 slices. If they divide the pizza equally, what fraction of the pizza would each friend get?

   _____

2. Mark is making a quilt with his grandmother. Each row of the quilt has 6 squares. There are 8 rows. $\frac{1}{2}$ of the squares are blue. How many blue squares are in the quilt?

   _____

3. Jane pulled weeds in the garden 7 times. She was paid $5 each time she pulled weeds for less than 1 hr and $6 each time she pulled weeds for more than 1 hr. If Jane received $39, how many times did she pull weeds for more than 1 hr?

   _____

   _____

4. Neil needs to cut 3 long boards into 9 smaller boards. The first is 10 ft, the second is 16 ft, and the third is 18 ft. The table lists the smaller boards Neil needs. Use a drawing to show how he can divide the 3 boards so there is no waste.

Length of Board	Number Needed
4 ft	3
5 ft	4
6 ft	2

10 ft

16 ft

18 ft

Equivalent Fractions

The fractions $\frac{3}{4}$ and $\frac{6}{8}$ both tell how much of the square is shaded. The fractions are equivalent.

You can find equivalent fractions using multiplication or division.

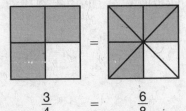

$$\frac{3}{4} = \frac{6}{8}$$

Using multiplication:

Write a fraction equivalent to $\frac{2}{7}$.

Multiply the numerator and denominator by the same number, but do not use zero.

$$\overset{\times 3}{\underset{\times 3}{\frac{2}{7} = \frac{6}{21}}}$$

So, $\frac{2}{7} = \frac{6}{21}$.

Using division:

Write a fraction equivalent to $\frac{8}{16}$.

Divide the numerator and denominator by the same number.

$$\overset{\div 2}{\underset{\div 2}{\frac{8}{16} = \frac{4}{8}}}$$

So, $\frac{8}{16} = \frac{4}{8}$.

Multiply or divide to find equivalent fractions.

1.

$$\overset{\times 5}{\underset{\times 5}{\frac{2}{3} = \boxed{}}}$$

2.

$$\overset{\div 2}{\underset{\div 2}{\frac{6}{12} = \boxed{}}}$$

3.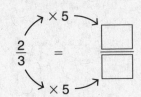

$$\overset{\times 10}{\underset{\times 10}{\frac{1}{4} = \boxed{}}}$$

4.

$$\overset{\div 5}{\underset{\div 5}{\frac{5}{20} = \boxed{}}}$$

5. $\frac{4}{5}$ _____

6. $\frac{8}{10}$ _____

7. $\frac{7}{9}$ _____

8. $\frac{12}{16}$ _____

Name_____

Equivalent Fractions

Multiply or divide to find equivalent fractions.

1.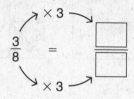

2.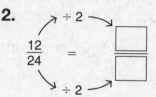

3.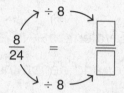

4.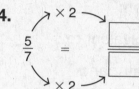

5. $\frac{11}{22}$ _____

6. $\frac{1}{5}$ _____

7. $\frac{5}{8}$ _____

8. $\frac{12}{30}$ _____

9. **Number Sense** Write two fractions that name the shaded part in the figure to the right. Explain how your fractions are equivalent.

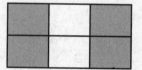

_____

_____

Test Prep

10. Which is NOT an equivalent fraction to $\frac{2}{3}$?

   A. $\frac{4}{6}$ **B.** $\frac{6}{9}$ **C.** $\frac{9}{12}$ **D.** $\frac{10}{15}$

11. **Writing in Math** 12 counters are arranged in 4 dishes as shown. How could you rearrange the shaded or white counters to clearly show two equivalent fractions? What are the fractions?

_____

_____

_____

© Pearson Education, Inc. 4

Use with Lesson 9-6. **115**

Fractions in Simplest Form

A fraction is in simplest form if the only common factor of the numerator and denominator is 1. $\frac{5}{20}$ in simplest form is $\frac{1}{4}$ because the numerator and denominator have no common factors other than 1.

Write $\frac{20}{30}$ in simplest form.

Step 1: Divide the numerator and denominator of the fraction by one of their common factors.	**Step 2:** Check to see if $\frac{10}{15}$ is in simplest form.	**Step 3:** Divide the numerator and denominator by the common factor.	**Step 4:** Check to see if $\frac{2}{3}$ is in simplest form.
A common factor of 20 and 30 is 2.	No, 10 and 15 have a common factor of 5.	$10 \div 5 = 2$	Yes, the only common factor of 2 and 3 is 1.
$20 \div 2 = 10$	Repeat division.	$15 \div 5 = 3$	So, $\frac{20}{30}$ in simplest form is $\frac{2}{3}$.
$30 \div 2 = 15$			

Write each fraction in simplest form. If it is in simplest form, write *simplest form*.

1. $\frac{6}{8}$ _____

2. $\frac{9}{10}$ _____

3. $\frac{10}{12}$ _____

4. $\frac{7}{8}$ _____

5. $\frac{25}{50}$ _____

6. $\frac{3}{15}$ _____

7. $\frac{15}{22}$ _____

8. $\frac{16}{20}$ _____

9. **Writing in Math** Kevin said that $\frac{300}{500}$ is in simplest form because 3 and 5 have only 1 as a common factor. Is he correct? Explain why or why not.

_____

_____

_____

Name_____

Fractions in Simplest Form

Write each fraction in simplest form. If it is in simplest form,
write *simplest form*.

1. $\frac{7}{8}$ _____

2. $\frac{2}{14}$ _____

3. $\frac{3}{9}$ _____

4. $\frac{7}{7}$ _____

5. $\frac{5}{30}$ _____

6. $\frac{20}{36}$ _____

7. $\frac{7}{15}$ _____

8. $\frac{16}{22}$ _____

9. $\frac{8}{12}$ _____

10. $\frac{27}{36}$ _____

11. Number Sense What fraction of the
region to the right is shaded? Write
your answer in simplest form.
Explain how you know.

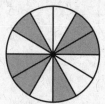

_____

_____

Give each fraction in simplest form.
What fraction of the farm to the right is

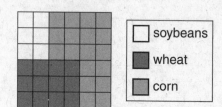

12. soybeans? _____

13. wheat? _____

14. corn? _____

Test Prep

15. Which fraction is in simplest form?

A. $\frac{6}{24}$ **B.** $\frac{7}{24}$ **C.** $\frac{8}{24}$ **D.** $\frac{9}{24}$

16. Writing in Math Is $\frac{11}{33}$ written in simplest form? How do you know?

_____

_____

Using Number Sense to Compare Fractions

Leanne wanted to compare $\frac{4}{6}$ and $\frac{3}{4}$. She used fraction strips to help.

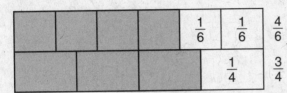

She compared the amounts that were shaded in each picture. Because the amount shaded in $\frac{3}{4}$ is more than the amount shaded in $\frac{4}{6}$, she knew that $\frac{3}{4}$ is greater than $\frac{4}{6}$.

So, $\frac{3}{4} > \frac{4}{6}$.

Write > or < for each $\bigcirc$. You may use fraction strips to help.

1. $\frac{5}{6}$ $\bigcirc$ $\frac{2}{3}$ **2.** $\frac{1}{5}$ $\bigcirc$ $\frac{2}{8}$ **3.** $\frac{9}{10}$ $\bigcirc$ $\frac{6}{8}$ **4.** $\frac{3}{4}$ $\bigcirc$ $\frac{1}{4}$

5. $\frac{8}{9}$ $\bigcirc$ $\frac{5}{10}$ **6.** $\frac{2}{5}$ $\bigcirc$ $\frac{2}{6}$ **7.** $\frac{6}{9}$ $\bigcirc$ $\frac{7}{9}$ **8.** $\frac{2}{10}$ $\bigcirc$ $\frac{3}{5}$

The same number of students attended school all week.

Day	Fraction of Students Buying Lunch
Monday	$\frac{1}{2}$
Tuesday	$\frac{2}{5}$
Wednesday	$\frac{3}{4}$
Thursday	$\frac{5}{8}$
Friday	$\frac{4}{6}$

9. Did more students buy lunch on Tuesday or on Wednesday?   _____

10. Did more students buy lunch on Thursday or on Friday?   _____

Using Number Sense to Compare Fractions

Write > or < for each $\bigcirc$. You may use fraction strips to help.

1. $\frac{1}{2}$ $\bigcirc$ $\frac{3}{13}$

2. $\frac{8}{9}$ $\bigcirc$ $\frac{5}{9}$

3. $\frac{3}{8}$ $\bigcirc$ $\frac{11}{22}$

4. $\frac{3}{3}$ $\bigcirc$ $\frac{7}{8}$

5. $\frac{3}{5}$ $\bigcirc$ $\frac{1}{3}$

6. $\frac{1}{4}$ $\bigcirc$ $\frac{2}{4}$

7. $\frac{5}{6}$ $\bigcirc$ $\frac{5}{8}$

8. $\frac{7}{12}$ $\bigcirc$ $\frac{4}{5}$

9. $\frac{3}{7}$ $\bigcirc$ $\frac{6}{7}$

10. **Number Sense** Explain how you know that $\frac{21}{30}$ is greater than $\frac{2}{3}$.

_____

_____

_____

11. Tina completed $\frac{2}{3}$ of her homework before dinner.
George completed $\frac{4}{7}$ of his homework before dinner.
Who completed a greater fraction of homework? _____

12. Jackson played a video game for $\frac{1}{6}$ hr. Hailey played
a video game for $\frac{1}{3}$ hr. Who played the video game
for a greater amount of time? _____

Test Prep

13. Which fraction is greater than $\frac{3}{4}$?

   A. $\frac{5}{9}$ B. $\frac{17}{24}$ C. $\frac{15}{20}$ D. $\frac{7}{9}$

14. **Writing in Math** James says that $\frac{5}{5}$ is greater than $\frac{99}{100}$.
Is he correct? Explain.

_____

_____

_____

Comparing and Ordering Fractions

Comparing fractions:

Compare $\frac{1}{4}$ and $\frac{3}{8}$.

Multiply or divide to make the denominators the same. Then compare the numerators.

$$\frac{1}{4} = \frac{2}{8} \quad \times 2$$

$$\frac{2}{8} < \frac{3}{8}$$

So, $\frac{1}{4} < \frac{3}{8}$.

Ordering fractions: Order $\frac{1}{2}$, $\frac{1}{4}$, and $\frac{3}{8}$ from least to greatest.

Use equivalent fractions.

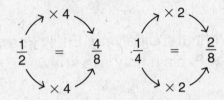

$$\frac{1}{2} = \frac{4}{8} \quad \times 4 \qquad \frac{1}{4} = \frac{2}{8} \quad \times 2$$

Compare the numerators. $\frac{2}{8} < \frac{3}{8}$ and $\frac{3}{8} < \frac{4}{8}$

The fractions in order are: $\frac{1}{4}$, $\frac{3}{8}$, $\frac{1}{2}$

Compare. Write >, <, or =.

1. $\frac{1}{6} \bigcirc \frac{2}{8}$ **2.** $\frac{3}{5} \bigcirc \frac{3}{10}$ **3.** $\frac{5}{7} \bigcirc \frac{6}{9}$ **4.** $\frac{1}{2} \bigcirc \frac{4}{6}$

Order the numbers from least to greatest.

5. $\frac{1}{2}$, $\frac{1}{3}$, $\frac{1}{4}$ _____   **6.** $\frac{2}{3}$, $\frac{3}{4}$, $\frac{2}{5}$ _____

7. $\frac{2}{9}$, $\frac{4}{5}$, $\frac{2}{8}$ _____   **8.** $\frac{1}{4}$, $\frac{7}{8}$, $\frac{5}{6}$ _____

9. Writing in Math Orlando wrote that $\frac{4}{5}$ is less than $\frac{4}{6}$. Is he correct? If not, explain how to find the correct answer.

_____

_____

_____

_____

Comparing and Ordering Fractions

Compare. Write >, <, or = for each $\bigcirc$.

1. $\frac{2}{5}$ $\bigcirc$ $\frac{5}{10}$ 2. $\frac{11}{16}$ $\bigcirc$ $\frac{5}{8}$ 3. $\frac{4}{5}$ $\bigcirc$ $\frac{8}{9}$

4. $\frac{3}{6}$ $\bigcirc$ $\frac{6}{12}$ 5. $\frac{2}{7}$ $\bigcirc$ $\frac{3}{10}$ 6. $\frac{1}{4}$ $\bigcirc$ $\frac{2}{11}$

7. **Number Sense** Without multiplying, Emily knew that $\frac{4}{9}$ was greater than $\frac{4}{10}$. Explain how she knew.

_____

_____

_____

Order the numbers from least to greatest.

8. $\frac{4}{15}, \frac{2}{5}, \frac{1}{3}$ _____   9. $\frac{4}{10}, \frac{2}{8}, \frac{1}{5}$ _____

10. $\frac{1}{9}, \frac{7}{8}, \frac{5}{6}$ _____   11. $\frac{3}{9}, \frac{1}{4}, \frac{5}{12}$ _____

12. $\frac{13}{16}, \frac{5}{8}, \frac{2}{8}$ _____   13. $\frac{1}{2}, \frac{7}{12}, \frac{4}{10}$ _____

Test Prep

14. Which fraction is greater than $\frac{1}{3}$?

A. $\frac{3}{6}$ B. $\frac{11}{36}$ C. $\frac{1}{4}$ D. $\frac{1}{12}$

15. **Writing in Math** Explain how you know that $\frac{31}{40}$ is greater than $\frac{3}{4}$, but less than $\frac{4}{5}$.

_____

_____

_____

_____

Mixed Numbers and Improper Fractions

How to write mixed numbers as improper fractions:

Write $3\frac{1}{5}$ as an improper fraction.

First multiply the denominator by the whole number.

$3\frac{1}{5}$ $5 \times 3 = 15$

Add the numerator to this sum. $15 + 1 = 16$

Write the sum as the numerator. $\longrightarrow \frac{16}{5}$

Use the denominator from the fraction. $\longrightarrow$

So, $3\frac{1}{5} = \frac{16}{5}$.

How to write improper fractions as mixed numbers:

Write $\frac{7}{4}$ as a mixed number.

First divide the numerator by the denominator.

$$4\overline{)7}$$
$$-\underline{4}$$
$$3$$

The quotient is the whole number.

The remainder is the new numerator. $\longrightarrow 1\frac{3}{4}$

The denominator stays the same.

So, $\frac{7}{4} = 1\frac{3}{4}$.

Write each mixed number as an improper fraction.

1. $2\frac{1}{3}$ _____

2. $4\frac{1}{5}$ _____

3. $2\frac{3}{4}$ _____

4. $5\frac{2}{6}$ _____

Write each improper fraction as a mixed number or a whole number.

5. $\frac{13}{12}$ _____

6. $\frac{50}{10}$ _____

7. $\frac{23}{10}$ _____

8. $\frac{17}{15}$ _____

9. Writing in Math Is $\frac{45}{5}$ equal to a whole number or a mixed number? Explain how you know.

_____

_____

_____

_____

Name_____

Mixed Numbers and Improper Fractions

Write each mixed number as an improper fraction.

1. $3\frac{2}{5}$ _____
2. $6\frac{1}{4}$ _____
3. $2\frac{1}{12}$ _____
4. $2\frac{7}{9}$ _____

Write each improper fraction as a mixed number or whole number.

5. $\frac{12}{5}$ _____
6. $\frac{27}{9}$ _____
7. $\frac{32}{3}$ _____
8. $\frac{20}{12}$ _____

9. **Number Sense** Matt had to write $3\frac{8}{24}$ as an improper fraction. Write how you would tell Matt the easiest way to do so.

_____

_____

_____

_____

10. Jill has 4 granola bars. Each bar weighs $\frac{2}{3}$ oz. Write the weight of Jill's granola bars as an improper fraction and as a mixed number. _____

11. Nick had $1\frac{3}{4}$ gal of milk. How many pints of milk does Nick have? (Hint: There are 8 pt in 1 gal.) _____

Test Prep

12. Which is NOT an improper fraction equal to 8?

   A. $\frac{24}{3}$ B. $\frac{49}{7}$ C. $\frac{56}{7}$ D. $\frac{64}{8}$

13. **Writing in Math** Write three different improper fractions that equal $4\frac{2}{3}$.

_____

Comparing Mixed Numbers

Here are some ways to compare mixed numbers.

Compare $1\frac{4}{8}$ **and** $3\frac{1}{5}$.

You can look at the whole numbers to decide which mixed number is larger.

$3 > 1$, so $3\frac{1}{5} > 1\frac{4}{8}$.

Compare $2\frac{1}{4}$ **and** $2\frac{6}{8}$.

Use a number line.

$$2\frac{2}{8} \quad 2\frac{4}{8} \quad 2\frac{6}{8}$$

$$2 \quad 2\frac{1}{4} \quad 2\frac{2}{4} \quad 2\frac{3}{4} \quad 3$$

Because $2\frac{6}{8}$ is to the right of $2\frac{1}{4}$, it is greater.

So, $2\frac{6}{8} > 2\frac{1}{4}$.

Compare $1\frac{2}{7}$ **and** $1\frac{9}{14}$.

Find fractions with the same denominators.

$$1\frac{2}{7} \xrightarrow{\times 2} = \xleftarrow{\times 2} 1\frac{4}{14}$$

$$1\frac{9}{14} > 1\frac{4}{14}$$

So, $1\frac{9}{14} > 1\frac{2}{7}$.

Compare. Write <, >, or = for each $\bigcirc$.

1. $3\frac{3}{4} \bigcirc 3\frac{5}{6}$

2. $1\frac{7}{8} \bigcirc 2\frac{7}{8}$

3. $2\frac{1}{2} \bigcirc 2\frac{2}{5}$

4. $5\frac{1}{5} \bigcirc 5\frac{2}{8}$

5. $5\frac{5}{25} \bigcirc 5\frac{4}{20}$

6. $6\frac{9}{10} \bigcirc 5\frac{8}{50}$

A large snowstorm hit northern New York in November, 2000. The table shows the number of feet of recorded snowfall in some areas during the storm.

Location	Feet of Snow
Central Buffalo	$1\frac{5}{6}$
Jamestown	$1\frac{1}{2}$
Buffalo	$2\frac{1}{12}$
West Monroe	$2\frac{1}{6}$

7. Which town got more snow, Jamestown or Central Buffalo?

_____

8. Which town got more snow, Buffalo or West Monroe?

_____

Name_____

Comparing Mixed Numbers

Compare. Write >, <, or = for each ◯.

1. $3\frac{1}{4}$ ◯ $2\frac{7}{8}$ 2. $2\frac{9}{16}$ ◯ $3\frac{1}{5}$ 3. $1\frac{7}{8}$ ◯ $1\frac{3}{4}$ 4. $5\frac{3}{8}$ ◯ $5\frac{1}{2}$

5. $3\frac{15}{16}$ ◯ $4\frac{1}{9}$ 6. $3\frac{2}{3}$ ◯ $3\frac{2}{14}$ 7. $5\frac{2}{3}$ ◯ $5\frac{3}{5}$ 8. $1\frac{9}{10}$ ◯ $1\frac{8}{9}$

Reasoning Write the missing numbers as mixed numbers. Write the fractional part in simplest form.

9.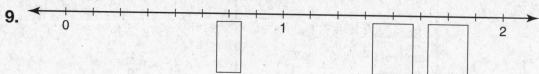

10.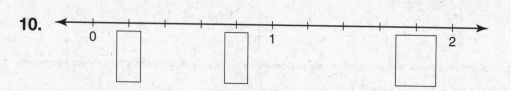

11. Jack and Callie are helping Mr. Harris by washing chalkboards at school. Before they take a lunch break, Jack has washed $3\frac{1}{3}$ chalkboards and Callie has washed $3\frac{5}{6}$ chalkboards. Who has washed more chalkboards? _____

Test Prep

12. Which is greater than $4\frac{2}{3}$?

   A. $4\frac{5}{8}$ **B.** $4\frac{3}{4}$ **C.** $4\frac{2}{5}$ **D.** $4\frac{1}{3}$

13. **Writing in Math** Explain how to find whether or not $2\frac{1}{3}$ is greater than $\frac{9}{4}$.

_____

_____

_____

_____

Circle Graphs

This circle graph shows what sport fourth-grade students liked best. $\frac{1}{2}$ of the students liked football the best. You know this because $\frac{1}{2}$ of the circle is shaded for football.

Because $\frac{1}{4}$ of the students liked soccer the best, $\frac{1}{4}$ of the circle is shaded for soccer. $\frac{1}{8}$ of the students liked hockey the best, and $\frac{1}{8}$ liked tennis the best.

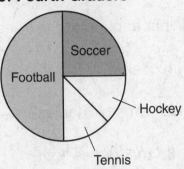

Favorite Sports of Fourth Graders

For 1–5, use the circle graphs below.

2002 Winter Olympics Medals, Italy

2002 Winter Olympics Medals, China

1. What fraction of the medals won by Italy was gold? _____

2. What fraction of the medals won by China was silver? _____

3. What fraction describes the number of silver medals won by Italy? _____

4. What fraction describes the number of bronze medals won by China? _____

5. **Number Sense** Did China win more gold or bronze medals? _____

Circle Graphs

Julie counted the 24 trees on her block. She wrote the data in a table and then made this circle graph.

Trees on Block

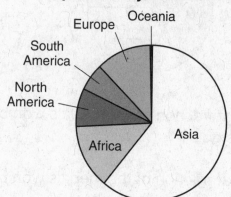

What fraction of the trees are

1. oaks? _____

2. elms or maples? _____

3. marked as "other"? _____

4. The table shows the type of table that Julie made to make her circle graph. Because you know that there are 12 oak trees on Julie's block, you can complete the entire table.

Tree	Number
Oaks	
Elms	
Maples	
Other	

5. About what fraction of the world's population lives in Asia?

_____

6. Name 2 continents that have about $\frac{1}{4}$ of the world's population.

_____

Population by Continent-2001

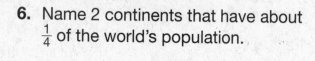

Test Prep

7. Two parts of a circle graph are each $\frac{1}{3}$ of the circle. The other two parts are equal in size. What fraction of the graph is each of the smaller parts?

A. $\frac{1}{6}$ B. $\frac{1}{4}$ C. $\frac{1}{3}$ D. $\frac{1}{2}$

8. **Writing in Math** John counted what people were drinking as he walked to school. He saw 3 people drinking coffee, 3 drinking juice, and 2 drinking water. John wants to put the data in a circle graph. How many equal parts should he divide his circle into? Explain your answer.

_____

_____

Writing to Explain

Pasta Gina and her brother Don made homemade pasta with their mother. Gina made $3\frac{1}{4}$ pans of pasta. Don made $3\frac{3}{8}$ pans. Which person made more pasta?

Writing a Good Math Explanation	**Example**
• Write your explanation in steps to make it clear.	• First I compared the whole numbers. Because they were the same, I knew I had to compare the fractions.
• Tell what the numbers mean in your explanation.	• Because $\frac{1}{4}$ and $\frac{3}{8}$ have different denominators, I multiplied the numerator and denominator of $\frac{1}{4}$ by 2 to get $\frac{2}{8}$.
• Tell why you took certain steps.	• Then I could compare the mixed numbers $3\frac{2}{8}$ and $3\frac{3}{8}$. Because $3\frac{3}{8}$ is greater than $3\frac{2}{8}$, I knew that Don made more pasta.

1. Humans usually have 20 baby teeth, which are replaced by 32 adult teeth. Raul said he has lost $\frac{6}{20}$ of his baby teeth. Write two fractions equivalent to this number. Explain how you came up with the fractions.

_____

_____

_____

_____

_____

PROBLEM-SOLVING SKILL

Writing to Explain

1. Mary has 23 marbles. $\frac{7}{23}$ of the marbles are yellow and $\frac{13}{23}$ of the marbles are blue. The rest of the marbles are green. How many marbles are green? Explain how you know.

_____

_____

_____

_____

2. Adam wants to compare the fractions $\frac{2}{5}$, $\frac{1}{6}$, and $\frac{1}{3}$. He wants to order them from least to greatest and rewrite them so they all have the same denominator. Explain how Adam can rewrite the fractions.

_____

_____

_____

_____

3. Adam used the three fractions to make a circle graph and colored each a different color. What fraction of the graph is not colored? Explain your answer.

_____

_____

_____

_____

Name_____

The Football Team

In a football game, there are a total of 22 players on the field at a time. One team plays offense and the other plays defense. What fraction of the players is on offense?

Offensive players → ⟶ [o] [o] [o] [o] [o] [o] [o] [o] [o] [o] [o]
Defensive players → ⟶ [d] [d] [d] [d] [d] [d] [d] [d] [d] [d] [d]

Because there are 22 players total, the denominator is 22. Because 11 of the players are on offense, the numerator is 11. So, $\frac{11}{22}$ players are on offense. In simplest form, $\frac{11}{22} = \frac{1}{2}$. So, $\frac{1}{2}$ of the players are on offense and $\frac{1}{2}$ are on defense.

1. The coaches made the players run sprints down the football field to get in shape. The running backs had to run down the field $6\frac{3}{4}$ times. The linemen had to run down the field $6\frac{5}{8}$ times. Which group ran more? Explain.

_____

_____

2. Because it was going to rain, the team covered the playing field with a tarp to keep it dry. About how much of the field has been covered with the tarp? _____

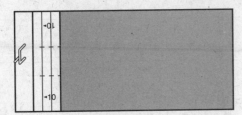

3. What fraction of players have their helmets on?

_____

4. The team played 16 games during the season. They won 4 games. So, the fraction that shows the number of games they won is $\frac{4}{16}$. Write this fraction in simplest form.

_____

Name_____

Fractional Orchards

Trees in an Orchard

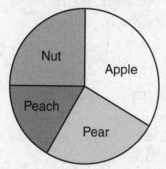

Tree	Acres
Apple	8
Pear	6
Peach	4
Nut	6

The circle graph and table show the acres for each tree grown in an orchard.

What fractional part of the orchard is

1. apple trees? _____

2. pear and peach trees combined? _____

3. nut trees? _____

4. NOT peach trees? _____

5. Explain how you knew what each fractional part was.

_____

_____

_____

_____

6. The part of the orchard for nut trees is divided into 3 equal parts for 3 different types of nut trees. What fractional part of the whole orchard is each nut tree? Explain.

_____

_____

_____

Estimating Fraction Sums

When you add two fractions, the sum is going to be less than, equal to, or greater than 1. An easy way to estimate the sum is to compare both of the fractions to $\frac{1}{2}$.

If both of the fractions are less than $\frac{1}{2}$, then the sum is going to be less than 1.

Example: $\frac{1}{5} + \frac{1}{3} < 1$

If both of the fractions are greater than $\frac{1}{2}$, then the sum is going to be greater than 1.

Example: $\frac{4}{5} + \frac{6}{7} > 1$

To compare a fraction to $\frac{1}{2}$, divide the denominator by 2. If the numerator is less than your quotient, the fraction is less than $\frac{1}{2}$. If it is greater than your quotient, the fraction is greater than $\frac{1}{2}$.

Write > or < for each $\bigcirc$.

1. $\frac{3}{4} + \frac{5}{6} \bigcirc 1$ **2.** $\frac{2}{7} + \frac{1}{3} \bigcirc 1$ **3.** $\frac{5}{16} + \frac{3}{10} \bigcirc 1$ **4.** $\frac{3}{12} + \frac{2}{12} \bigcirc 1$

5. $\frac{4}{5} + \frac{5}{7} \bigcirc 1$ **6.** $\frac{6}{10} + \frac{9}{10} \bigcirc 1$ **7.** $\frac{1}{3} + \frac{1}{4} \bigcirc 1$ **8.** $\frac{2}{3} + \frac{7}{12} \bigcirc 1$

Estimate to decide whether each sum is greater than 1 or less than 1. If you cannot tell, explain why.

9. $\frac{9}{12} + \frac{2}{5}$ _____

_____

10. $\frac{1}{4} + \frac{7}{16}$ _____

11. **Number Sense** Is $\frac{2}{4} + \frac{8}{16}$ greater than, equal to, or less than 1? Explain.

_____

_____

_____

Name_____

Estimating Fraction Sums

Write $>$ or $<$ for each ◯.

1. $\frac{2}{6} + \frac{1}{3}$ ◯ 1   2. $\frac{2}{3} + \frac{4}{5}$ ◯ 1   3. $\frac{3}{4} + \frac{7}{10}$ ◯ 1   4. $\frac{2}{7} + \frac{1}{6}$ ◯ 1

5. $\frac{4}{10} + \frac{3}{8}$ ◯ 1   6. $\frac{8}{10} + \frac{5}{6}$ ◯ 1   7. $\frac{1}{4} + \frac{3}{12}$ ◯ 1   8. $\frac{3}{7} + \frac{1}{16}$ ◯ 1

Estimate to decide whether each sum is greater than 1 or less than 1. If you cannot tell, explain why.

9. $\frac{2}{3} + \frac{5}{6}$ _____

_____

10. $\frac{1}{16} + \frac{8}{20}$ _____

_____

11. $\frac{8}{9} + \frac{1}{7}$ _____

_____

12. Three quarters are worth $\frac{3}{4}$ of a dollar and 4 dimes are worth $\frac{4}{10}$ of a dollar. Are 3 quarters and 4 dimes worth more than or less than a dollar?

13. A half dollar is worth $\frac{1}{2}$ of a dollar and 5 nickels are worth $\frac{5}{20}$ of a dollar. Are 1 half dollar and 5 nickels worth more than or less than a dollar?

_____   _____

Test Prep

14. Which of the following is greater than 1?

   A. $\frac{1}{2} + \frac{1}{3}$ B. $\frac{7}{8} + \frac{6}{10}$ C. $\frac{2}{5} + \frac{5}{12}$ D. $\frac{6}{18} + \frac{3}{7}$

15. **Writing in Math** Explain how to estimate if $\frac{3}{5} + \frac{5}{8}$ is greater than or less than 1.

_____

_____

Adding Fractions with Like Denominators

How to add fractions that have the same denominator:

$\frac{2}{3} + \frac{2}{3}$

Step 1

Estimate.

$\frac{2}{3} > \frac{1}{2}$, so $\frac{2}{3} + \frac{2}{3} > 1$.

Step 2

Add the numerators. Keep the denominator the same. Write the sum of the numerators over the denominator.

$\frac{2}{3} + \frac{2}{3} = \frac{4}{3}$

Step 3

Simplify, if necessary.

$\frac{4}{3} = 1\frac{1}{3}$

So, $\frac{2}{3} + \frac{2}{3} = 1\frac{1}{3}$

The answer is reasonable since $1\frac{1}{3} > 1$.

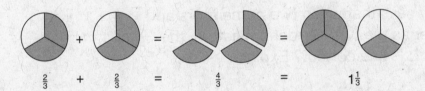

Find each sum.

1. $\frac{2}{5} + \frac{1}{5} =$ _____

2. $\frac{1}{3} + \frac{1}{3} =$ _____

3. $\frac{2}{4} + \frac{3}{4} =$ _____

4. $\frac{6}{10} + \frac{2}{10} =$ _____

5. $\frac{1}{5} + \frac{3}{5} =$ _____

6. $\frac{9}{16} + \frac{3}{16} =$ _____

7. $\frac{4}{12} + \frac{9}{12} =$ _____

8. $\frac{6}{7} + \frac{6}{7} =$ _____

9. $\frac{3}{15} + \frac{5}{15} =$ _____

10. $\frac{5}{10} + \frac{9}{10} =$ _____

11. Number Sense Jake estimates that $\frac{12}{19} + \frac{18}{19}$ is less than 1, since both fractions are less than 1. Is he correct?

_____

_____

Adding Fractions with Like Denominators

Find each sum.

1. $\frac{7}{10} + \frac{2}{10} = $ _____

2. $\frac{4}{5} + \frac{4}{5} = $ _____

3. $\frac{1}{6} + \frac{2}{6} = $ _____

4. $\frac{3}{8} + \frac{2}{8} = $ _____

5. $\frac{2}{5} + \frac{2}{5} = $ _____

6. $\frac{3}{6} + \frac{1}{6} = $ _____

7. $\frac{4}{6} + \frac{4}{6} = $ _____

8. $\frac{2}{3} + \frac{2}{3} = $ _____

9. $\frac{1}{8} + \frac{1}{8} = $ _____

10. $\frac{4}{12} + \frac{6}{12} = $ _____

11. **Number Sense** Cindy says that when two numerators add up to the same number as the two like denominators, the answer will always be 1. Is she correct? Explain.

_____

_____

_____

There are 8 pencils in a box: 2 are red, 2 are blue, 3 are yellow, and 1 is brown. What fraction of the pencils are

12. red?   13. yellow?   14. red and blue combined?

_____   _____   _____

Test Prep

15. Which is the sum of $\frac{8}{12} + \frac{1}{12}$?

   A. $\frac{9}{24}$ **B.** $\frac{5}{12}$ **C.** $\frac{7}{12}$ **D.** $\frac{9}{12}$

16. **Writing in Math** Explain how you know your answer to Exercise 10 is reasonable.

_____

_____

Name_____

Adding Fractions with Unlike Denominators

To change fractions to like denominators, you write equivalent fractions.

Example: $\frac{1}{8} \times \frac{2}{2} = \frac{2}{16}$

So, $\frac{1}{8} = \frac{2}{16}$.

$$\frac{2}{6}$$
$$+ \ \frac{1}{4}$$
_____

Step 1

First estimate.

$\frac{2}{6} < \frac{1}{2}$ and
$\frac{1}{4} < \frac{1}{2}$, so
$\frac{2}{6} + \frac{1}{4} < 1$.

Step 2

Find equivalent fractions with like denominators.

$$\frac{2}{6} = \frac{8}{24}$$
$$+ \ \frac{1}{4} = \frac{6}{24}$$
_____

Step 3

Add the numerators. Write the sum over the denominator. Simplify, if necessary.

$$\frac{8}{24}$$
$$+ \ \frac{6}{24}$$
_____
$$\frac{14}{24} = \frac{7}{12}$$

The sum is reasonable since
$\frac{7}{12} < 1$.

---

1. $\frac{5}{6}$
   $+ \ \frac{1}{3}$

2. $\frac{1}{4}$
   $+ \ \frac{4}{5}$

3. $\frac{3}{10}$
   $+ \ \frac{1}{20}$

4. $\frac{3}{4}$
   $+ \ \frac{1}{6}$

5. $\frac{1}{2}$
   $+ \ \frac{3}{8}$

6. $\frac{1}{9}$
   $+ \ \frac{2}{3}$

7. **Reasoning** Carl says that since the sum of 3 and 5 is 8, he can use 8 as a denominator to add $\frac{1}{3} + \frac{1}{5}$. Is he correct? Explain.

_____

_____

Name _____

Adding Fractions with Unlike Denominators

Find each sum.

1. $\frac{1}{3} + \frac{1}{4} =$ _____

2. $\frac{1}{5} + \frac{1}{3} =$ _____

3. $\frac{5}{8} + \frac{1}{4} =$ _____

4. $\frac{3}{10} + \frac{5}{6} =$ _____

5. $\begin{array}{r} \frac{3}{4} \\ + \frac{4}{5} \\ \hline \end{array}$

6. $\begin{array}{r} \frac{1}{12} \\ + \frac{3}{4} \\ \hline \end{array}$

7. $\begin{array}{r} \frac{1}{8} \\ + \frac{1}{4} \\ \hline \end{array}$

8. $\begin{array}{r} \frac{2}{3} \\ + \frac{2}{9} \\ \hline \end{array}$

9. $\begin{array}{r} \frac{1}{7} \\ + \frac{2}{5} \\ \hline \end{array}$

10. $\begin{array}{r} \frac{5}{6} \\ + \frac{1}{3} \\ \hline \end{array}$

11. $\begin{array}{r} \frac{1}{14} \\ + \frac{2}{7} \\ \hline \end{array}$

12. $\begin{array}{r} \frac{1}{3} \\ + \frac{4}{15} \\ \hline \end{array}$

A class was asked how many siblings each student had. The results are listed in the table.

Number of Siblings

0	1	2	3 or more
$\frac{11}{30}$	$\frac{1}{3}$	$\frac{1}{5}$	$\frac{1}{10}$

13. What fraction of the class has fewer than 2 siblings?

_____

14. What fraction of the class has more than 1 sibling? _____

Test Prep

15. Which is the sum of $\frac{5}{7} + \frac{1}{2}$?

A. $\frac{3}{7}$　　　　B. $\frac{6}{7}$　　　　C. $1\frac{1}{7}$　　　　D. $1\frac{3}{14}$

16. **Writing in Math** Is Amanda's work correct? Explain why or why not.

_____

_____

_____

$$\begin{array}{r} \frac{3}{4} = \frac{3}{12} \\ + \frac{1}{3} = \frac{4}{12} \\ \hline \frac{7}{12} \end{array}$$

Subtracting Fractions with Like Denominators

When two fractions with the same denominator are being subtracted, the denominator in the difference remains the same and the numerators are subtracted.

Find $\frac{9}{12} - \frac{3}{12}$.

Step 1	**Step 2**
Subtract the numerators. Write the difference over the denominator.	Simplify, if necessary.
$\frac{9}{12} - \frac{3}{12} = \frac{6}{12}$	$\frac{6}{12}$ is not in simplest form.
Note that the denominator stays the same.	6 is a common factor of 6 and 12, so divide each number by 6.
	$\frac{6 \div 6}{12 \div 6} = \frac{1}{2}$
	So, $\frac{9}{12} - \frac{3}{12} = \frac{1}{2}$

1. $\frac{3}{5} - \frac{1}{5} = $ _____   2. $\frac{5}{9} - \frac{2}{9} = $ _____   3. $\frac{6}{12} - \frac{5}{12} = $ _____   4. $\frac{2}{3} - \frac{1}{3} = $ _____

5. $\quad\frac{4}{8}$ 6. $\quad\frac{4}{7}$ 7. $\quad\frac{7}{8}$ 8. $\quad\frac{9}{12}$

$-\frac{1}{8}$ $-\frac{3}{7}$ $-\frac{1}{8}$ $-\frac{1}{12}$

9. **Estimation** Is $\frac{5}{8} - \frac{3}{8}$ more or less than $\frac{1}{2}$? Explain.

_____

_____

_____

_____

_____

_____

Name_____

Subtracting Fractions with Like Denominators

Find each difference.

1. $\frac{5}{6} - \frac{4}{6} =$ _____

2. $\frac{4}{6} - \frac{1}{6} =$ _____

3. $\frac{4}{5} - \frac{2}{5} =$ _____

4. $\frac{7}{8} - \frac{2}{8} =$ _____

5. $\frac{3}{4} - \frac{2}{4} =$ _____

6. $\frac{4}{5} - \frac{1}{5} =$ _____

7. $\frac{7}{9} - \frac{1}{9} =$ _____

8. $\frac{9}{12} - \frac{7}{12} =$ _____

9. $\begin{array}{r} \frac{5}{6} \\ - \frac{1}{6} \\ \hline \end{array}$

10. $\begin{array}{r} \frac{7}{8} \\ - \frac{3}{8} \\ \hline \end{array}$

11. $\begin{array}{r} \frac{2}{5} \\ - \frac{1}{5} \\ \hline \end{array}$

12. $\begin{array}{r} \frac{9}{15} \\ - \frac{4}{15} \\ \hline \end{array}$

13. Mr. Brown had $\frac{4}{5}$ tbsp of salt. He used $\frac{1}{5}$ tbsp of salt in a recipe. How much is left?

_____

14. In Mrs. DeLong's class, $\frac{5}{9}$ of her class are boys and $\frac{4}{9}$ of her class are girls. What is the difference between the fraction of boys and the fraction of girls?

_____

15. **Estimation** Is $\frac{11}{12} - \frac{7}{12}$ more than or less than $\frac{1}{2}$? Explain.

_____

Test Prep

16. Which is the difference of $\frac{7}{15} - \frac{3}{15}$?

   A. $\frac{4}{30}$　　　　**B.** $\frac{4}{15}$　　　　**C.** $\frac{1}{2}$　　　　**D.** 4

17. **Writing in Math** Frank says that $\frac{6}{12} - \frac{1}{12}$ is less than $\frac{1}{2}$. Is he correct? Explain your answer.

_____

_____

Subtracting Fractions with Unlike Denominators

When the denominators are not easily found for both of the fractions, you can multiply the denominators together.

$$\frac{3}{7}$$
$$-\frac{1}{6}$$

Take the denominator from the second fraction, and multiply both the numerator and the denominator of the first fraction.	Take the denominator from the first fraction, and multiply both the numerator and the denominator of the second fraction.	After the fractions have like denominators, subtract the numerators. Simplify the answer if necessary.

$\frac{3}{7}\frac{\times 6}{\times 6} = \frac{18}{42}$

$-\frac{1}{6}$

$\frac{3}{7} = \frac{18}{42}$

$-\frac{1}{6}\frac{\times 7}{\times 7} = -\frac{7}{42}$

$\frac{3}{7} = \frac{18}{42}$

$-\frac{1}{6} = \frac{7}{42}$

$18 - 7 = \frac{11}{42}$

1. $\frac{3}{4} - \frac{5}{8} =$ _____

2. $\frac{7}{10} - \frac{1}{2} =$ _____

3. $\frac{7}{8} - \frac{2}{16} =$ _____

4. $\frac{3}{5} - \frac{3}{10} =$ _____

5. $\frac{5}{6}$
$-\frac{3}{4}$

6. $\frac{2}{3}$
$-\frac{1}{2}$

7. $\frac{4}{7}$
$-\frac{3}{14}$

8. $\frac{5}{6}$
$-\frac{7}{10}$

9. **Number Sense** Simon ran $\frac{3}{4}$ of a mile on Monday, $\frac{1}{3}$ of a mile on Tuesday, and $\frac{1}{2}$ a mile on Wednesday. How much farther did Simon run on Monday than on Wednesday? _____

Name_____

Subtracting Fractions with Unlike Denominators

Find each difference. Simplify if necessary.

1. $\frac{5}{6} - \frac{1}{3} =$ _____

2. $\frac{4}{5} - \frac{2}{3} =$ _____

3. $\frac{7}{8} - \frac{1}{2} =$ _____

4. $\frac{11}{12} - \frac{3}{4} =$ _____

5. $\frac{7}{12} - \frac{1}{3} =$ _____

6. $\frac{1}{2} - \frac{2}{7} =$ _____

7. $\frac{2}{3} - \frac{1}{4} =$ _____

8. $\frac{5}{8} - \frac{1}{3} =$ _____

9. $\begin{array}{r} \frac{7}{10} \\ - \frac{2}{5} \\ \hline \end{array}$

10. $\begin{array}{r} \frac{9}{10} \\ - \frac{1}{2} \\ \hline \end{array}$

11. $\begin{array}{r} \frac{5}{9} \\ - \frac{2}{5} \\ \hline \end{array}$

12. $\begin{array}{r} \frac{7}{12} \\ - \frac{1}{10} \\ \hline \end{array}$

The background of the flag of Chile is $\frac{1}{6}$ blue, $\frac{1}{3}$ white, and $\frac{1}{2}$ red.

13. How much more of the flag is red than blue?

White
Blue
Red

_____

14. How much more of the flag is white than blue?

_____

15. What fraction of the flag is blue and
white combined?   _____

Test Prep

16. Which is the difference of $\frac{1}{2} - \frac{1}{16}$?

   A. $\frac{1}{16}$ B. $\frac{1}{8}$ C. $\frac{3}{8}$ D. $\frac{7}{16}$

17. **Writing in Math** Explain how you know that $\frac{7}{8} - \frac{1}{4}$ will be more than $\frac{1}{2}$.

_____

_____

Name_____

Use Logical Reasoning

Sports Alan, Jack, Todd, and Trent play baseball, basketball, football, and soccer. Alan does not play a sport that begins with the letter b. Todd plays football. Jack does not play basketball. What sport does Trent play?

Read and Understand

Step 1: What do you know?

Alan does not play baseball or basketball. Todd plays football. Jack does not play basketball.

Step 2: What are you trying to find?

What sport Trent plays

Plan and Solve

Step 3: What strategy will you use?

You know that Todd is playing football, so you then know that Alan, Jack, and Trent do not play football. You also know that Todd is not playing baseball, basketball, or soccer.

Answer: Trent plays basketball.

Strategy: Use logical reasoning

	Baseball	Basketball	Football	Soccer
Alan	No	No	No	Yes
Jack	Yes	No	No	No
Todd	No	No	Yes	No
Trent	No	Yes	No	No

Look Back and Check

Step 4: Is your work correct? Yes, I filled in the information I was given and made the right conclusions.

1. Joleen, Cori, and Bethany are cousins, but they each have a different last name. None of the cousins have a last name that begins with the same letter as their first name. Bethany is not a Carson. What is each cousin's full name?

	Butcher	Carson	Jacobson
Bethany			
Cori			
Joleen			

Name_____

Use Logical Reasoning

Solve each problem. Write the answer in a complete sentence.

1. Jennifer and her four friends, Anna, Debra, Mary, and Sue, were born in different months of the same year. The girls were born in January, March, April, September, and December. None of the girls were born in a month that begins with the same letter as their first name. Sue is the youngest, and Debra is the oldest. Jennifer was born in September. In what month was Mary born?

   _____

2. What figure comes next?

   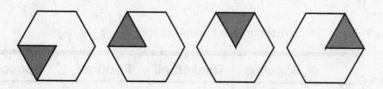

3. John, Ben, and Thomas each brought a different kind of sandwich for lunch. The boys had bologna, ham, and turkey sandwiches. John does not like ham, and Thomas brings bologna every day. What kind of sandwich did each boy bring for lunch?

   _____

   _____

   _____

   _____

4. Randall has a meeting this afternoon. He knows it is on the half hour, but he cannot remember which half hour. The meeting is after 1 P.M. and before 6 P.M. The sum of the digits in the time is 7. What time is Randall's meeting?

   _____

Length and Customary Units

Unit	Example
inch	width of a U.S. quarter
1 foot (ft) = 12 inches (in.)	gym shoes
1 yard (yd) = 3 feet	height of a desk
1 mile (mi) = 5,280 feet	distance between school and home

How to measure an object:

To measure an object, make sure one end of the object begins at the zero unit.

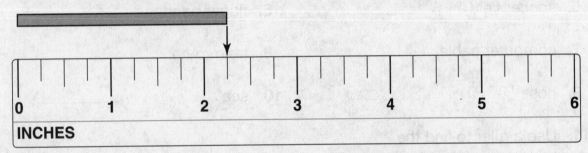

The rectangle is closest to the 2 in. mark, so we can say the rectangle is 2 in. long to the nearest inch.

Estimate first. Then find each length to the nearest inch.

1. ⊢————————————————⊣   _____

2. ⊢————⊣   _____

Choose the most appropriate unit to measure the length of each. Write in., ft, yd, or mi.

3. cat _____   4. lake _____

5. hallway _____   6. basketball court _____

Length and Customary Units

Estimate first. Then, measure each length to the nearest inch.

1. ├─────────────────────────┤   _____

2. ├──────────┤   _____

Choose the most appropriate unit to measure the length of each. Write in., ft, yd, or mi.

3. boat   _____   4. wallet   _____

5. soccer field   _____   6. finger bandage   _____

7. computer cable   _____   8. train route   _____

9. nose   _____   10. sea   _____

11. Use a ruler to find the perimeter of the triangle.

_____

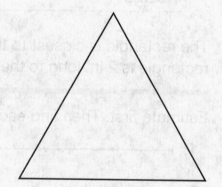

12. Eileen needs 9 ft of fabric to make a skirt. How many yards of fabric does she need?

_____

Test Prep

13. Which unit would be most appropriate for measuring the length of a barn?

    A. Inches   **B.** Pounds   **C.** Yards   **D.** Miles

14. **Writing in Math** Explain how you would decide which unit is best for measuring your math book.

_____

_____

Fractions of an Inch

The nail is just over $2\frac{1}{8}$ in. long.

To the nearest inch, the nail is 2 in.

To the nearest $\frac{1}{2}$ in., the nail is also 2 in. long, because it is closer to 2 in. than it is to $2\frac{1}{2}$ in.

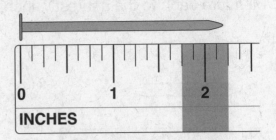

To the nearest $\frac{1}{4}$ in., the nail is $2\frac{1}{4}$ in. long, because the length is over $2\frac{1}{8}$, which is the halfway point between 2 and $2\frac{1}{4}$.

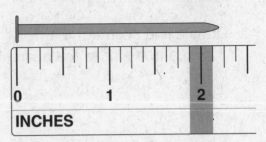

To the nearest $\frac{1}{8}$ in., the nail is $2\frac{1}{8}$ in. long.

The measurement to the nearest $\frac{1}{8}$ in. is the closest to the actual measurement.

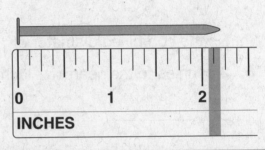

Measure each segment to the nearest $\frac{1}{2}$, $\frac{1}{4}$, and $\frac{1}{8}$ in.

1.

_____ , _____ , _____

2.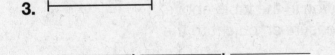

_____ , _____ , _____

3. ├────────────┤

_____ , _____ , _____

4. Number Sense A beetle is just over $1\frac{5}{8}$ in. long. How long is the beetle to the nearest $\frac{1}{2}$ in.?

_____

Name_____

Fractions of an Inch

Measure each to the nearest $\frac{1}{2}$ inch, $\frac{1}{4}$ inch, and $\frac{1}{8}$ inch.

1.

    _____, _____, _____

2.

    _____, _____, _____

3. CRAYON

    _____, _____, _____

4. Draw a line segment that is $4\frac{5}{8}$ in. long to the nearest $\frac{1}{8}$ inch and $4\frac{3}{4}$ in. to the nearest $\frac{1}{4}$ inch.

What is the combined diameter of

5. 2 pennies to the nearest $\frac{1}{4}$ inch?

_____

6. 1 nickel and 1 dime to the nearest $\frac{1}{8}$ inch?

_____

Diameter of Coin to Nearest $\frac{1}{8}$ in.	
Penny	$\frac{3}{4}$ in.
Nickel	$\frac{7}{8}$ in.
Dime	$\frac{3}{4}$ in.
Quarter	1 in.

Test Prep

7. Find the length to the nearest $\frac{1}{4}$ in.

    |————————————|

    A. 1 in.   **B.** $1\frac{1}{4}$ in.   **C.** $1\frac{1}{2}$ in.   **D.** 2 in.

8. **Writing in Math** Use the information in the table above. Which coin would be useful to measure an object to the nearest inch? Explain.

_____

_____

_____

Capacity and Customary Units

Capacity is the amount that a container can hold. Capacity is measured in teaspoons, tablespoons, fluid ounces, cups, pints, quarts, and gallons, from smallest to largest.

    1 tablespoon (tbsp) = 3 teaspoons (tsp)

    1 fluid ounce (fl oz) = 2 tbsp

    1 cup (c) = 8 fl oz

    1 pint (pt) = 2 c

    1 quart (qt) = 2 pt

    1 gallon (gal) = 4 qt

A container that holds 2 gal will hold more than 2 qt. A container that holds 20 c will hold less than 20 pt.

Choose the most appropriate unit or units to measure the capacity of each. Write tsp, tbsp, fl oz, c, pt, qt, or gal.

1. eye dropper _____

2. bathtub _____

3. milk carton _____

4. water tower _____

5. teacup _____

6. flour in a recipe _____

7. Reasoning Would a teaspoon be a good tool for measuring the amount of water in a bathtub? Explain why or why not.

_____

_____

Blood The adult human body contains about 5 qt of blood.

8. Are there more or less than 5 pt of blood in a human adult?

9. Are there more or less than 5 gal of blood in a human adult?

_____   _____

Capacity and Customary Units

Choose the most appropriate unit or units to measure the
capacity of each. Write tsp, tbsp, fl oz, c, pt, qt, or gal.

1. teacup _____

2. juice box _____

3. motor oil _____

4. pepper in a recipe _____

5. carton of creamer _____

6. lake _____

7. **Number Sense** Would a teaspoon be a good way to
measure the capacity of a milk carton? Explain.

_____

_____

8. A refreshment jug for the baseball team holds
20 gal of water. To make an energy drink, 1 c
of mix is used for every 2 gal of water. How many
cups of the mix are needed to fill the jug with
energy drink?   _____

Test Prep

9. Which unit has the greatest capacity?

   A. Tablespoon   **B.** Quart

   C. Pint   **D.** Teaspoon

10. **Writing in Math** Cassidy says that capacity is the same as
    the amount. Do you agree? Explain why or why not.

_____

_____

_____

_____

Name_____

Weight and Customary Units

There are 16 ounces (oz) in 1 pound (lb).

There are 2,000 lb in 1 ton (T).

| You use ounces to weigh smaller things, like a tomato. | You use pounds to weigh things like a heavy box. | You use tons to weigh very large or heavy things, like a rocket. |

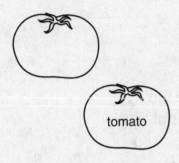

tomato

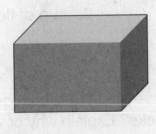

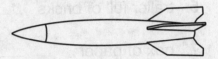

Choose the most appropriate unit to measure the weight of each. Write oz, lb, or T.

1. car _____

2. computer _____

3. bowling ball _____

4. onion _____

5. dinosaur _____

6. vacuum cleaner _____

7. Reasoning A hippo weighs about 5,000 lb. Does the same hippo weigh more or less than 5,000 oz?

_____

8. Would you most likely measure a leaf using ounces, pounds, or tons? Explain.

_____

_____

_____

Weight and Customary Units

Choose the most appropriate unit to measure the weight of each. Write oz, lb, or T.

1. truck _____

2. can of vegetables _____

3. person _____

4. desk _____

5. trailer full of bricks _____

6. cup of flour _____

7. box of paper _____

8. CD _____

9. **Reasoning** Would a scale that is used to weigh food be the best tool to weigh concrete blocks? Explain why or why not.

_____

_____

_____

10. Jen wants to weigh her cat. Should she weigh the cat with ounces, pounds, or tons? _____

11. What unit would you use to measure the weight of your house? _____

Test Prep

12. Which animal would it be appropriate to measure in ounces?

    A. Mouse   **B.** Elephant   **C.** Horse   **D.** Cow

13. **Writing in Math** Dezi says that there are more ounces in 1 T than there are pounds. Do you agree? Explain.

_____

_____

_____

Changing Units and Comparing Measures

How to change customary units:

To change larger units to smaller units, multiply.	To change smaller units to larger units, divide.
12 yd = ☐ ft	20 qt = ☐ gal
Think: 1 yd = 3 ft	Think: 1 gal = 4 qt
$12 \times 3 = 36$	$20 \div 4 = 5$
So, 12 yd = 36 ft.	So, 20 qt = 5 gal.

How to compare measures:

Compare 2 mi ◯ 11,000 ft.

Step 1
Change to the same units.

2 mi ☐ 11,000 ft
1 mi = 5,280 ft
Think: $5,280 \times 2 = 10,560$
2 mi = 10,560 ft

Step 2
Compare.

10,560 ft < 11,000 ft
So, 2 mi < 11,000 ft.

Find each missing number.

1. 50 pt = _____ qt

2. 10 tbsp = _____ fl oz

3. 2 lb 1 oz = _____ oz

4. 9 yd = _____ ft

5. 3 gal = _____ qt

6. 12 tsp = _____ tbsp

Compare. Write > or < for each ◯.

7. 8 qt ◯ 3 gal

8. 10 lb ◯ 100 oz

9. 2 mi ◯ 5,000 yd

10. Reasoning The heart of a giraffe is 2 ft long and can weigh as much as 24 lb. How many ounces can the heart of a giraffe weigh?

_____

Name_____

Changing Units and Comparing Measures

Find each missing number.

1. 2 ft = _____ in.

2. 8 qt = _____ pt

3. 2 gal = _____ qt

4. 9 ft = _____ yd

5. 64 oz = _____ lb

6. 10,560 ft = _____ mi

7. 20 T = _____ lb

8. 4 lb, 6 oz = _____ oz

Compare. Write > or < for each $\bigcirc$.

9. 20 pt, 2 c $\bigcirc$ 12 qt

10. 10 lb $\bigcirc$ 200 oz

11. 13 ft, 6 in. $\bigcirc$ 5 yd

12. 100 in. $\bigcirc$ 2 yd

13. 3 gal $\bigcirc$ 10 qt

14. 9 oz $\bigcirc$ 9 lb

15. How many inches long is the longest car?

_____

16. How many ounces does the lightest car weigh?

_____

Car Records

Lightest car	21 lb
Heaviest car	7,353 lb
Longest car	100 ft

Test Prep

17. How many fluid ounces are in 6 c?

A. 32   **B.** 40   **C.** 48   **D.** 54

18. Writing in Math Explain why you cannot convert fluid ounces to pounds.

_____

_____

_____

Exact Answer or Estimate

The Fundraiser There are 296 students signed up to attend a fundraiser at the school gym. Each student will receive an 8 oz bag of popcorn and a drink. Sheri is making the popcorn, and has made 3,000 oz so far. Does she need to make more?

What are you trying to find?

Is 3,000 oz enough popcorn for 296 students to each receive 8 oz?

Do you need an exact answer or an estimate?

You don't need to know the exact amount of popcorn needed for 296 students. You just need to know if there is enough already, so an estimate is OK. Since $300 \times 8 = 2,400$; 3,000 oz is enough.

Tell whether an exact answer is needed or if an estimate is enough. Then solve.

1. A picture measures 11 in. $\times$ 14 in. Michael wants to make a frame for the picture out of wood. He has a 5 ft piece of wood he would like to use. Is the wood long enough to make a frame?

   _____

   _____

2. Theo is a schoolteacher. He needs to order buses for a third-grade field trip. Each bus can hold 70 students. There are a total of 97 third graders. If Theo ordered 2 buses for the trip, will all of the students be able to fit?

   _____

   _____

3. Jane bought 7 notebooks. If each notebook costs $2, how much did Jane spend?

   _____

PROBLEM-SOLVING SKILL   **P 10-12**
Exact Answer or Estimate

For 1–4, tell whether an exact answer is needed or if an
estimate is enough. Then solve.

1. You have 100 lb of green beans. Each canning jar holds
    14 oz of the beans. You have 100 jars. Do you have enough
    jars to hold all the beans?

    _____

    _____

Grace is making a dress to enter as a craft fair project. The
pattern says that she needs 6 yd of fabric, 1 spool of thread,
and 8 one-inch buttons.

2. Grace has 20 ft of fabric that she really likes. Is there
    enough to make the dress?

    _____

    _____

3. The buttons that Grace likes are $4.25 for a package of
    4 buttons. The right color thread is $2.35. If Grace pays for
    the supplies with a $20.00 bill, how much change should
    she receive?

    _____

    _____

4. You need to add 2 gal of apple juice to a fruit punch. You
    only have a container that measures quarts. How many
    quarts should you add?

    _____

    _____

PROBLEM-SOLVING APPLICATION

Facts Galore!

A full-sized whale needs to eat more than 2 T of food every day. Is 3,750 lb of food a day enough for a full-sized whale?

Remember, to compare measures you must first change to the same units.

> 1 T = 2,000 lb, so 2 T = 4,000 lb.
>
> 3,750 lb < 4,000 lb

So, 3,750 lb is not enough food for the whale.

Solve.

The Eiffel Tower is 984 ft tall and weighs 7,300 T.

1. How many yards tall is the Eiffel Tower? _____

2. How many pounds does the Eiffel Tower weigh?

_____

3. Presidents Cleveland, Coolidge, Eisenhower, Lincoln, and Nixon were from the states of California, Kentucky, New Jersey, Texas, and Vermont. Coolidge and Cleveland were not from California, Kentucky, or Texas. Lincoln was from Kentucky. Nixon was not from Texas. Cleveland's home state was New Jersey. Complete the chart to find out what state Eisenhower was from.

	CA	NJ	TX	VT	KY
Cleveland					
Coolidge					
Eisenhower					
Lincoln					
Nixon					

© Pearson Education, Inc. 4

PROBLEM-SOLVING APPLICATION

Measurements Abound!

Solve each problem. Write your answer in a complete sentence.

1. Ted has 20 ft of rope and Lou has 42 ft of rope. They need to have at least 12 yd of rope between the two of them. Do they have enough? Explain your answer.

   _____

   _____

2. Arnold, Cathy, Derrick, and Eldon each have a different pet. They have a dog, a cat, a bird, and an iguana. Arnold is allergic to anything with fur. Cathy's pet can say some words, and likes to eat sunflower seeds. Derrick does not have a cat. What kind of animal is Eldon's pet?

   _____

Christie runs every morning before school. This week she ran $\frac{2}{3}$ mi each on Monday, Wednesday, and Thursday. She ran $\frac{1}{2}$ mi on Tuesday and $\frac{7}{9}$ mi on Friday.

3. How far did Christie run on Monday, Wednesday, and Thursday combined?

   _____

   _____

4. Christie wants to run at least 3 mi each week. Did she meet her goal this week? Explain how you decided.

   _____

   _____

   _____

   _____

Decimals and Fractions

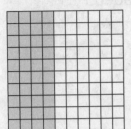

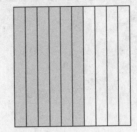

Fraction: $\frac{40}{100}$　　Decimal: 0.40

Fraction: $\frac{6}{10}$　　Decimal: 0.6

Writing fractions as decimals:

Write $\frac{4}{5}$ as a decimal.

$$\overset{\times\,20}{\frac{4}{5} = \frac{80}{100}}_{\times\,20}$$

80 parts out of 100 is 0.80.

So, $\frac{4}{5} = 0.80$.

Writing decimals as fractions:

Write 0.8 as a fraction in simplest form.

0.8 is eight tenths or $\frac{8}{10}$.

$$\overset{\div\,2}{\frac{8}{10} = \frac{4}{5}}_{\div\,2}$$

So, $0.8 = \frac{4}{5}$.

Write a fraction and a decimal for the part of each grid that is shaded.

1.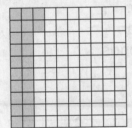

2.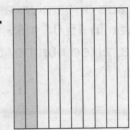

_____

_____

Write each fraction as a decimal.

3. $\frac{6}{10}$ _____

4. $\frac{75}{100}$ _____

5. $1\frac{1}{10}$ _____

Write each decimal as a fraction or a mixed number in simplest form.

6. 0.3 _____

7. 0.95 _____

8. 7.7 _____

Decimals and Fractions

Write a fraction and a decimal for the part of each grid that is shaded.

1.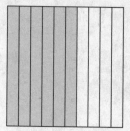

_____

2.

_____

Write each number as a decimal.

3. $\frac{1}{10}$ _____

4. $\frac{4}{5}$ _____

5. $3\frac{1}{2}$ _____

6. $1\frac{1}{50}$ _____

7. $\frac{11}{20}$ _____

8. $\frac{19}{100}$ _____

Write each decimal as a fraction or mixed number, in simplest form.

9. 0.77 _____

10. 0.6 _____

11. 3.75 _____

12. 2.9 _____

13. 36.36 _____

14. 6.65 _____

Kari and Timothy made origami swans and timed each other.
Kari finished her swan in 15.04 sec. Timothy finished his swan
in 17.82 sec. Write a mixed number to show how many seconds
it took each of them.

15. Kari _____

16. Timothy _____

Test Prep

17. Which fraction has the same value as 0.15?

A. $\frac{3}{10}$

B. $\frac{3}{15}$

C. $\frac{3}{20}$

D. $\frac{3}{25}$

18. Writing in Math Explain how saying the decimal can help
you to write the decimal as a fraction.

_____

_____

Decimal Place Value

There are different ways to represent the decimal 1.35.

Number line:

1.30 1.31 1.32 1.33 1.34 1.35 1.36 1.37 1.38 1.39

Place-value chart:

Ones		Tenths	Hundredths
1		3	5

Expanded form: 1 + 0.3 + 0.05

Standard form: 1.35

Word form: one and thirty-five hundredths

Write each number in standard form.

1. Two and seventeen hundredths _____

2. 80 + 7 + 0.09 _____

Write the word form and tell the value of the underlined digit for each number.

3. 4.<u>1</u>6 _____

_____

4. <u>2</u>.08 _____

_____

5. 9.9<u>4</u> _____

_____

The world's largest dog biscuit measured 2.35 m long, 577 cm wide, and 2.54 cm thick.

6. Write the thickness of the dog biscuit in expanded form.

_____

138 Use with Lesson 11-2.

Name _____

Decimal Place Value

Write each number in standard form.

1. Two and three tenths

_____

2. 200 + 8 + 0.5 + 0.06

_____

Write the word form and tell the value of the underlined digit for each number.

3. 2.1<u>9</u>   _____

_____

4. 40.<u>6</u>2   _____

_____

5. Number Sense How many tenths are there in twenty hundredths?

_____

To make one quarter, the cost is 4.29 cents. It costs 1.88 cents to make one dime. Write the word form for the number of cents it costs to make one of each coin.

6. quarter   _____

7. dime   _____

Test Prep

8. Which is 60 + 5 + 0.09 in standard form?

A. Sixty-five and nine hundredths   **B.** 65.09

C. 65.9   **D.** 659

9. Writing in Math Explain how to write eight and nineteen hundredths in standard form.

_____

_____

Comparing and Ordering Decimals

Compare 0.87 to 0.89.

First, begin at the left. Find the first place where the numbers are different.

0.87

0.89

The numbers are the same in the tenths places, so look to the next place.

The first place where the numbers are different is the hundredths place. Compare 7 hundredths to 9 hundredths.

$0.07 < 0.09$, so $0.87 < 0.89$

Compare. Write $>$, $<$, or $=$ for each $\bigcirc$.

1. 0.36 $\bigcirc$ 0.76   **2.** 5.1 $\bigcirc$ 5.01   **3.** 1.2 $\bigcirc$ 1.20

4. 6.55 $\bigcirc$ 6.6   **5.** 0.62 $\bigcirc$ 0.82   **6.** 4.71 $\bigcirc$ 4.17

Order the numbers from least to greatest.

7. 1.36, 1.3, 1.63   **8.** 0.42, 3.74, 3.47

_____   _____

9. 6.46, 6.41, 4.6   **10.** 0.3, 0.13, 0.19, 0.31

_____   _____

11. Number Sense Which is greater, 8.0 or 0.8? Explain.

_____

_____

_____

_____

Name_____

Comparing and Ordering Decimals

Compare. Write >, <, or = for each ◯.

1. 0.31 ◯ 0.41   **2.** 1.9 ◯ 0.95   **3.** 0.09 ◯ 0.1

4. 2.70 ◯ 2.7   **5.** 0.81 ◯ 0.79   **6.** 2.12 ◯ 2.21

Order the numbers from least to greatest.

7. 0.37, 0.41, 0.31   **8.** 1.16, 1.61, 6.11

_____   _____

9. 7.9, 7.91, 7.09, 7.19   **10.** 1.45, 1.76, 1.47, 1.67

_____   _____

Margaret has three cats. Sophie weighs 4.27 lb, Tigger weighs
6.25 lb, and Ghost weights 4.7 lb.

11. Which cat has the greatest weight?   _____

12. Which cat weighs the least?   _____

Test Prep

13. Which group of numbers is ordered from least to greatest?

    A. 0.12, 1.51, 0.65   **B.** 5.71, 5.4, 0.54

    C. 0.4, 0.09, 0.41   **D.** 0.05, 0.51, 1.5

14. Writing in Math Darrin put the numbers 7.25, 5.27, 7.52,
and 5.72 in order from greatest to least. Is his work
correct? Explain.
7.25, 7.52, 5.72, 5.27

_____

_____

Rounding Decimals

Here is how to round decimals:

		Round 5.23 to the nearest whole number.	Round 3.67 to the nearest tenth.
Step 1	Find the rounding place.	5.23 ↑ 5 is in the ones place.	3.67 ↑ 6 is in the tenths place.
Step 2	Look at the digit to the right. If it is 5 or more, change to the next greatest digit. If it is less than 5, leave the number as it is.	5.23 ↑ Leave the number as it is because 2 < 5. 5.23 rounds to 5.	3.67 ↑ Change 6 to 7, because 7 > 5. 3.67 rounds to 3.7.

Round each number to the nearest whole number.

1. 27.93 _____   **2.** 0.8 _____   **3.** 7.49 _____   **4.** 63.1 _____

Round each number to the nearest tenth.

5. 63.25 _____   **6.** 0.47 _____

7. 11.14 _____   **8.** 1.92 _____

9. 33.08 _____   **10.** 27.64 _____

11. Number Sense Ashley was asked to round 79.37 to the nearest tenth. She answered 79.3. Is her answer correct? Explain.

_____

_____

_____

_____

_____

Rounding Decimals

Round each number to the nearest whole number.

1. 15.2 _____   **2.** 0.79 _____   **3.** 1.50 _____   **4.** 6.47 _____

5. 10.23 _____   **6.** 2.75 _____   **7.** 9.32 _____   **8.** 32.58 _____

Round each number to the nearest tenth.

9. 5.62 _____   **10.** 11.47 _____

11. 0.73 _____   **12.** 1.88 _____

13. Number Sense What is the greatest decimal with hundredths
that will round to 0.5 when rounded to the nearest tenth? _____

For each age group in the data file, round the part of the
population to the nearest tenth.

14. under 18

_____

15. over 64

_____

**U.S. Population
by Age, 2000**

Age Group	Part
Under 18	0.26
18 to 64	0.62
Over 64	0.12

Test Prep

16. Which number below is 8.3 when rounded to the tenths place?

A. 7.35   **B.** 8.27   **C.** 8.35   **D.** 8.39

17. Writing in Math Explain how to round 1.342 to the nearest tenth.

_____

_____

_____

_____

Estimating Decimal Sums and Differences

To estimate, you change numbers to ones that are easier to add and subtract.

Estimate 11.7 + 3.8.

Estimate by rounding to the nearest whole number.

11.7 + 3.8
↓   ↓
12   +   4   =   16

So, 11.7 + 3.8 is about 16.

Estimate 12.9 − 7.1.

Estimate by rounding to the nearest whole number.

12.9 − 7.1
↓   ↓
13   −   7   =   6

So, 12.9 − 7.1 is about 6.

Estimate each sum or difference.

1. 7.12 + 8.64 _____

2. 12.74 − 6.11 _____

3. 22.91 + 4.86 _____

4. 17.4 − 12.8 _____

5. 19.8 + 7.12 _____

6. 31.22 − 18.3 _____

7.
```
   9.3
+ 6.27
```

8.
```
   8.4
− 3.1
```

9.
```
   4.13
− 1.68
```

10.
```
   0.31
+ 0.74
```

11.
```
   24.7
+   3.88
```

12.
```
   51.99
+ 11.11
```

13.
```
   24.24
− 12.81
```

14.
```
   0.79
+ 1.88
```

15. Number Sense Explain why 20 is NOT a reasonable estimate for 33.71 − 17.25.

_____

_____

Estimating Decimal Sums and Differences

Estimate each sum or difference.

1. 1.45 + 0.6 _____   **2.** 8.91 + 1.16 _____   **3.** 7.09 − 5.11 _____

4. 6.59 − 3.84 _____   **5.** 8.54 + 9.01 _____   **6.** 6.11 − 0.15 _____

7.   18.05   **8.**   11.45   **9.**   8.65   **10.**   9.50
     +   0.85   −   0.9   − 5.1   + 6.8

11. Reasoning Cheryl had $86.51. She bought 6 cases of fruit drink and had $50.67 left. About how much did Cheryl pay for each case of fruit drink?

12. Jean walked 19.87 mi last week, 17.15 mi the week before, and 18.92 mi this week. About how many miles has Jean walked in the 3 weeks?

13. William drives 14.81 mi to work each day. Kathy drives 2.6 mi to work each day. About how much farther does William drive each day?

Test Prep

14. Which is the best estimate for the sum of 22.36 + 19.6?

   A. 41   **B.** 42   **C.** 43   **D.** 44

15. Writing in Math Kayla needs $15.00 to buy a CD. She has $8.18 in her wallet, $3.19 in her pocket, and $5.42 in her piggy bank. Does Kayla have enough? Explain.

Using Grids to Add and Subtract Decimals

Adding decimals using a hundredths grid:

Add 0.32 + 0.17.

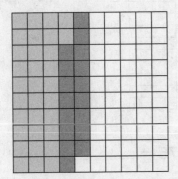

Step 1: Shade 32 squares to show 0.32.

Step 2: Use a different color. Shade 17 squares to show 0.17.

Step 3: Count all the squares that are shaded. How many hundredths are shaded in all? Write the decimal for the total shaded squares: 0.49.

So, 0.32 + 0.17 = 0.49.

Subtracting decimals using a hundredths grid:

Subtract 0.61 − 0.42.

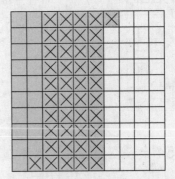

Step 1: Shade 61 squares to show 0.61.

Step 2: Cross out 42 squares to show 0.42.

Step 3: Count the squares that are shaded but not crossed out. Write the decimal: 0.19.

So, 0.61 − 0.42 = 0.19.

Add or subtract. You may use grids to help.

1. 0.22 + 0.35 = _____

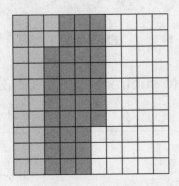

2. 0.52 − 0.41 = _____

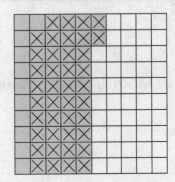

Name _____

Using Grids to Add and Subtract Decimals

Add or subtract. You may use grids to help.

1. 0.12 + 0.56 = _____

2. 0.27 − 0.09 = _____

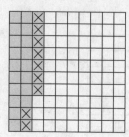

3. 0.86 + 0.54 = _____

4. 1.27 + 0.75 = _____

5. 0.93 − 0.25 = _____

6. 1.07 − 0.61 = _____

7. 1.13 − 1.02 = _____

8. 0.28 + 1.96 = _____

9. Number Sense Is the difference of
1.45 − 0.12 less than or greater than 1? _____

10. A bottle of nail polish holds 0.8 oz. A bottle of perfume
holds 0.45 oz. How many more ounces does a bottle
of nail polish hold? _____

Test Prep

11. Add.
1.18 + 1.86 =

A. 2.04   **B.** 2.94   **C.** 3.04   **D.** 3.14

12. Writing in Math Explain how you can use a grid to subtract 1.65 − 0.98.

_____

_____

_____

_____

Name _____

Adding and Subtracting Decimals

Add 12.8 + 52.64.

First, estimate 13 + 53 = 66.

Step 1	**Step 2**	**Step 3**	**Step 4**
Line up the decimal points. Write zeros as place holders, if necessary.	Add the hundredths. Regroup if necessary.	Add the tenths. Regroup if necessary.	Add the ones, then the tens. Place the decimal point.
$\begin{array}{r} 12.80 \\ +52.64 \\ \hline \end{array}$	$\begin{array}{r} 12.80 \\ +52.64 \\ \hline 4 \end{array}$	$\begin{array}{r} {}^{1} \\ 12.80 \\ +52.64 \\ \hline 44 \end{array}$	$\begin{array}{r} {}^{1} \\ 12.80 \\ +52.64 \\ \hline 65.44 \end{array}$
Remember, 12.8 = 12.80.			

The sum 65.44 is reasonable because it is close to the estimate of 66.

Subtract 68.2 − 41.05.

First, estimate 70 − 40 = 30.

Step 1	**Step 2**	**Step 3**	**Step 4**
Line up the decimal points. Write zeros as place holders, if necessary.	Subtract hundredths. Regroup if necessary.	Subtract tenths. Regroup if necessary.	Continue subtracting ones and tens, regrouping as necessary. Place the decimal point.
$\begin{array}{r} 68.20 \\ -41.05 \\ \hline \end{array}$	$\begin{array}{r} {}^{1\;10} \\ 68.2\!\!\!/0 \\ -41.05 \\ \hline 5 \end{array}$	$\begin{array}{r} {}^{1\;10} \\ 68.2\!\!\!/0 \\ -41.05 \\ \hline 15 \end{array}$	$\begin{array}{r} {}^{1\;10} \\ 68.2\!\!\!/0 \\ -41.05 \\ \hline 27.15 \end{array}$
Remember, 68.2 = 68.20.			

The difference 27.15 is reasonable because it is close to the estimate of 30.

---

1. $\begin{array}{r} 12.51 \\ +\ \ 6.43 \\ \hline \end{array}$ **2.** $\begin{array}{r} 5.8 \\ +\ 0.65 \\ \hline \end{array}$ **3.** $\begin{array}{r} 8.97 \\ -\ 5.61 \\ \hline \end{array}$ **4.** $\begin{array}{r} 15.8 \\ -\ 12.15 \\ \hline \end{array}$

5. Estimation Estimate the sum of 35.67 and 9.51.

_____

Name_____

Adding and Subtracting Decimals P 11-7

1. 4.52
      + 8.61

2. 52.36
      + 9.74

3. 7.54
      − 4.64

4. 92.56
      − 13.8

5. 1.54 + 5.67 = _____

6. 1.56 − 0.42 = _____

7. 0.64 − 0.08 = _____

8. 92.22 + 64.53 = _____

9. 65.12 − 37.88 = _____

10. 73.12 + 77.69 = _____

11. 0.54 − 0.48 = _____

12. 0.61 + 0.88 = _____

13. 37.8 − 18.27 = _____

14. 11.94 + 7.19 = _____

15. There are two records for the greatest distance traveled by a model car in 24 hr. The larger scale model car traveled 305.94 mi, and the smaller scale model car traveled 213.07 mi. How many more miles did the larger car travel in 24 hr? _____

Sara and Jessica are twins. At birth, Sara weighed 5.42 lb and Jessica weighed 6.8 lb.

16. How much was their combined weight? _____

17. How much more did Jessica weigh than Sara? _____

Test Prep

18. Which is the difference of 8.97 − 7.8?

A. 0.17   **B.** 0.89   **C.** 1.17   **D.** 1.89

19. Writing in Math Heather added 9.42 + 6.3. Is her answer correct? Explain.

      9.42
    + 6.3
    ──────
    10.05

_____

_____

_____

PROBLEM-SOLVING STRATEGY   **R 11-8**

Solve a Simpler Problem

Squares A student is making a pattern of squares out of cotton balls. Each unit on a side of the pattern is made up of 2 cotton balls. How many cotton balls will the student need to make a pattern that is 4 units high and 4 units wide?

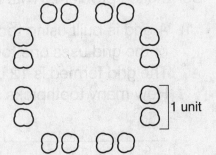

1 unit

Read and Understand

Step 1: What do you know?

There are 2 cotton balls in each unit. The square is 4 units high and 4 units wide.

Step 2: What are you trying to find?

How many cotton balls are needed in all

Plan and Solve

Step 3: What strategy will you use?   **Strategy:** Solve a simpler problem

Problem 1: How many cotton balls are needed for a 1-unit by 1-unit square?

8 cotton balls are needed for a 1-unit square.

Problem 2: How many cotton balls are needed for a 2-unit by 2-unit square?

16 cotton balls are needed for a 2-unit square.

There are 2 cotton balls for each unit on the side. There are always 4 sides, so the pattern is the number of units in each side, multiplied by 2 cotton balls, multiplied by 4 sides.

Answer: 32 cotton balls are needed.

Look Back and Check

Step 4: Is your work correct?

Yes, all of my computations are correct, and I saw the correct pattern.

---

1. Joan works for 6 hr each weekday, and 8 hr total on the weekends. She earns $6 an hour on weekdays and $9 an hour on weekends. How much money does she earn each week?

Name_____

Solve a Simpler Problem

Solve each problem. Write the answer in a complete sentence.

1. A grid is built using toothpicks. Each square
   of the grid uses one toothpick on each side.
   The grid formed is 12 units long and 1 unit high.
   How many toothpicks are needed to make the grid?

_____

2. At the end of the volleyball season, the 4 top teams hold a
   tournament. Each team plays each other team twice. How
   many games are played at the tournament altogether?

_____

3. Ben is cutting a round piece of bread dough into equal pie-
   shaped sections. If he keeps the circle together and makes
   cuts across the diameter, how many sections will he have
   when he has made 6 cuts?

_____

4. Doris bought 2 magazines for $1.79 each. Her dad had
   given her $2.50 for cleaning the car, and she already had
   saved $3.88. How much did Doris have left after she
   bought the magazines?

_____

5. Norman is folding a square piece of paper. Each fold he
   makes divides the folded paper in half. When he unfolds
   the paper, it is divided into equal sections. How many
   sections will there be if Norman has folded the paper
   8 times?

_____

Length and Metric Units

Metric units are used to estimate and measure length.

Metric Units of Length

    1 cm = 10 mm

    1 dm = 10 cm

    1 m = 100 cm

    1 km = 1,000 m

Find the length to the nearest centimeter.

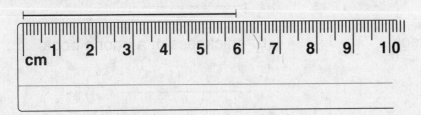

Measured to the nearest centimeter, the segment is 6 cm long.

Estimate first. Then find each length to the nearest centimeter.

1. _____   _____

2. _____   _____

Choose the most appropriate unit to measure each. Write mm, cm, dm, m, or km.

3. length of a finger _____

4. length of a football _____

5. width of a big toe _____

6. length of the lunchroom _____

7. distance between Paris and London _____

8. Number Sense The distance across a field is 20 m. Is the distance across the same field greater than or less than 20 km?

_____

Name _____

Length and Metric Units

Estimate first. Then find each length to the nearest centimeter.

1. |————————————|

2. |————————|

Choose the most appropriate unit to measure each. Write mm, cm, dm, m, or km.

3. width of a house

_____

4. distance across Lake Erie

_____

5. width of a thumbtack

_____

6. thickness of a phone book

_____

Find each missing number.

7. 10 mm = _____ cm

8. 10 cm = _____ dm

9. 1 m = _____ dm

10. **Number Sense** Which would you be more likely to measure in centimeters, a fish tank or a swimming pool?

_____

11. Which is longer, a 12 cm pencil or a 1 dm pen? _____

12. Find the area of a square with sides 2 cm long. _____

Test Prep

13. Which is the most appropriate measure for the length of a skateboard?

A. 5 mm **B.** 5 cm **C.** 5 dm **D.** 5 m

14. **Writing in Math** Explain how to give the measurement in centimeters of a 56 mm object.

_____

_____

Capacity and Metric Units

Capacity is the amount of liquid that an object can hold. The metric system of measurement uses the units liter (L) and milliliter (mL).

You would use liters to measure the amount of water in a water bottle or the amount of gasoline in a gas can.

A milliliter is a very small unit of measurement. There are 5 mL of liquid in a teaspoon. You would use milliliters to measure small amounts of liquid, such as measuring how much medicine to give a baby.

1 L is the same as 1,000 mL.

Choose the most appropriate unit to use to measure the capacity of each.

1. thimble   _____

2. kitchen sink   _____

3. coffee cup   _____

4. bucket of water for a horse   _____

5. **Number Sense** A container holds 5 L of fluid. Does it hold more than or less than 5 mL of fluid?

_____

6. Mr. Burke has a 1 L container of oil. He poured 750 mL of oil into his lawn mower. How many mL are left in the container?

_____

7. A bottle is filled with saline solution for eyes. Is the bottle more likely to hold 15 mL of solution or 1 L of solution?

_____

_____

Capacity and Metric Units

Choose the most appropriate unit to measure the capacity of each. Write L or mL.

1. water in a bathtub   **2.** perfume in a bottle   **3.** soup in a can

_____   _____   _____

4. Number Sense Which will be less, the number of liters or the number of milliliters, of the water in a pool? _____

5. Name something you might measure in liters.

_____

6. Name something you might measure in milliliters.

_____

7. A gallon of milk is the same as 3.78 L of milk. How many liters of milk are there in 2 gal?   _____

8. A small can of tomato juice contains 56.8 mL of juice. A large can of tomato juice contains 202.62 mL of juice. How much juice is there in the large and small can combined?   _____

Test Prep

9. Which capacity would you be most likely to measure in milliliters?

A. Gas in a car   **B.** Water in a dam

C. Tea in a cup   **D.** Detergent in a bottle

10. Writing in Math Would you be more likely to measure the amount of water in your kitchen sink in liters or milliliters? Explain.

_____

_____

_____

Mass and Metric Units

The metric units for mass are grams (g) and kilograms (kg).

    1 kg = 1,000 g

A paper clip might have the mass of 1 g.

A kitten or watermelon might have the mass of 1 kg.

Choose the most appropriate unit to measure the mass of each.
Write g or kg.

1. lawn mower _____   **2.** pumpkin _____

3. child _____   **4.** gold ring _____

5. robin's egg _____   **6.** cannonball _____

7. cement block _____   **8.** spool of thread _____

9. Number Sense Which is greater, 850 g or 1 kg?

_____

10. The mass of a certain window is 18.6 kg. What is the mass
of 2 of the same windows together?

_____

11. The mass of a horse is 180.82 kg. The mass of the horse's
sister is 275.6 kg. How much larger is the mass of the
sister than that of the first horse?

_____

_____

Mass and Metric Units

Choose the most appropriate unit to measure the mass of each.
Write g or kg.

1. Banana _____
2. Tractor _____
3. Coin _____

4. Bowling ball _____
5. Letter _____
6. Encyclopedia _____

7. **Number Sense** Which is a greater number, the mass of a
cat in grams or the mass of the same cat in kilograms?

_____

8. The *Dromornis stirtoni* was the largest bird
ever. It is now extinct. The ostrich is the
largest living bird. What is the difference
in mass between the *Dromornis stirtoni*
and the ostrich?

Bird	Mass
Ostrich	156 kg
Andean condor	9 kg
Eurasian eagle owl	4.2 kg
Dromornis stirtoni	454 kg

_____

9. Which has a larger mass, an Andean condor or a Eurasian
eagle owl?

_____

10. **Reasoning** A decigram is related to a gram in the same
way a decimeter is related to a meter. How many
decigrams are there in a gram? _____

Test Prep

11. Which object would be most likely to have a mass of 2 kg?

A. A truck   **B.** An orange   **C.** A mosquito   **D.** A math book

12. **Writing in Math** Would you be more likely to find the mass
of a pen in grams or in kilograms? Explain.

_____

_____

Name _____

Changing Units and Comparing Measures

How to change metric units:

To change larger units to smaller units, multiply.

6 kg = ☐ g

Think: 1 kg = 1,000 g

6 × 1,000 = 6,000

So, 6 kg = 6,000 g.

To change smaller units to larger units, divide.

200 mm = ☐ cm

Think: 1 cm = 10 mm

200 ÷ 10 = 20

So, 200 mm = 20 cm.

How to compare measures:

Compare 2 m 73 cm to 285 cm.

Step 1: Change to the same units.

Think: 1 m = 100 cm

200 + 73 = 273 cm

2 m 73 cm = 273 cm

Step 2: Compare.

273 cm < 285 cm

So, 2 m 73 cm < 285 cm.

Find each missing number.

1. 32,000 g = _____ kg

2. 9 cm 3 mm = _____ mm

3. 1 m 45 cm = _____ cm

Compare. Write > or < for each.

4. 90 g ◯ 9 kg

5. 1,750 mL ◯ 2 L

6. 12 m 6 cm ◯ 126 cm

7. **Number Sense** How many meters are in 13 km? _____

Changing Units and Comparing Measures

Find each missing number.

1. 4,000 mL = _____ L

2. 51 kg = _____ g

3. 7,000 dm = _____ m

4. 600 cm = _____ m

Compare. Write > or < for each ◯.

5. 70 g ◯ 7 kg

6. 890 cm ◯ 9 dm

7. 6 L ◯ 900 mL

8. 98 mm ◯ 9 cm 9 mm

	Great Gray Owl	Elf Owl	Great Horned Owl
Length	84 cm	160 mm	63 cm
Wingspan	152 cm	380 mm	152 cm
Mass	1.45 kg	4 g	1,800 g

9. Write the owls in order from the least to the greatest mass.

_____

10. How many centimeters long is the elf owl? _____

Test Prep

11. How many milliliters are there in 32 L?

   A. 32,000   B. 3,200   C. 320   D. 32

12. **Writing in Math** The bird with the longest beak is the
   Australian pelican. The pelican's beak is up to 47 cm long.
   Explain how to find the number of millimeters long the beak is.

_____

_____

PROBLEM-SOLVING SKILL

Writing to Explain

Airplanes The Paper Airplane Club at school was having a contest to see whose paper airplane could fly the farthest. Before the contest started, students were allowed two practice flights to test their planes. The results are shown at the right.

Student	Flight 1	Flight 2
Cheryl	3 m	2 m 10 cm
Kenya	6 m 3 cm	7 m
Mario	36 cm	1 m 5 cm

Use the data in the table to predict who will win the contest.

Writing a Math Explanation

- Make sure your prediction is stated clearly.

- Use steps to make your explanation clear.

- Show and explain carefully how you used the numbers to make your prediction.

Example

I think Kenya will win. Here is why.

1. I looked at the results of the two test flights. Her plane flew over 6 m both times.

2. Cheryl's and Mario's planes both flew much less each flight. Mario's plane barely flew more than 1 m.

3. When they fly their planes in the contest, Kenya's plane will likely fly around 6 m and the other planes will fly less than that, so Kenya's plane should win.

---

1. The softball league is going to have a playoff. All 4 teams are included. During the season, each team played 30 games. Team A won 17 games, Team B won 29, Team C won 16, and Team D won 7. Predict which team will win the championship. Tell why.

_____

_____

_____

Name_____

Writing to Explain

Write to explain.

1. Explain the relationship between a liter and a milliliter.

_____

_____

2. Explain how to find the perimeter of
   the rectangle in two different ways.

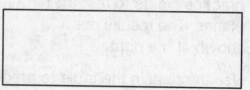

_____

_____

_____

3. Explain how the number of shaded
   triangles needed in the design
   compares to the number of
   triangles not shaded.

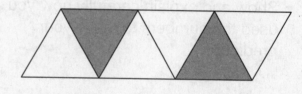

_____

_____

4. Explain how to take three different metric measurements of
   a can of fruit cocktail.

_____

_____

_____

Temperature

Thermometers are used to measure the temperature. Often thermometers will have both the degrees Celsius (°C) and the degrees Fahrenheit (°F) scales on them.

Reading a thermometer:

The scale on the right side of the thermometer is the Celsius scale. The temperature is about 15°C.

The scale on the left side of the thermometer is the Fahrenheit scale. The temperature is about 58°F.

Read each thermometer. Write the temperature in °C and in °F.

1. _____

2. _____

3. _____

4. **Number Sense** Are you more likely to ice skate on a lake when the temperature outside is 30°C or 30°F? Explain.

_____

_____

_____

Name_____

Temperature

Read each thermometer. Write the temperature in °C and in °F.

1.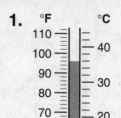

_____

2.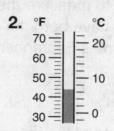

_____

3.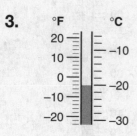

_____

4.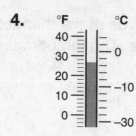

_____

5. Number Sense Name one activity you are likely to do outdoors if the temperature is 15°F.

_____

_____

6. A storm front went through and the temperature dropped 10°C in 3 hr. If the temperature started at 6°C, what was the temperature after the 3 hr? _____

Test Prep

7. Which temperature would be best for a day at the beach?

A. 110°F   **B.** 60°C   **C.** 60°F   **D.** 32°C

8. Writing in Math Which temperature scale are you more familiar with? Explain why.

_____

_____

_____

PROBLEM-SOLVING APPLICATION

Shark!

About how long is a basking shark to the nearest whole meter?

First find the rounding place.

12.3

2 is in the ones place.

Then look at the digit to the right.

12.3

3 < 5, so leave the number as it is.

So, the basking shark is about 12 m long.

Sharks

Shark	Length (meters)
Whale shark	15 m
Basking shark	12.3 m
Great white shark	6.4 m
Piked dogfish shark	1.6 m
Spined pygmy shark	21 cm
Pygmy ribbontail cat shark	16 cm

Use the chart above to solve each problem.

1. How many centimeters longer is the great white shark than the spined pygmy shark?

   _____

2. How many millimeters longer is the spined pygmy shark than the pygmy ribbontail cat shark?

   _____

3. Write the length of the whale shark in centimeters and millimeters.

   _____

4. The piked dogfish shark is the most common shark. Is the piked dogfish shark more likely to weigh 200 kg or 200 g?

   _____

5. If 2 great white sharks were placed end to end, what would their total length be?

   _____

PROBLEM-SOLVING APPLICATION

Take Out Dinner

Lynn bought a container of Chinese food and brought it home to eat. The container the rice came in was a cardboard folded box with a metal handle. Its measurements were 8 cm deep, 10 cm wide, and 12 cm tall.

1. What is the volume of the box the rice came in? _____

2. Is the container more likely to hold 20 g of rice or 20 kg of rice? Explain.

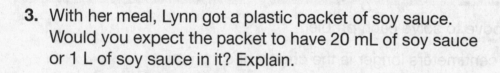

_____

_____

3. With her meal, Lynn got a plastic packet of soy sauce. Would you expect the packet to have 20 mL of soy sauce or 1 L of soy sauce in it? Explain.

_____

_____

4. Lynn also ordered an extra large iced tea. The iced tea fills a 2 L container. How many milliliters of tea will the container hold? _____

5. Ruth had $10.54 and paid $2.75 to Taylor for a notebook. At a garage sale, Ruth sold a stuffed fish for $5.50 and a plastic panda bank for $0.75. How much money does Ruth have now? _____

6. Blocks are used to build a pyramid in the pattern shown. How many blocks are needed to build a pyramid that has 7 layers?

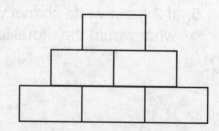

_____

Inequalities on a Number Line

To solve an inequality, you must find the value that makes the inequality true.

For example: $x < 4$ is an inequality. This means "x is less than 4."

What numbers make the inequality true? What numbers are less than 4?

0, 1, 2, and 3 are all less than 4. They can solve the inequality.

5, 6, and 7 are greater than 4. They cannot solve the inequality.

To graph the solutions to the inequality $x < 4$, first draw an open circle at 4 on the number line. Then draw an arrow over the solutions.

Name three solutions to each inequality and graph all the solutions on a number line.

1. $b > 5$

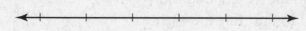

_____

2. $a < 9$

_____

3. $d > 0$

_____

4. $m < 13$

_____

5. Number Sense Could $7 - 4$ be a solution to the inequality $c < 2$? Explain.

_____

Inequalities on a Number Line

Name three solutions to each inequality and graph all the
solutions on a number line.

1. $b < 8$ _____

2. $y > 15$ _____

3. $n > 5$ _____

4. $c < 10$ _____

5. A weatherman said the high temperature today will be
above 90°F. Name three temperatures that could be the
high temperature if the weatherman is correct.

_____

6. A ride at the fair says that riders must weigh less than
120 lb. Use the inequality $c < 120$ to find three weights
of people that could go on the ride.

_____

Test Prep

7. Which is a solution to the inequality $x < 16$?

A. 15   **B.** 16   **C.** 17   **D.** 18

8. Writing in Math Is 15.6 a solution to the inequality $b < 15$?
Explain why or why not.

_____

_____

_____

Translating Words to Equations

When you are translating words to equations, the words give clues about which operation you should use in the equation.

The words *plus*, *added*, and *more* tell you that you should use addition.

Sentence	Equation
y plus 9 is equal to 17.	$y + 9 = 17$

The words *minus*, *less than*, and *difference* tell you that you should use subtraction.

Sentence	Equation
8 less than *m* is 7.	$m - 8 = 7$

Divided by and *equally between* refer to division, and *product*, *times*, and *each* refer to multiplication.

Sentence	Equation
16 split equally between *n* is 4.	$16 \div n = 4$
5 times *n* is 25.	$5n = 25$

Write an equation for each sentence.

1. 12 times *t* is 132.

_____

2. 8 minus *r* equals 2.

_____

3. 70 plus *w* is 102.

_____

4. 100 divided by *x* is 10.

_____

Write an equation for the problem.

5. Number Sense Harry had $45 and gave $5 to his brother. How much money does Harry have left?

_____

Translating Words to Equations

Write an equation for each sentence.

1. g minus 6 leaves 4.   _____

2. 5 times t = 40.   _____

3. d divided by 7 is 4.   _____

4. r less than 16 is 12.   _____

5. 7 cars plus f cars equal 21 cars.   _____

6. 22 birds less than h birds is 50 birds.   _____

Write an equation for each problem.

7. The life span of a swan is up to 50 years
   in captivity. In the wild, a swan lives up
   to 19 years. How much longer can a
   swan live in captivity than in the wild?   _____

8. In a conference room, seats are arranged
   with 6 people around each table. There
   is seating for 96 in a conference room.
   How many tables are in the room?   _____

Test Prep

9. Which equation matches the sentence?

   12 more than y is 19.

   A. $12y = 19$ **B.** $\frac{y}{12} = 19$ **C.** $y - 12 = 19$ **D.** $y + 12 = 19$

10. **Writing in Math** Gary has a rope that is 9 ft long. He wants to
    find out how many inches long the rope is. He uses the equation
    $\frac{x}{12} = 9$. Will Gary's equation find the correct answer? Explain.

    _____

    _____

    _____

Name _____

Equations and Graphs

Use the equation $y = x + 2$. Find the value of y if $x = 3$.

First substitute 3 for x. $y = 3 + 2$

Then add. $y = 5$

So when $x = 3$, $y = 5$.

x	y
0	2
1	3
2	4
3	5

Here is a table of values made from the equation $y = x + 2$.

The table of values can be used to make a graph of the line $y = x + 2$. Plot each ordered pair from the table. For example, (0, 2).

Then connect the plotted points with a straight line.

Other ordered pairs on the graph of the equation are (4, 6), (5, 7), and (6, 8).

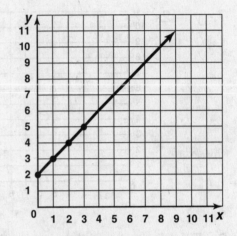

Use the equation $y = 3x + 1$ to find the value of y for each value of x.

1. $x = 0$ _____

2. $x = 2$ _____

3. $x = 4$ _____

4. $x = 6$ _____

5. Graph the equation $y = x - 2$ on the coordinate grid at the right.

6. List five ordered pairs on the graph of the equation $y = x + 9$.

_____

_____

_____

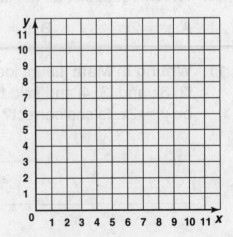

Equations and Graphs

Use the equation $y = 2x + 4$. Find the value of y for each value of x.

1. $x = 3$ _____

2. $x = 1$ _____

3. $x = 10$ _____

4. $x = 25$ _____

5. $x = 0$ _____

6. $x = 7$ _____

Graph each equation on the given coordinate graph.

7. $y = 2x$

8. $y = x - 3$

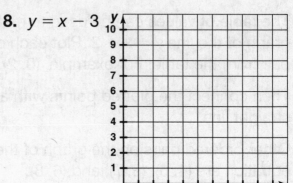

9. Find five ordered pairs on the graph of the equation $y = 3x - 1$.

_____

Test Prep

10. Which equation has the ordered pair (3, 5) as a solution?

A. $y = 2x$ **B.** $y = 2x + 1$ **C.** $y = 2x - 1$ **D.** $y = 3x - 5$

11. Writing in Math Laura looked at the ordered pairs (1, 2), (2, 3), and (3, 4) and said that $1 \times 2 = 2$, so the rule must be $y = 2x$. Is she correct? Explain.

_____

_____

_____

PROBLEM-SOLVING SKILL
Extra or Missing Information

Butterflies The largest butterfly is the female Queen Alexandra Birdwing butterfly, which has a wingspan of 32 cm. The next largest butterfly is the Goliath Birdwing, which has a wingspan of 28 cm. The smallest butterfly is the Western Pygmy Blue, which has a wingspan of only 1.5 cm. How many centimeters longer is the wingspan of the largest butterfly than that of the smallest?

Read and Understand

Step 1: What do you know?

The Queen Alexandra Birdwing is the largest and has a 32 cm wingspan.
The Western Pygmy Blue is the smallest and has a wingspan of 1.5 cm.

Step 2: What are you trying to find?

How much longer is the wingspan of the largest butterfly than that of the smallest butterfly?

Plan and Solve

Step 3: Find and use the needed information.

32 cm − 1.5 cm = 30.5 cm. The difference between the longest wingspan and the shortest wingspan is 30.5 cm.

The wingspan of the Goliath Birdwing was extra information.

Decide if the problem has extra information or not enough information. Tell any information that is not needed or that is missing. Then solve the problem if you have enough information.

1. A group of 12 teens went skiing. Three of them took a chairlift up the hill, and the rest used the T-bar. The chairlift ticket costs $3.00 more than the T-bar ticket. How many teens used the T-bar?

_____

_____

Extra or Missing Information

Decide if each problem has extra information or not enough information. Tell any information that is not needed or that is missing. Solve the problem if you have enough information.

1. Angie wrote 5 letters and 7 e-mails on Monday. On Tuesday, she sent the same number of e-mails as she did on Monday, but she wrote 2 fewer letters. On Wednesday, she wrote 4 letters and did not send any e-mails. How many letters did Angie write from Monday through Wednesday?

_____

_____

2. Darrell has 4 boxes of screws that he uses for building wooden toy cars. Each box weighs 10 kg. The cars weigh 200 kg when they are finished. How many screws does Darrell have altogether?

_____

_____

3. Nigel and Cynthia went to the movies. They each had a large drink and they shared a large popcorn. How much did they spend altogether, including their admission?

MOVIES!		
Admission:		$6.00
Drinks:	Large	$2.00
	Small	$1.25
Popcorn:	Large	$3.00
	Medium	$2.25
	Small	$1.75

_____

4. Jessica went to the theater with $10.00. She wants a popcorn and a drink. The movie is 1 hr 44 min long. If she buys a large drink, what is the largest size popcorn Jessica can purchase?

_____

_____

Understanding Probability

Probability is the chance that a certain event will happen.
Events can be likely, unlikely, impossible, or certain.

Spinner A

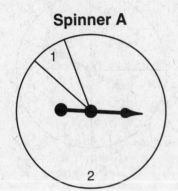

Spinner B

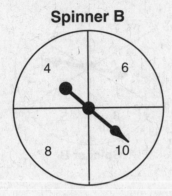

In Spinner A, it is likely that the number 2 will be spun. Over half
of the spinner area is number 2.

In Spinner A, spinning a 1 is unlikely.

In Spinner A, spinning a 3 is impossible. There is no 3 on the spinner.

In Spinner B, spinning an even number is certain. All of the
numbers are even.

Tell whether each event is likely,
unlikely, impossible, or certain.

Spinner C

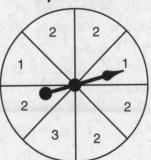

Spinner D

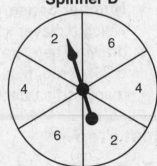

1. Spinning a 2 on Spinner C

   _____

2. Spinning a 2 on Spinner D

   _____

3. Spinning an even number on Spinner D   _____

4. Spinning a 4 on Spinner C   _____

5. **Reasoning** Describe an event using Spinner D that would
   be impossible.

   _____

Understanding Probability

Tell whether it is likely, unlikely, impossible, or certain to get each number when each spinner is spun.

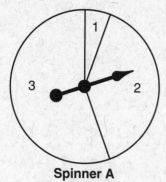
Spinner A

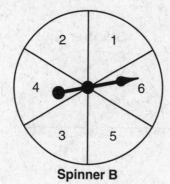
Spinner B

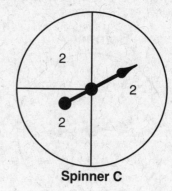
Spinner C

1. 1 on Spinner A

_____

2. 2 on Spinner B

_____

3. 3 on Spinner A

_____

4. 4 on Spinner C

_____

5. 2 on Spinner C

_____

6. Number Sense A fair game is played in which a player wins if his or her color card is drawn. There are three players and a 30-card deck of red, blue, and green cards. How many red cards are there?

_____

Test Prep

7. How many red marbles must there be in a bag of 12 marbles for it to be likely that a red marble is drawn?

A. 4   **B.** 5   **C.** 6   **D.** 7

8. Writing in Math Explain the difference between a fair game and an unfair game.

_____

_____

Listing Outcomes

List all the possible outcomes for the spinners shown.

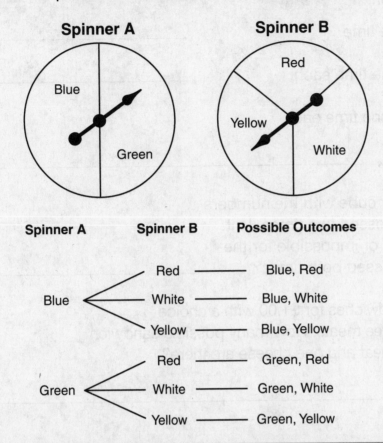

Spinner A	Spinner B	Possible Outcomes
Blue	Red	Blue, Red
	White	Blue, White
	Yellow	Blue, Yellow
Green	Red	Green, Red
	White	Green, White
	Yellow	Green, Yellow

List all the possible outcomes for selecting a marble from each box, without looking.

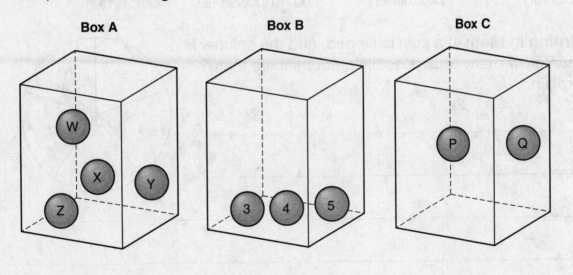

1. Box A _____

2. Boxes B and C

Listing Outcomes

A coin has two sides, heads and tails. List all the possible outcomes for each situation.

1. Flipping one coin, one time _____

2. Flipping two coins, one time each _____

3. Flipping three coins, one time each

_____

4. **Reasoning** A number cube with the numbers 1, 2, 3, 4, 5, and 6 is tossed two times. Is it likely, unlikely, certain, or impossible for the same number to be tossed both times? _____

5. A deli offers lunch sandwiches for $1.00 with a choice of two cheeses and three meats. How many possible sandwich combinations of one meat and one cheese are there?

_____

Test Prep

6. A coin is flipped twice. Which is the probability that both will be heads?

   A. Likely 　　**B.** Unlikely 　　**C.** Impossible 　　**D.** Certain

7. **Writing in Math** If a coin is flipped, and the spinner is spun, how many total possible outcomes are there? Explain.

   _____

   _____

   _____

   _____

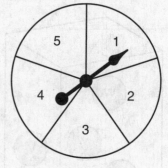

Finding Probability

You can write a fraction to describe the probability of an event.

Probability = $\dfrac{\text{number of favorable outcomes}}{\text{number of possible outcomes}}$

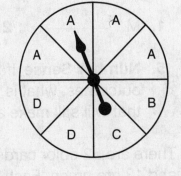

The probability of spinning an A is $\frac{4}{8}$ or $\frac{1}{2}$.

The probability of spinning a B is $\frac{1}{8}$.

The probability of spinning a D is $\frac{2}{8}$, or $\frac{1}{4}$.

The probability of spinning a letter between A and D is $\frac{8}{8}$, or 1. It is certain you will spin a letter between A and D.

The probability of spinning an L is $\frac{0}{8}$, or 0. It is impossible to spin an L, because there isn't one on the spinner.

Write the probability of drawing each letter when the letters from the word MATHEMATICS are drawn without looking.

1. a vowel _____

2. not a vowel _____

3. a capital letter _____

4. the letter *M* _____

5. the letter *L* _____

6. the letter *C* _____

7. **Number Sense** In the problem above, is the event of drawing a vowel likely, unlikely, impossible, or certain? Explain.

_____

_____

_____

8. **Reasoning** Complete the spinner at the right by drawing and labeling to show that the probability of spinning a red is $\frac{3}{4}$.

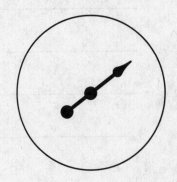

Finding Probability

Write the probability of drawing each letter out of a bag
containing the letters in the word MISSISSIPPI.

1. M _____   2. I _____   3. S _____   4. P _____

5. **Number Sense** If there are 12 possible
   outcomes, what is the lowest probability
   that will still make an outcome likely?   _____

There are 52 color cards. 13 are red, 13 are blue, 13 are yellow,
and 13 are green. Each color has cards numbered from 0 to 12.

6. What is the probability of a card being drawn
   at random that is red?   _____

7. What is the probability of a card being drawn
   at random that is a 12?   _____

Test Prep

8. If the letter tiles are randomly selected,
   which is the probability of selecting A?

   A. $\frac{3}{10}$ B. $\frac{2}{10}$

   C. $\frac{3}{20}$ D. $\frac{1}{10}$

9. **Writing in Math** A game is played by
   flipping two coins. One player wins if
   both are heads. The other player wins
   if both are tails. Is this a fair game?
   Explain.

_____

_____

_____

_____

Making Predictions

Predict the number of times the letter *p* will be drawn when you pick a letter 15 times. The letter is returned to the bag after each pick.

To make the prediction, take the probability, $\frac{1}{3}$, and find an equivalent fraction with the number of picks in the denominator.

$$\frac{1}{3} = \frac{\overline{}}{15}$$

To go from a 3 to a 15, you multiply by 5. To make an equivalent fraction, you must multiply the numerator and denominator by the same number. $1 \times 5 = 5$

$$\frac{1}{3} = \frac{5}{15}$$

The prediction is that out of 15 draws, a *p* will be drawn 5 times.

Use the spinner to predict how many times each letter will be spun.

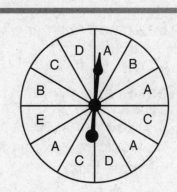

1. *D* when you spin 12 times

_____

2. *E* when you spin 48 times

_____

3. *A* when you spin 9 times _____

4. *B* when you spin 60 times _____

5. *C* when you spin 100 times _____

6. Reasoning A meteorologist predicted that it would rain 1 out of 3 days this month. If there are 30 days in the month, about how many days would you expect it to rain? _____

Name_____

Making Predictions

Use the number tiles for 1–6. Predict how
many times you would pick each number.
You put the number back after each pick.

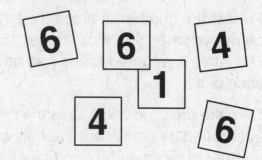

1. 6 when you pick a number 50 times

_____

2. 1 when you pick a number 12 times

_____

3. 4 when you pick a number 30 times   _____

4. 5 when you pick a number 10 times   _____

5. An even number when you pick a
    number 60 times   _____

6. An odd number when you pick a number
    36 times   _____

Test Prep

7. When three coins are tossed, how many times out of 100
    would you expect the result to be either three heads or
    three tails?

    A. 10   **B.** 20   **C.** 25   **D.** 30

8. **Writing in Math** Jennifer used a three-color
    spinner 100 times. Her results are shown.
    Do you think the spinner was fair? Explain.

Red	Green	Blue
30	29	41

_____

_____

_____

Name _____

Morning Routine Brenda takes 30 min to get dressed for school. She eats breakfast for 20 min more, then walks to school. It takes Brenda 15 min to walk to school. Brenda needs to be at school by 8:55 A.M. What time is the latest she should get out of bed in the morning?

Read and Understand

Step 1: What do you know?

Brenda takes 30 min to get ready, 20 min for breakfast, and 15 min to walk to school. She must be at school by 8:55 A.M.

Step 2: What are you trying to find?

What time is the latest Brenda should get up?

Plan and Solve

Step 3: What strategy will you use?

Strategy: Work backward

Work backward from the end, doing the opposite of each step.

I need to move backward, or subtract from the school arrival time, one step at a time.

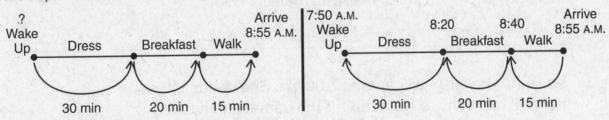

Brenda must get up by 7:50 A.M. at the latest to make it to school in time.

Look Back and Check

Step 4: Is your work correct?

Yes. If I follow the times forward, I end at 8:55 A.M.

1. When Christopher Columbus was 41 years old he sailed across the Atlantic Ocean for the first time. He went on his final expedition 10 years later, which took 2 years. He died 2 years after his final expedition ended, in 1506. What year was Columbus born?

PROBLEM-SOLVING STRATEGY
Work Backward

Solve by working backward. Write the answer in a complete sentence.

1. There are 21 students in Travis's fourth-grade class. Four new students joined his class after school began this year, and 2 moved away. One student was transferred to another fourth-grade teacher. How many students were in Travis's class at the beginning of the school year?

_____

_____

_____

2. Sir John Franklin was an explorer who traveled in Canada and the United States. He was 33 years old when he began exploring northwestern Canada. In a second expedition 17 years later, he explored as far as Alaska. 11 years later, Franklin died in an expedition in search of a Northwest Passage in 1847. In what year was Franklin born?

_____

3. Tessie has a volleyball game at 7:00 P.M. She needs to be there 20 min early to warm up for the game, and it takes her 45 min to get to the gym. What time should she leave her house?

_____

4. Frank bought lunch for $5.60 at a diner. He spent $2.00 to ride the bus to the mall and back, and spent $6.50 while he was at the mall. His friend Bill paid him back $5.00 that he had borrowed last week. If Frank arrived at home with $10.50 in his pocket, how much did he have when he left home that morning?

_____

© Pearson Education, Inc. 4

Name_____

Veronica's Monday

Veronica rides the train every day to work. She needs to arrive at work by 9:00 A.M. It takes her 1 hr and 20 min to get ready for work. Her train ride lasts 30 min. What time is the latest that Veronica can get out of bed and still make it to work on time?

First, identify the time Veronica must arrive: 9:00 A.M.

Then work backwards using the information you know. Her train ride takes 30 min, and it takes her 1 hr 20 min to get ready. That is a total of 1 hr 50 min. One hour before 9:00 A.M. is 8:00 A.M., and 50 min before 8:00 A.M. is 7:10 A.M. So Veronica must get up by 7:10 A.M.

1. Veronica bought lunch, 2 sets of earrings, and a pair of tennis shoes at the mall. The earrings were $4.29 for each set and her tennis shoes were on sale for $22.79. She had $6.21 left when she was finished shopping. How much did she begin with?

   _____

   _____

   _____

   _____

2. In the afternoon, Veronica's coworker Keisha asked to borrow one of Veronica's pens. Veronica had 12 pens in her desk drawer. Three of them were black, 7 were blue, and 2 were red. What is the probability that Veronica will pick a red pen from her drawer?

   _____

3. Veronica worked 8 hr. Her manager asked her to work 3 more hours Tuesday than she did on Monday. Write an equation for *3 more than 8 hr.*

   _____

Name _____

Duck Pond Game

Solve. Write the answer in a complete sentence.

In the duck pond game, players draw plastic ducks out of the pond to win a prize. Every player wins a prize. If you draw out a duck with a red mark on the bottom, you win a small prize. If you draw out a duck with a black mark, you win a large prize. If you draw out a duck with a green star, you win an extra large prize. There are 60 ducks in the pond. Two of them have green stars, 6 have black marks, and the rest have red marks.

1. What is the probability of drawing a duck with a red mark?

   _____

   _____

2. Is it likely, unlikely, impossible, or certain that you will win a prize when you draw out a duck?

   _____

3. Each time a duck is drawn, it is returned to the duck pond. Out of 300 draws, how many do you predict will have green stars?

   _____

   _____

4. As soon as Jack finished dinner last night he spent 2 hr working on his science report, then another 30 min studying for a math test, and 45 min reading a mystery book before he fell asleep. If Jack fell asleep at 10:30 P.M., what time did he finish his dinner?

   _____

5. Write an equation for the sentence. Nine years more than Tina's age is 27. Solve the equation for Tina's age.

   _____